LIONS AND SHADOWS

NEL SIGNET MODERN CLASSICS

Lions and Shadows

An Education in the Twenties

CHRISTOPHER ISHERWOOD

THE NEW ENGLISH LIBRARY

To
William Robson-Scott

First published in Great Britain by The Hogarth Press in 1938
Subsequently published by Methuen & Co. in 1953

*

FIRST NEL SIGNET EDITION JANUARY 1968
This new edition October 1974

*

NEL Books are published by New English Library Limited from Barnard's Inn, Holborn, London, EC1. Made and printed in Great Britain by Love & Malcomson Ltd., Redhill, Surrey.

450021645

TO THE READER

I had better start by saying what this book is not: it is not, in the ordinary journalistic sense of the word, an autobiography; it contains no 'revelations'; it is never 'indiscreet'; it is not even entirely 'true.'

Its sub-title explains its purpose: to describe the first stages in a lifelong education—the education of a novelist. A young man living at a certain period in a certain European country, is subjected to a certain kind of environment, certain stimuli, certain influences. That the young man happens to be myself is only of secondary importance: in making observations of this sort, everyone must be his own guinea-pig.

Because this book is about the problems of a would-be writer, it is also about conduct. The style is the man. Because it is about conduct, I have had to dramatize it, or you would not get farther than the first page. Read it as a novel. I have used a novelist's licence in describing my incidents and drawing my characters: 'Chalmers,' 'Linsley,' 'Cheuret' and 'Weston' are all caricatures: that is why—quite apart from the fear of hurt feelings—I have given them, and nearly everybody else, fictitious names.

C. I.

September 1937

CHAPTER I

To look at, Mr. Holmes was a short, stout, middle-aged man with reddish hair just beginning to get thin on the crown. He had closely folded, rather prim clergyman's lips and a long astute pointed nose which was slightly crooked. His glance was cold, friendly and shrewd. When he had made a successful joke and the whole form was laughing, he would clasp his hands behind his back under his gown and look primly down his nose at his small neat brown shoes.

I can hear him now:

"Napoleon the Third *an*gled for war with the greatest a-acumen and subtlety. Unfortunately for himself, he was soon to discover the highly r-regrettable fact that you cannot serve both M-Mars and M-Mammon. . . ."

He spoke quietly and deliberately, with an instant's hesitation—too slight to be described as a stammer—in pronouncing certain words. These words usually occurred with increasing frequency towards the climax of one of his anecdotes or the springing of one of his aphorisms, and as he said them he would screw his head comically to one side, as if ducking under some invisible obstacle. The head movement and the instant's hesitation may have been the traces of a nervous tic: more probably they were quite deliberate. They produced a pleasingly pedantic effect which charmed many of us; and we often tried to imitate them. I sometimes catch myself trying the pseudo stammer on strangers, even to-day.

Almost everything Mr. Holmes did or said contributed to a deliberate effect: he had the technique of a first-class clergyman or actor. But unlike most clergymen, he was entirely open and shameless about his methods. Having achieved his object—which was always, in one way or another, to startle,

7

shock, flatter, lure or scare us for a few moments out of our schoolboy conservatism and prejudice—he would explain to us gleefully just how this particular trap, bait or bomb had been prepared. His behaviour thus became a parody of itself; and this continually disconcerted us. We liked the staff to have its mannerisms, of course—there was the Boss's snort, Johnny's roar, Jimmy's wail; there were Hutchinson's fancy waistcoats, Butcher's sermons, Capel-Williams' conversations with the grocer's horse: all these, we knew, were genuine. We could laugh at them safely, wholeheartedly, unkindly, as spectators. We couldn't laugh wholeheartedly at Mr. Holmes, because even laughter would put us, we felt, under a kind of obligation to him; would, in some way, subtly involve us in his plans. Besides, we were never quite sure that he mightn't be laughing at us.

Quiet, astute, disconcertingly witty, he was never widely popular. His brand of humour, and indeed his whole personality, was an acquired taste. A large percentage of his pupils bored him and he showed it, unobtrusively but most insultingly. He had arrived at our school a couple of terms after the end of the War. It was a difficult period for a new master, proposing to begin work on untraditional lines. The Sixth was still composed of boys who had only just missed being conscripted, potential infantry officers trained to expect the brief violent career of the trenches: they had outgrown their school life long before they left it. And now, suddenly, the universal profession of soldiering was closed to them; and the alternatives seemed vague and dull. So the Sixth-formers let things drift and didn't much care. They regarded the school curriculum with benevolent amusement, broke bounds, ragged work and games, cut chapel, wrote daring love-poetry, strolled about the place in various forms of mild fancy dress or lolled round their study fires with their feet on the mantelpiece, smoking their pipes like grandfathers. There was a story of how Ponds, the head of our house, was visited by our housemaster one evening for a serious discussion of house politics. The house-master, warming to his subject, talked and talked. Ponds, muscular, lazy, untidy and profoundly bored, agreed with every word: "Oh, quite definitely, sir . . ." he kept repeating: " . . yes, quite definitely. . . ." Presently, with the utmost sang-froid, he fell asleep.

Such was Mr. Holmes' audience when he entered the Sixth Form room to deliver his first history lecture—faintly patronizing, not unfriendly, prepared to be comfortably amused. Mr. Holmes had not, however, come to amuse his hearers; and he seems to have made this plain, mildly but firmly, from the very beginning. He expected them to attend to what he was saying—worse still, to remember it. Breaking an unwritten law, he asked them direct questions in turn, saying: "Next . . . Next . . . Next . . ." as though he were taking a class in the Lower School. The Sixth was first dazed, then resentful. Its self-conceit had been wounded and its lack of knowledge brutally exposèd. Nor was this all. It was said that Mr. Holmes, in the Masters' Common Room, had actually referred to his pupils as "idle and ignorant." Indignation against him reached boiling-point and I seem to remember that there was even some sort of overt demonstration. If so, Mr. Holmes crushed it, no doubt, efficiently enough. Later, several members of that Sixth became his personal friends. But all this was before my time.

As for myself, I accepted Mr. Holmes' influence all the more readily because, during the first four or five terms of my school life, I had scarcely any personal contacts with the staff at all. I had arrived at my public school thoroughly sick of masters and mistresses, having been emotionally messed about by them at my preparatory school, where the war years had given full licence to every sort of dishonest cant about loyalty, selfishness, patriotism, playing the game and dishonouring the dead. Now I wanted to be left alone. The boys I could deal with, more or less, as long as I kept my wits about me. The masters I deeply distrusted: remembering those "fatherly" pi-jaws and the resultant floods of masochistic tears. So I made friends with a very tough character named Dock—a black-haired Liverpool boy with a pale goatish face, older than myself, who wore thick pebble glasses on gold wires. Dock did me a great deal of good. He restored my self-respect. Through knowing him, I ceased gradually to believe that I was—as my preparatory school headmaster had done his best to persuade me—greedier, lazier, more selfish, less considerate and in general more unpleasant than anybody else. I certainly wasn't lazier than Dock, nor such a liar, nor half as greedy: yet he would have been the very last person to regard his own character with disgust or remorse. He was highly satisfied with himself.

In the Officers' Training Corps, Dock played an important if unobtrusive part: he was one of a group of saboteurs whose

9

influence was out of all proportion to its numbers. Alone, he was capable of demoralizing an entire platoon. Because of Dock, I never disliked O.T.C. parades: as for field days, they were among the happiest of my school life. But it was during the period of the O.T.C. summer camp that Dock and his friends really came into their own. I can see them now —loosening the guy-ropes of the big canteen tent, scaring the horses of nervous masters unaccustomed to riding, creeping up behind a smartly turned-out sentry from another school and suddenly planting a large melon on the point of his bayonet. They were caught, of course, and reprimanded, but nothing more. The authorities were embarrassed: they didn't want to spoil the jolly holiday atmosphere with punishments. The Guards officer who interviewed them, a very nice man, talked unhappily about the team spirit and looked far more distressed than his prisoners, whose faces were as expressionless as their ill-polished buttons. "Private Dock," ran the official report, "failed, for the third time, to obey orders." That was it —Dock just failed. There was nothing to be done with him and his kind—unless you were prepared to shoot them. The school contingent left camp with a bad name.

During my third year, I became attached to the History Sixth. This was in 1921. From that time onwards, Mr. Holmes was the director of my studies. Except for divinity and a little classics, I worked for him entirely. It had been decided that I should try for a history exhibition at Cambridge at the end of the autumn term.

The History Sixth shared with the other branches of the Sixth Form the important privilege of doing its private work in the school library. Here we were supposed to read text-books, write essays and copy out our notes. The library was a handsome room, thickly carpeted and furnished with most comfortable arm-chairs. In addition to the standard works of history, literature, biography and science, there was plenty of miscellaneous stuff to be dipped into, including five or six of those rare flowers of semi-pornography which always contrive to bloom (like the edelweiss, in some high inaccessible nook) amongst even the most carefully pruned collections. There was no actual supervision; though from time to time, one of the masters might enter, quietly and unexpectedly. However, a number of small bookcases standing about the room provided excellent cover, and it was nearly impossible, if you were awake at all, to be taken by surprise. Dozing in one of the arm-chairs, with Lord Acton's lectures open and the right way up upon your lap, you might pass a very agreeable hour, and only once in a while a sudden well-placed kick, probably from the Headmaster, would remind you painfully that you were not already a grown-up member of a London club.

The library privilege was abused in a number of ways. There were those, like Sargent, who simply ragged—launching gliders across the room, lobbing ink-bombs over the bookcases or trying to hurl each other from the tops of the ladders. We, the quiet ones, disapproved of these: they might easily have got us all turned out, to sit on a hard bench in a classroom, for good. Then there were the idlers who chatted, wrote letters and slept. And there were the studious few who were really busy—but for the wrong reasons. Chief among these was Linsley. He had long been engaged in writing a novel of public school life. The novel was no secret. Plump, smiling, always affable, never in the least upset by criticism however adverse, Linsley was at all times perfectly willing to answer any questions, show us the manuscript and outline the forthcoming phases of the plot. *Donald Stanton* soon became our common property: gleefully we searched its pages for spelling mistakes, *double entendres* and marvels of grammar. We were seldom disappointed. Mrs. Stanton, who is packing, tells her son: "I've put you in four tins of fruit and two tins of sardines." A page or two later, she succeeds in getting "a wry smile" into a suitcase already very full. "Mrs. Stanton," ran a favourite passage, "knew the organist very well—though Donald did not know it, he was almost his son." Linsley had undoubtedly been influenced by *David Blaize,* his soliloquies were in Mr. E. F. Benson's most luscious manner and, lacking the polish of their original, considerably more embarrassing. I myself had revelled in *David Blaize* (though by this time, already, I would have died rather than admit it): my sarcasms at the expense of *Donald Stanton* were all the more bitter in consequence. I even covered the margins of the patient Linsley's manuscript with didactic or would-be humorous notes: ". . . and so the matter dropped." (*Where? Into the Thames?*) We thought ourselves very clever, but not one of us could do what Linsley was doing: he provided the library with almost daily entertainment for two whole terms. *Donald Stanton* flourished, despite the brutality of its literary foster-parents; by the time its author left the school, it was 123 pages long.

One day Linsley was caught at work upon his novel by Mr. Paddington. We expected trouble. but Paddington merely asked: "Did you write all this yourself?" "Yes, sir," said Linsley, much discomforted. "Indeed?" said Paddington, without a trace of sarcasm, and obviously meaning to be kind: "very creditable indeed." And he walked away. Mr. Paddington was the Maths master and Linsley was reading modern languages, so perhaps his lack of indignation may be explained.

Another library author was Chalmers. But Chalmers wrote poetry and, unlike Linsley, didn't show his work to the public; unless, as sometimes happened, it was published in the school magazine. He had recently won the school poetry prize on the set subject: "The Surrender of the German Fleet at Scapa Flow." Chalmers' poem began: "The Prussian watched the sombre winter sea." This was its first and last reference, throughout, to anything German: as for the fleet itself, it was never mentioned at all. Chalmers filled the remainder of his six Spenserian stanzas with his favourite properties: wan blood-red mists, meaningless cries of invisible sea birds and the inaudible moanings of the drowned. But his entry was so unquestionably the best that it got the prize, nevertheless; despite the suspicion that it was merely one more expression of the author's limitless quiet contempt for the authorities and all their works.

Chalmers was a pale, small, silent boy, a year older than myself, strikingly handsome, with dark hair and dark blue eyes. On the rare occasions when he got excited and began to talk, his face became flushed; he spoke so quickly and indistinctly, with nervous fumblings of his fingers against his lips, that it was very difficult to understand what he was saying. His nervous energy made him extremely good at football; and, if he had taken more trouble, he might easily have got into the school eleven. People in his house liked him but didn't altogether understand him. He was rather isolated there and had no intimate friends.

No sooner had I come into contact with Chalmers than I determined to get to know him well. Never in my life have I been so strongly and immediately attracted to any personality, before or since. Everything about him appealed to me. He was a natural anarchist, a born romantic revolutionary;

12

I was an upper-middle-class Puritan, cautious, a bit stingy, with a stake in the land. Chalmers had refused to be confirmed, explaining quite simply to his housemaster that he was an agnostic. I had been through the confirmation process a few months earlier, working up all the emotions prescribed in my little black leather "companion" and delighting the master who prepared me by the complexity and ingenuity of my religious "difficulties." Now already I had to admit to myself that, as far as I was concerned, the entire ceremony had been altogether meaningless. If only I had been more honest with myself and avoided it, like Chalmers, from the very start!

Above all things, Chalmers loathed the school to which he invariably referred as "Hell." His natural hatred of all established authority impressed me greatly and I felt that it was a weakness in myself not to share it; to be guilty, indeed, of having sometimes kissed the rod. It wasn't as if I had been a success as a public schoolboy. I only fitted uneasily into the system. But I was adaptable; I could always find my feet. And, on the whole, I quite enjoyed my life in a community where cunning and diplomacy could always so easily defeat brute force.

One of the most admirable things about Mr. Holmes was his attitude towards Chalmers. Mr. Holmes can only have viewed with impatience his pupil's contempt for the public school system: he himself belonged to the system body and soul. He did not care much for poetry, and Chalmers' Francis-Thompsonish verses must have struck him as painfully puerile. But he was a true connoisseur; he knew a good thing when he saw it. So he intrigued to secure Chalmers for the History Sixth and, having got him there, artfully curbed and spurred him on by turns, preaching now revolution, now moderation, and encouraging him to write anything and everything which came into his head. On the whole, the treatment was a great success. Chalmers soon ceased to be on the defensive; he even became cautiously friendly. Under Mr. Holmes' supervision, his school essays began more and more to resemble prose poems; they were filled with weird dream-like phrases such as "After 1848, Europe became a filmy hospital of dishonoured causes." Most schoolmasters would have waxed very caustic over the "filmy hospital" and perhaps enquired whether the surgeons were opaque or transparent; but Mr. Holmes merely smiled. He was perfectly satisfied. He was working along his own peculiar lines for a certain definite result. And nobody could better appreciate than he the market value of the Odd.

Mr. Holmes' methods of teaching are, I am sure, much more generally employed to-day. To us, they appeared startlingly unconventional. Mr. Holmes fairly staggered us by the impudence of his generalizations: "All revolutions occur when the worst period is over and things are improving . . . . All revolutions are followed by a military dictatorship. . . . All military dictatorships are followed by a restoration of constitutional monarchy . . . Every constitutional monarch . . ." He would continue like this, absurdly, preposterously, until he had wrung a protest from one or other of us: "But, surely, sir, that isn't always true?" Then he would pounce upon the heckler at once, delighted: "Of c-course it isn't Tell me an exception." He liked us to have historical prejudices and loved to bait them: "This morning I propose to p-pronounce a eulogy of Oliver Cromwell—for the benefit of Carrick." Carrick was supposed to be an ardent Royalist. In the same way, with equal fervour, he would attack or defend Gladstone's Irish policy, the character of Napoleon or the career of Frederick the Great. He was the first person to make clear to most of us the connection between history and geography: "Look at this chain of mountains, now look at this river-mouth. You see, of course, why the people on this side have always been Catholics. Well, I mean to say, simply inevitable——"

We were now busily preparing for the Cambridge scholarship exams. Chalmers and myself were among the first batch of entrants sent up by our school to Cambridge since the War and there was a good deal of general interest in the possible results. Mr. Holmes, himself a Cambridge man, was popularly supposed to have friends at court; certainly, his advice to us showed an almost uncanny knowledge of the examiners' mentality. As usual, he played the frankly cynical charlatan. The Essay, we were told, was the most important paper of the lot. Historical knowledge was absolutely unnecessary: all you had to do was to sparkle and startle. In the Viva, you merely had to keep calm and be gentlemanly (dozens of brilliant scholars, said Mr. Holmes, were rejected because of their provincial accents); and, above all, you must display curious and interesting literary tastes. As for the mere matter of book-learning, Mr. Holmes had his shock tactics here, too. He advised us to memorize a few lines of

Dante, preferably out of the *Inferno,* in the original Italian, and quote them casually somewhere in the middle of an answer. I learnt:

> *e la lor cieca vita è tanto bassa,*
> *che invidiosi son d'ogni altra sorte*

—which fits in well almost anywhere, in a paper on the Middle Ages. Whatever you do, Mr. Holmes added, never despair if you find you've forgotten something; never be at a loss. And he told the story of how, when he himself was taking the Tripos, he had set a question on the religious problems of Tudor England. The question was *his* question: he had all the facts ready and all the epigrams, he was prepared to be brilliant, he couldn't, on any account, afford to pass it by. But suddenly, with horror, he realized that he couldn't, for his life, remember whether Edward VI came before or after Mary! For a moment he lost his head entirely. He saw the whole examination, his whole future, slipping away from him. And then the simple solution presented itself. Throughout his answer he referred ambiguously to "the Monarch"!

The day arrived. Chalmers and I had arranged to travel up to Cambridge by ourselves. We had got to stick together, we told each other. We were venturing, like spies, into an enemy stronghold. "They," our adversaries, would employ other tactics down there; they would be sly, polite, reassuring; they would invite us to tea. We should have to be on our guard. "They'll do everything they can to separate us," I said darkly, for I had adopted Chalmers' phraseology and ideas, lock, stock and barrel, and now talked exactly like him: "every possible bribe will be offered." The train clanked through the iron-coloured fen landscape, with its desolate pointing spires, infinitely mournful in the fading December afternoon. Chalmers said: "Arrival at the country of the dead."

Cambridge exceeded our most macabre expectations. It seemed a city of perpetual darkness, for we spent the few hours of winter daylight almost entirely in the examination hall. When we emerged, the shop lamps were already blurred in the icy fog which stole out of the marshes into the town, bicycles veered shrilly hither and thither in the gloom, and the outlines of college buildings, half seen, half suggested, were massive and shadowy as the architecture of the night itself. Within doors, all was luxury: the arm-chairs, the crumpets, the beautifully-bound eighteenth-century volumes, the fires roaring in stoked grates. Each of us had the loan of an absent undergraduate's room—bedroom, sittingroom and pantry; all fitted up in a style which, after the spartan simplicity of a public school study, seemed positively sinful. Each of us was called, every morning, by a college servant with a cup of tea. Both Chalmers and myself were overpowered, by the leisure, by the politeness, by the extravagance, by the abundance of alcohol and rich food. Nobody attempted to separate us, as I had predicted; but the whole establishment seemed to offer an enormous tacit bribe. We fortified ourselves against it as best we could, in the privacy of our rooms; swearing never to betray each other, never to forget the existence of "the two sides" and their eternal, necessary state of war.

Of the examination itself I remember very little; for me, it was the least important feature of that memorable expedition. But I can see clearly the faces of the other candidates— dazed, earnest, pushing, scared, shy, pimply, reckless. They seemed strangely isolated from us. We took a special interest in one boy, who looked intelligent and rather lost; we nick-named him "the man with the soul." We spoke to nobody and discussed our examination papers very little. It seems to me that I knew we should succeed. This was Mr. Holmes' doing. By virtue of his extraordinary hypnotism he was with us, in spirit, throughout; guiding us over every obstacle warning us of every pitfall. Subconsciously, we knew he couldn't fail us. Our defeat would have been his own.

He didn't fail us. Chalmers got a sixty-pound scholarship, I got an exhibition worth forty pounds, and Browne, the school's prize history scholar, got the best scholarship of his year. Chalmers left at the end of the term, to go to a *pension* at Rouen and learn French. I had to stay on another whole year at a school, because I was so young. It seemed an un-attractive prospect.

Seven months later, on August 3rd, 1922, I woke up on board a cross-channel steamer from Southampton, to find that Le Havre was already in sight. It was my first unfor-gettable view of anywhere abroad. The boat stole in towards the land across a flat grey sea, spreading heavy whitish ripples, as if through milk. The coast rose solemn behind the town.

The tall houses were like shabby wings of stage scenery which had been left out of doors all night, propped against the cliffs. As we approached the quay, we heard the faint vigorous shouting of the inhabitants, the crowing of cocks and the clanging of the bells of trams. Bolsters were hung out from the windows to air in the pale sunshine. It seemed to me that the people here got up very early.

Mr. Holmes was beside me at the rail, and Queensbridge, another member of the History Sixth, a freckled jolly boy with a bright red nose. Mr. Holmes had arranged this trip; we were on our way to a walking tour in the French Alps. He wore a cloth cap which made him look more than ever like a Renaissance cardinal on holiday, and a surprisingly loud suit of pepper-and-salt tweeds.

We crossed Havre in a tram, crushed together with crowds of workmen going to their daily jobs, and found ourselves in the great gloomy shabby platformless station, where grass grew between the rails and the grimy locomotives looked so rusty and ancient that one expected them at any moment to blow themselves to bits. Havre had not yet been tidied up after the War. I was duly shocked and remarked on all this to Mr. Holmes, who retorted that every European country looked like that just now, except England, where a lot of money was wasted on coats of paint, most uneconomically, since we were every bit as much in debt as the others. We sat down in the waiting-room and ordered coffee and *brioches*. Mr. Holmes was enthusiastic about the prospect of eating *brioches* again. I thought they tasted of cardboard and cheese, and the coffee was dirty water full of floating wisps of skin. But I was not disappointed, for I had never for a moment expected that I should like French food. I was very pink and young and English; and quite prepared for a Continent complete with poisonous drains, roast frogs, bed-bugs and vice.

Our train stopped at Rouen, where Chalmers, it had been arranged, would join us. It was strange to see him standing there, puffing at his pipe, placid and vague as usual, and seeming perfectly at home amidst these alien porters and advertisements. He had grown a small moustache and looked exactly my idea of a young Montmartre poet, more French than the French. Now he caught sight of us, and greeted me with a slight wave of the hand, so very typical of him, tentative, diffident, semi-ironical, like a parody of itself.

17

Chalmers expressed himself habitually in fragments of gestures, abortive movements, half-spoken sentences; and if he did occasionally do something decisive—take off his hat to a lady, buy a tin of tobacco, tell a stranger the correct time—he would immediately have to cover it with a sarcasm or a little joke. Getting into the carriage, he was received by Queensbridge and Mr. Holmes with congratulations and witicisms on the moustache. Mr. Holmes was, of course, delighted, and only sorry, I think, that Chalmers wasn't also wearing a velvet jacket, corduroy trousers and a floppy tie. Meanwhile, Chalmers glanced at me with a faint mysterious smile and I had the feeling, as so often, that we were conspirators.

In Paris it was terrifically hot. We visited Les Invalides; I was secretly very much impressed by the coloured lighting, but I wasn't going to show it. Chalmers had denounced the building in advance—a shrine to war! And, of course, one couldn't admit that a shrine to war was anything but vulgar and ugly. As we leaned on the parapet, looking down at Napoleon's shiny tomb, we reminded each other of H. G. Wells' verdict in the *Outline of History*:

> Against this stormy and tremendous dawn appears this dark little archaic personage, hard, compact, unscrupulous, imitative and neatly vulgar.

Chalmers suggested that the only adequate comment was to spit. Mentally, we spat.

The Sainte-Chapelle I privately thought hideous, but Mr. Holmes told us that it is one of the wonders of Europe, so I dutifully noted in my diary (needless to say, I was keeping a diary of our tour; how I wish I had put down in it one interesting, one sincere, one genuinely spiteful remark): "a marvellous example of the colouring of medieval cathedrals." Finally, after a glance at Notre-Dame and a brisk trot through the Louvre, we sat down at a café on the Place de l'Opéra and watched the people. They were amazing—never had we seen such costumes, such make-up, such wigs; and, strangest of all, the wearers didn't seem in the least conscious of how funny they looked. Many of them even stared at us and smiled, as though we had been the oddities, and not they. Mr. Holmes no doubt found it amusing to see that pageant of prostitution, poverty and fashion reflected in our callow faces and wide-open eyes.

We were to travel all night, third class, on wood. The Gare du Lyon was crammed with yelling porters and frantically jostling travellers, like a station in a nightmare. Mr. Holmes hired a pillow for each of us. People were settling into the compartments as though they meant to inhabit them for a month: fathers of families were heating up food on stoves, a baby had been slung in a miniature hammock, everybody had changed into shirt-sleeves and bedroom slippers. One man was preparing to sleep in the corridor, on a mattress, with sheets and blankets complete. We got a carriage to ourselves and dozed uneasily while the train dashed screaming through the darkness, towards the Alps. As its speed increased, the jolts lengthened out into jumps, until we seemed to leave the rails altogether for seconds at a time. Chalmers murmured sleepily that his people at the Rouen *pension* had told him P.L.M. stood for *"Pour les Morts."*

But in the morning we were still alive; we changed at Aix-les-Bains and by breakfast time we were in Annecy. The sun was shining on the lake. The mountains rose, steep and wooded, sheer out of the bluish-green water; high above, they were black and veined with snow. It was the most beautiful place I had seen in my whole life. I wrote in my diary: "There is an impressive château and a clerical school, with a long stone staircase approaching it, where Rousseau was educated for a time."

During the afternoon we made a trip round the lake in a steamer. As we passed Sévrier, Menthon, Talloires, Duingt, with their white vine-covered houses and gay crowds waving from the little piers, Chalmers told me, in bits of sentences and with silent ambiguous gestures toward the shore, how he had discovered *Les Fleurs du Mal*: ". . . it's the very greatest . . . I shall never forget the first time I . . . you see, he exposes once and for all, the tremendous sham . . . the thing we never realized while we were at school . . ." His suppressed excitement set me, as always, instantly on fire. We got back late, and I had to run through the streets to buy my first copy of Baudelaire before the bookshops closed. Without it, that night, I should not have slept a wink.

The stay at Rouen was, as I was to discover later, one of the most important periods of Chalmers' life. His *pension* was nothing out of the ordinary—a typical coaching

19

establishment kept by a typical Lycée professor, pedantic, underpaid, a martinet on the irregular verbs, with a high starched collar and a beard which smelt of cheese. But Chalmers was in the city of Flaubert and de Maupassant; his imagination supplied everything that was lacking. He strolled along the quays and bicycled through the forest, thinking of the murder of La Petite Roque and of Madame Bovary being seduced in the closed black cab. The Pension Dubois provided him with an interior setting for all those anecdotes of frustrated bourgeois longings, adulteries and illicit loves: the tea-urn, the coloured sliding glass doors, the tiny greenhouse which was used as a study, the little garden on the ramparts and the sham marble pillars which supported the slippery polished staircase composed into a romantic vision of late nineteenth-century France. Chalmers, like many of the English writers whom he then most admired, felt a strong natural sympathy with everything French. At Rouen he imagined himself as having escaped into a world in which it was possible to speak openly and unaffectedly of all those subjects which in England must be introduced by an apology or guarded with a sneer—poetry, metaphysics, romantic love. Like all shy people, he enjoyed a freedom from his inhibitions in speaking a foreign language; and his French was already fluent. I heard later that Madame Dubois and her friends had found him charming.

Next morning, the walking tour started. We took the steam-tram, with its enormous funnel, to Thônes; and then set off on foot, up the road which led to the Col des Aravis. Mr. Holmes and Queensbridge stopped frequently to take photographs; they were both experts.

Chalmers and I refused to look at the view at all, much less to admire it; we had passed a resolution that morning consigning mountains to the great rubbish-heap of objects and ideas admired by our adversaries, "the other side," and therefore automatically condemned. "Not that we dislike mountains as mountains," Chalmers was careful to add, "but we decline to subscribe to the loathsome alpine blague." ("Blague" was a prominent word in the new Rouen vocabulary, we had used it several hundred times already during the last forty-eight hours.) Mr. Holmes, without being in a position to appreciate these fine shades of disapproval, was delighted. As usual, he asked nothing better than that we should behave with the maximum of eccentricity.

Presently the mountains disappeared into the clouds; it began to drizzle. We stopped at a chalet where drinks were sold. Queensbridge tried to order beer and was given byrrh instead, an opportunity for Mr. Holmes to read us a little lecture on the correct pronunciation of the two words. We were learning all the time. A few kilometres higher, we sat down on a fence which broke, tipping us over backwards into a field of potatoes. Mr. Holmes pretended to be afraid that the farmer would claim damages, and hurried us on for the next twenty minutes. Actually, I think, he saw that we were tired and wanted to create a diversion by providing some bogus adventure. He was endlessly considerate and sly.

From the Col des Aravis, in fine weather, the tourist gets his first view of Mont Blanc. But now, as we climbed the last loop of the road to the summit, we were enveloped suddenly in a clammy mist. When we reached the chalet at the top there was nothing to be seen—not even the cows, whose clanging bells were moving invisibly all around us. This, as far as I remember, was the only one of Mr. Holmes' effects which failed to come off. However, we none of us much cared; we were glad of our supper. Mr. Holmes, I read in my diary, "was very gay at the expense of Queensbridge, who stared too hard at the waitress."

Next morning the sunshine woke us early. Chalmers, with whom I shared a room, was the first out of bed; yawning, stretching himself, he hobbled over to the window, started back in mock horror: "Good God! It's arrived!"

Mont Blanc confronted us, dazzling, immense, cut sharp out of the blue sky; more preposterous than the most baroque wedding cake, more convincing than the best photograph. It fairly took my breath away. It made me want to laugh.

"I don't believe it!"

"Neither do I."

After breakfast we started off down the pass. The cows were being driven out to pasture; their bells made a continuous jangle, pretty and metallic, like a musical-box. Peasants were cutting hay in the steep upland meadows. There was a village called Giettaz with a gaudy toy church, whose golden weather-vane sparkled in the sun. In front of the dark pinewood chalets grew ash trees with thick gnarled oak-like trunks; on top of one of the trees stood a little windmill. Here and there, on the gigantic mountain-side, clearings had been made in the forest; the felled trees lay scattered like a box of matches. Long rays of light struck downwards through the tall solemn conifers, as if through cathedral windows, exploring the darkness of the gorge below. Chalmers quoted: ". . . *des pins qui ferment leur pays.*"

The gorge grew narrower and deeper. Cables from a slate quarry spanned the ravine, high above our heads. Waterfalls sprayed the ruins of the precipice; we remembered how Tennyson had described them as "downward smoke." Charabancs came tearing round the corkscrew corners, missing death by inches, and girls waved their handkerchiefs to us and screamed. Mr. Holmes waved back, encouraging us to do likewise. Throughout the trip he lost no opportunity for facetiousness, even skittishness, where the opposite sex was concerned. This naughtiness seemed rather forced, it didn't suit him. No doubt he was trying to continue our education in yet another direction. If so, his problem was certainly a difficult one; he couldn't, as a respectable master in an English public school, have taken us to a brothel. Yet how I wish he had! His introduction to sexual experience would, I feel sure, have been a masterpiece of tact; it might well have speeded up our development by a good five years. As it was, he merely joked and giggled, unsure of his ground, and we, reflecting that Mr. Holmes belonged, after all, to an older and more innocent generation, felt superior and amused and slightly pained. For Chalmers, thanks to Baudelaire, knew all about l'affreuse Juive, opium, absinthe, negresses, Lesbos and the metamorphoses of the vampire. Sexual love was the torture-chamber, the loathsome charnel-house, the bottomless abyss. The one valid sexual pleasure was to be found in the consciousness of doing evil. Its natural and honourable conclusion was in general paralysis of the insane. Needless to say, Chalmers and myself were both virgins, in every possible meaning of the word.

The rest of the tour is best described by a series of snapshots. I see our little party at Chamonix, on the terrace of a café beside the shallow mountain river. The snow-peaks have turned green, then crimson, then orange; now they are black against the stars. A few yards from where we sit, Saussure's statue points towards the ice-fields of Mont Blanc—or, as Mr. Holmes insists, towards the servants' bedroom windows of the Hotel de la Poste. We are arguing about the public school system: Chalmers and myself on one side, Mr. Holmes on the other, Queensbridge neutral, egging us on.

22

Chalmers pauses in the middle of a sentence to light his pipe.
I only wish that mine would go out. It is my very first pipe,
large and light brown and highly varnished, bought that
morning, together with a lilac bow-tie and a copy of *La
Dame aux Camélllias*. I am perspiring freely and my mouth
is unnaturally full of saliva. Chalmers says: "All institutions
are bad." And Mr. Holmes retorts: "That depends, doesn't
it, on how you define an institution?" I do not hear Chalmers'
definition because I have to return to the hotel in order to
be sick.

Here we are at La Flégère, a chalet high up the mountain
side opposite the Mont Blanc range. We have walked up here
from Chamonix for lunch, and on the way Mr. Holmes has
told us stories about Oscar Browning, whose lectures he attended in his Cambridge days. We look through telescopes
at the aiguilles and are thrilled to see two men perched on
the very top of the Dru. Just below us, a party of French boy
scouts is eating sandwiches. Somebody loosens a small stone
with his foot, it gathers momentum, becomes a deadly missile,
all but hits a scout on the back of the head. The boys look up
furiously; they decide, quite unjustly, that we are the culprits.
There are murmurs against the dirty English. We are indignant, our tentative internationalism withdraws aggrieved into
its shell. Very well, we are English. We will be very English
indeed. We return from our walk in an isolationist mood.

The next picture is out of focus, because I am rather drunk.
We are having supper at a little hamlet called Les Chapieux;
it has been a long day, we have walked over the Col du Bon-
homme, from Les Contamines, where the Feast of the As-
sumption was being celebrated and we had to sleep on the
floor. Crossing the Col was quite an adventure: the guide-
book describes it as being dangerous in bad weather—we
feel like mountaineers. To celebrate the achievement, Mr.
Holmes has ordered Asti Spumanti. What a marvellous drink!
Here, at last, is something alcoholic which I don't merely
have to pretend to like, it is nicer, even, than the best
lemonade; so cool and fizzy and sweet. It makes me wonderfully happy and full of love and romantically sad. That
young officer over there in the corner, for instance—how
utterly I understand everything he is feeling! He is dreadfully
bored up here, in this tiny mountain barracks; he is thinking of his girl, down in Bourg-St.-Maurice, and wondering
if she is thinking of him, and if she really loves him at all.

Well, I am clairvoyant this evening, and I *know* that she is thinking of him; she loves him very much. Later, perhaps, I will give him a message from her which I have just telepathically received. But now I find that we are all wandering along the edge of a lake, in the dark. I try to tell Chalmers about the officer, but I can't get him to stop reciting the *Voyage à Cythère*. Mr. Holmes says it is time to go to bed.

Now comes the most vivid scene in my collection. Chalmers and I are sitting on the edge of a small grassy cliff overlooking the village of Val d'Isère and the steep fertile valley leading up to the Col du Mont-Iseran, which we shall cross next day. We have chosen this spot with care; trees and bushes protect us from all sides. There is nobody to hide from—Mr. Holmes and Queensbridge have gone out for a walk and will not be back till supper—but a certain air of conspiracy is fitting to the occasion. Chalmers is going to read me the poem on which he has been working since he left Rouen, and which he finished last night. It is the longest and most ambitious thing he has so far written. He talks about it first, deprecating, making excuses in advance, then getting excited: "There're one or two bits, perhaps, which come off . . . you'll see . . . my idea really was to . . ." He loses confidence again, his voice drops, he mumbles: "Oh well . . ." At length he clears his throat, grins apologetically: "It's called *Stranger in Spring*. . . ."

> The wind that surges from the wold
>   Crested with cloud and filled
> With groping passion for crude wastes
>   The man has scored and tilled,
> Quiver about the Spring flowers
>   That tremble in the field.
>
> As She goes from the cobble ways
>   And from the echoing town,
> Sunlight is purer than white wine,
>   The hills are pranked with brown,
> The Devil's Bowl is filled with sky
>   Upon a far green down.
>
> Her sudden eyes that brim with flame
>   Of life, are not less clear
> Than those swift stars of sunlight lithe
>   That flit above her hair.

And then it seems her lips are ghosts
    Of shadows that once were.

This is the death of all despair—
    A kiss of Spring at heart,
To rest with her quite secretly
    As she turns to depart.

I think the hills are made with light
    Drawn from a turquoise sky.
And the woodland is thronged with voices
    Of Life; and daws that cry
Seem phantoms of withheld delight
    Made in bright mimicry
Of the unseen, birdlike soul of Spring
    That is eternity.

The wind from wraithlike tarns of sky
    Is a torrent that bears
Music and impulse to the leaves
    Glinting above, and fares
Dimly with her amongst dwarf trees
    Lapped round with low grass spears.

There is a thought that she will long
    To pause tiptoe and creep
Into the brooding, shadowy trees,
    And rest, and go to sleep
So that she does not hear the leaves
    Above her head that weep.

Surely there is no kiss at all
    Deep as this kiss the Spring
Wreathed with all brightness takes away
    From her heart quivering
For joy of the beauty that seems
    In wandering.

And the strayed hound lurks silently
    Under those trees, and lies
Couched with the weevil and the worm,
    Gazing from sheenless eyes,
Where in that latticed gloom of boughs
    The leprous sunlight dies . . .

There is a pause. Then Chalmers says abruptly: "That's
all." Hastily stuffing the papers back into his pocket, he be-

gins to light his pipe with nervous fingers; the mouthpiece between his lips, he mutters: "What do you think of it?"

I forget what words I used. I tell him that this is his best poem and that now I am certain, absolutely convinced, that he is going to be a really great poet, the greatest of our generation. My voice trembles with excitement; I keep my eyes fixed on the roofs of the distant village, because they are full of tears. Chalmers is moved, too. "Do you honestly like it? I'm glad. . . ." After this, we are too happy and excited to say any more. From the top of our little cliff, we gaze into the future. The vision of Chalmers' destiny, on that wonderful afternoon, seems quite impersonal. It is a triumph in which we can both equally share.

There are several more pictures—of dreary Modane, where our luggage, which had been on a trip by itself across the Italian frontier, had to be opened at the Customs; of Briançon, surrounded by Vauban's fortifications, which I couldn't properly admire because I had eaten a bad prawn at a restaurant on the Col du Galibier; of Grenoble, where we stopped only a few hours, *en route* for Paris—but all these are merely old photographs, faded and quite dead. I had lost the first freshness of my interest in the Continent. My British digestion, accustomed to watery junket and school meat, had at length registered the inevitable protest against properly cooked, tasty food; after my return to England I was ill for some weeks. The only two memories I can rescue from our final three days in Paris are of a water-closet without a seat and of a man trying to pull a sword out of a tree. The latter was at the Opéra, during a very long performance of *Die Walküre*, towards the end of which I fell uneasily asleep.

The autumn term which followed this holiday was the twelfth and last of my public school life. Now, for the first time, I had a study of my own, and two fags to keep it clean. The fags were both new boys, their names were Berry and Darling. I caused my friends much amusement whenever I shouted down the passage: "Berry, darling!" or *"Darling Berry!"* Darling was one of the smallest boys in the whole school; his hair stood on end and his voice squeaked. He and Berry were both very intelligent; they used to help me with secretarial work for the school magazine, of which I was literary editor.

During my own first term at the school I had fagged for

26

Ponds, that almost legendary figure whose name I have mentioned already. It was Ponds' lazy, absent-minded benevolence which had made my life as a new boy tolerable and even enjoyable. From the very first moment, when he had found me in his study, seated dolefully upon a suitcase, and had drawled: "Tell me, somebody, who is this *curious* little creature?" my admiring gratitude towards him had known no bounds. "When I have fags of my own," I had often told myself, "I shall treat them as Ponds treated me."

But, alas, I was not Ponds. I was as little fitted for authority as the majority of my fellow study-holders; less so, indeed, than most. Starting with the friendliest intentions, I soon became peevish, resented fancied symptoms of "side," puzzled my unfortunate fags by alternations of good humour and ill temper, and generally behaved like any petty office boss. Study-holders in our house, even when they were not prefects, had the power of caning their fags, and we were rather encouraged to exercise our privilege. One day Darling lost my football boots (he played already in the Second house game, while I myself had never risen above the Third); here, according to precedent, was my sufficient opportunity and excuse. There was an ugly, cold-blooded little ceremony, I used the words "afraid" and "sorry" with an hypocrisy worthy of a grown-up man; then I let him wait three hours—a traditional refinement of torture—through prep and supper; finally I sent for him, told him to bend over a chair and gave him the allowed maximum, three strokes. I don't suppose I hurt him much; next day, of course, the whole thing was elaborately turned into a joke. Nevertheless, a certain confidence had been broken between us, we shared a sense of humiliation like an indecent secret; our relations could never be quite the same again.

I was very busy that term. In addition to my work on the school magazine, I wrote occasional poems, a beginning of a novel and a paper for the literary society on Chivalry in English Literature. The keynote of the paper was anti-industrialism and hurrah for the bold decorative Middle Ages before the machines, when Life (I quoted) was "colour and warmth and light." Suitably polished up, this essay might well be acceptable to the editor of any literary-historical magazine in Germany to-day. I also proposed a motion before the debating society that "in the opinion of this House, patriotism is an obstacle to civilization." We won our motion,

27

thanks chiefly to a discreet speech by Mr. Holmes, who began by agreeing with both sides and went on to lead the House gently round to the reflection that patriotism had been all very well in 1914, but that now we were in 1922 the days of national competition were over, we must work together for co-operation in the future world state. Nearly everybody agreed with him, though there were growls from one or two die-hard members of the staff. Mr. Holmes was lecturing to the civics class that term on the causes of the war and had considerably startled most of us by pointing out that the Central Powers were not the only ones to blame. In the meanwhile, we were getting ready for the Cambridge examinations. I was to go up again in December and try, if possible, to convert my exhibition into a sixty-pound scholarship. Mr. Holmes thought I might manage this, with luck. In any case, however much I disgraced myself, my exhibition would still hold good.

Such was the official half of my life; the other, smaller, more exciting half was nourished by Chalmers' letters. He was up at Cambridge now. "If school was unmitigated hell, then Cambridge is insidious hell! Cambridge is a monster, a blood-supping blasé monster. It attacks you when you are off your guard, and before you know where you are all poetry and individuality have been drained out of you, and you become a motor-bike or history maniac. Beware of the dæmon of history: it is merciless, it casually eats the flesh and heart and leaves the bleaching bones. History, history, hysteria!" There was a great deal of this sort of thing, mixed up with over-generous criticism of my poems (Mr. Holmes once referred to us, in a moment of slight exasperation, as "the mutual admiration society"), exclamations against politicians, the team-spirit and "religious emporiums," and quotations from Baudelaire and Wilfred Owen, who had lately been added to our extremely select pantheon. The letters had neither beginning nor ending; we had abolished both, as being intolerably conventional. Actually, I think, we were still shy—such was the influence of public school convention upon two declared rebels—of using each other's christian names. It was years before I could call Chalmers "Allen" or he could call me "Christopher" without a trace of self-consciousness. We generally finished with a quotation: "Out of the pit that covers me," "O Life, Life, let me breathe!" "Fail not our feast!"; or simply with the word "Amen."

28

Chalmers had peculiarly exciting handwriting—sharply pointed, vivid, impatient, with an occasional romantic flourish;
his poems gained enormously by being read in manuscript.
The mere sight of my address on the envelope would thrill
me in anticipation. I sometimes carried the letter about with
me for hours, waiting for a quiet moment to enjoy it to the
full.

A couple of days before the end of term, the telegram
from Cambridge arrived. I had won an eighty-pound scholarship, my marks were the highest of all the scholars in my
future college; I had, in fact, very nearly repeated the epoch-
making achievement of Browne himself. We were all frankly
amazed. There were more jokes made about Mr. Holmes'
influence than ever, and many speculations as to the amount
of the cheque which had passed between him and the University authorities.

On the last day of term, Mr. Holmes invited me to lunch
at his house. We were both in high spirits yet inclined to be
sentimental, for we were fond of each other in our different,
peculiar ways, and this was a parting. Now that Chalmers
had left, Mr. Holmes meant far more to me than any of my
school contemporaries. I told him this, with many rather
tactless qualifications, for, of course, I was delighted to be
leaving and didn't attempt to conceal my joy. As for Mr.
Holmes himself, he was experiencing, no doubt, that sense
of weariness and depression common to all schoolmasters
when they say good-bye to a favourite pupil. It isn't so much
the pupil himself whom they will miss; what is saddening is
the thought that now they have got to start all over again,
from the beginning, with somebody else. But if Mr. Holmes
felt this, he didn't tell me so; he merely smiled his cold
friendly smile and plied me with claret till I was mildly
drunk and had to rest on his sofa with my feet up. Viewed
from this position, the future seemed very bright indeed. I
told Mr. Holmes that I wanted to be a writer. He agreed,
cautiously, that this might be possible. Then, for the first time,
I confided to him that I didn't want to read History at Cambridge at all. I wanted to do English. "After all," I argued,
"you yourself admit that I must have got my scholarship
chiefly on the English essay. I'm not really an historian at all."
"I k-know you're not," he retorted smiling; and went on to
give me a lecture, half-mocking, half-serious, on the value

of drudgery, the need for breadth, the necessity of getting inside the minds of people differently constituted from myself: "you butterfly, you cobweb, you s-skimmer of other people's cookery!" His advice was to take Part One of the Tripos in History, Part Two in English, if I still wished. "I wouldn't have you miss a single one of the home-truths you'll get from Gorse," he added, gleefully, "you'll wriggle and shed several s-skins and be quite a respectable animal at the end of it; whereas, from the English people, you'll get nothing but a-adulation and d-damnation." He paused, pretended to wipe the perspiration from his forehead. "But I declaim in vain!"

He was right. For Chalmers' voice kept whispering in my ear. I privately decided to write at the earliest possible opportunity and lay my difficulties before the college tutor. I felt perfectly sure I could persuade him to let me have my own way.

That night, in Hall, before the assembled school, the Headmaster referred to the scholarships in the course of his farewell speech. When my turn came to be applauded, a member of the staff, who had hitherto regarded me with marked disapproval, clapped and smiled across at me with special warmth. And Mr. Holmes, who was sitting beside me, bent over and hissed into my ear. "You see? N-nothing succeeds like s-success!"

This, and no phrase from the chapel sermon or my Housemaster's parting pi-jaw, was the message I carried away with me next day, out into the great treacherous flattering world.

CHAPTER II

THE college authorities, considerate as always in such matters, had arranged to give me rooms on the same staircase as Chalmers: his were on the ground floor, mine were on the second. I disliked my sitting-room from the first moment I saw it. It was chilly, bare and high; and the walls had been newly papered and painted, a bright unfriendly brown. My few books huddled together, quite lost in the tall built-in bookcase; and I had no photographs or menu-cards to break the long bleak black line of the mantelpiece. The grate didn't draw properly: the fire was difficult to keep alight and the chimney smoked. There were eight hard, leather-padded brown chairs, none of which I ever used. They had to be ranged along the wall or grouped round the table; making you feel, in either case, that you were surrounded by stiff invisible presences. Altogether, the place was like an old-fashioned dentist's waiting-room.

We preferred to sit downstairs in Chalmers' room, which was low-ceilinged and snug. It seemed to me that Chalmers had strongly impressed his personality upon it; though more by accident than by design, and with a minimum of properties. There were lots of books, of course; the old favourites and the latest acquisitions of his first year—Baudelaire, Poe, Whitman, Owen, Sir Thomas Browne, Donne, Katherine Mansfield, Flaubert, Villon, Tchekhov, Dunbar and the Elizabethans. There were only three pictures: the Dürer engravings —"Melencolia," "St. Jerome" and "The Knight, Death and the Devil." On the mantelpiece were a pair of long-stemmed clay pipes and a little china skull, which Chalmers had seen one day in one of the many curiosity shops of the the town. A big inverted lamp-shade, like a half-pumpkin, filled the room with warm red light. Chalmers hadn't many

31

personal belongings ; but, such as they were, they lay scattered about in the most unlikely places. His untidiness made his two rooms seem homely and inhabited. I recognized this, with admiration and occasional irritation: my own tidiness was hopelessly ingrained—in my sitting-room, even the matchbox had its proper position; a position which Chalmers never failed to disturb. With an absent-mindedness which was too consistent to be entirely unintentional, he would knock out his pipe on to my hearth-rug, catch my pained glance (for I hated to check the flow of our conversation), smile guiltily, mumble an apology, and make the feeblest of efforts to sweep up the mess with his hand. In the end, of course, I had to get out of my chair and tidy things up with my little hearth-brush, under Chalmers' ironical, mock-apologetic eyes. And by the time I had finished, we had both forgotten what it was that we had been talking about.

If we used my sitting-room at all, it was chiefly to escape from intrusions. Chalmers lived in perpetual terror, half sham, half genuine, of the visits of his college friends. At our very first meeting, he confessed to me, rather shamefacedly, that he had been playing soccer and had actually been given his college colours. This season, he added, he was determined not to play at all. Scarcely were the words out of his mouth, when somebody knocked at the door: it was the college captain, smiling, persuasive, very polite, a list in his hand. (One more striking contrast, I reflected, between public school and university: here was the ex-prefect, accustomed to giving orders, having to *ask* people to play football as a favour!) "No," I said aloud, "I was sorry—I'd really no idea when Chalmers would be back. Yes, I'd tell him, of course." When the captain had gone, I went through into the bedroom. Chalmers was hiding under the bed. "Christ!" he gasped, crawling out, "that was a near thing! I suppose this means I shall never be able to use these rooms again." Finally, of course, he was cornered and smilingly badgered into promising to play; but only in two or three of the most important matches.

Then there were his first-year boon companions, Queensbridge, Sargent and Black. Black was "the man with the soul," whom we had noticed but not spoken to during the scholarship examination, two years before. Black had won a scholarship then, but it didn't seem likely that he would keep it after the first part of the Tripos—for, like Chalmers himself, he had done badly in the Mays. He was a rowing man, tall and handsome, with pale innocent blue eyes, and wavy brown hair of the kind which girls admire. I rather liked him, but he didn't like me; finding me affected, highbrow and a bad, because mysterious, influence upon "our Al.". When sober, he was very careful not to show this, for fear of offending Chalmers, to whom he was genuinely and touchingly attached. But it came out, in occasional sarcasms, when he was drunk.

Throughout their first year, these four, surrounded by a group of hearties from the fifteen and the college boat, had spent most of their time together. During the winter, they played poker, dashed round the countryside in Sargent's car, assisted at all the more violent rags and did some dangerous climbs along the neighbouring roofs. In summer, they had taken shopgirls up the river in punts, returned after midnight without their gowns and scrambled back into college over a private garden wall. Chalmers, whatever he tried to pretend to the contrary, had enjoyed these adventures. His noisy hearty friends accepted him without question; he was old Al, our Al, who played soccer and got drunk and ran after the girls ; he was one of the gang. Nobody minded his being a poet—that sort of thing was quite usual up here; even Anderson, the left back, had contributed a sonnet about rose gardens to the College magazine. Literature had its recognized place—as long as you weren't highbrow about it and could play some game as well. Black and his friends rather made fun of the B.M. colleges which tried to be spartan and tough. Even if Al did know which end of the pen Shakespeare used, he was all right —aren't you, Al, old boy? And Al grinned at them faintly as they slapped his back. Black's world was, for Chalmers, a world of escape, like the Pension Dubois at Rouen—escape from shyness, self-consciousness, but not always from "The Watcher in Spanish."

"The Watcher in Spanish" was the latest of our conceits. The phrase came, I believe, from a line in a poem, about: "The Watcher in Spanish cape. . . ." We imagined him as a macabre but semi-comic figure, not unlike Guy Fawkes, or a human personification of Poe's watching raven. He appeared to us, we said, at moments when our behaviour was particularly insincere; one might, for example, be telling a boastful story, or pretending an interest in heraldry, or flattering the wife of a don—and there, suddenly, he would be standing, visible only to ourselves. He made no gesture, never spoke. His mere presence was a sufficient reminder and warning.

33

Mutely, he reminded us that the "two sides" continued to exist, that our enemies remained implacable, beneath all their charming, expensive, scholarly disguises; he warned us never to betray ourselves by word or deed. He was our familiar, our imaginary mascot, our guardian spirit. We appealed to him, made fun of him, tried to deceive him. Often, when we were alone together, we spoke to him aloud. "Come out of that corner!" Chalmers would shout. "You needn't think we can't see you! Now, leave us alone—do you hear? We're busy."

It was the Watcher, we said, who disapproved of my presence at Black's poker parties and vetoed all Ashmeade's invitations to bring Chalmers with me to coffee after Hall; in other words, we were jealous of each other's friends. On the rare occasions when we attempted jointly to entertain, the Watcher immediately put in his appearance; our whole behaviour, when a third party was in the room, became so strained and falsified that we seemed to each other to be acting in a disgraceful kind of charade. Every word, every laugh rang sham as a bad penny, every smile or gesture was an act of treason to our dearest beliefs. As soon as the visitors had gone, our mutual accusations would begin, half in joke, half in earnest. Very soon, we both agreed to keep our respective acquaintances to ourselves.

Chalmers was particularly alarmed by what he regarded as my dangerous weakness for the society of the college "Poshocracy"—a word he had coined to designate the highest of our social circles. In our college, Chalmers pointed out, people were far too subtle to admit openly that they admired titles, Blues, money, good looks or academic successes; they preferred simply to say that a young man was "nice" (or, as we put it, "posh"). A group was therefore formed of all the "nicest" people—each of whom possessed one or more of the required characteristics. "Niceness" was written all over every member of this favoured caste; you heard it in the tones of his voice, it shone from his clear kind eyes, it animated his negligent yet graceful movements, it was tactfully expressed in the colour-scheme of his tie, pullover and socks. We used to watch the Poshocracy from our window as they walked about the court, met, waved gaily, exchanged suitably jolly greetings. "Look, look!" Chalmers would mutter, rubbing his hands together in gleeful ecstasies of hate: "Did you see that?

34

Did you see the way he handed him that book? Look at the way he's kicking that stone! Christ, how *electrically* vile!"

When Chalmers had first arrived at the college, the Poshocracy were prepared to welcome him into their midst. He was "nice" on three counts—a scholar, a footballer and good-looking. Black was "nice," too ; but not *quite* so "nice"—presumably because his public school was socially inferior to ours. Both of them, however, were invited to an inspection coffee party. Neither made a good impression. Black simply could not be bothered with his hosts, and showed it. Chalmers' behaviour was more complicated. He was, he admitted, mildly flattered and even prepared to associate with these people—on his own terms. He advanced a couple of millimetres from his shell, sensed some faint suggestion of an insult (probably imaginary) and immediately withdrew. The Poshocracy, who were no fools, were rather intrigued; this was the first time they had had to deal with a man who actually did not *want* to get to know them, and was yet so clearly eligible for their favours. (Black, I suppose, they dismissed as a mere ill-bred boor ; in any case, he was only a border-liner.) Good-natured, indolently curious, they pursued Chalmers for a little, teasing him with invitations, accepting his obviously insincere excuses with a knowing, forgiving smile. Then they left him to himself —a certified eccentric, not ostracized, perfectly understood. "Chalmers?" they would have murmured, if asked: "Oh yes— the world's nicest man . . . such a pity he's so shy. . . ."

And now, a year later, it was my turn to be dealt with. As senior scholar among the freshmen, I had, at any rate, the right to an inspection, and as it happened, I was quite presentable. I didn't look like a midnight swotter, hadn't pimples or a grammer-school accent, didn't wear boots; further enquiries (exceedingly tactful) disclosed a minor "county" family with the background of an Elizabethan "place." So I was all right— even, perhaps, an agreeable surprise. One invitation led to another.

And really, I secretly thought—whatever Chalmers might say—however disloyal it might be to admit it—the Poshocracy could be very nice indeed. Or so I felt while I was actually with them. Their civilized, flattering laughter went to my head. The truth was, in my heart, I really enjoyed society: I could talk their language, I could make jokes, I could strike the right note—and if the Watcher appeared, well, he was merely an addition to my audience. Later, of course, in the sobering at-

35

mosphere of Chalmers' room, I mimicked and sneered, hypo-
critically describing my sayings and doings as a spy's ruses in
the midst of the enemy camp. I thus enjoyed a repetition of
my social success; for Chalmers laughed too. He didn't suspect me, at first, of the slightest breach of good faith.

But the Poshocracy knew that I was Chalmers' friend, and
it wasn't very long before they began to suggest, in their
kindly way, that I should help to bring him back to the fold.
Couldn't I use my influence? Wouldn't he, perhaps, come
along with me on Thursday night? It would be so nice. "Tell
him we're all very fond of him." Not only did I mention this
invitation to Chalmers himself, I was rash enough to press the
point. "After all, I don't see why you shouldn't. Really, you
behave as if they'd eat you. . . . When you got there, you'd
probably enjoy it." At this, he became angry; we had our
first serious quarrel—a long, heated argument, in the course
of which I maintained that "one's got to cultivate one's social
side"; an unluckily chosen phrase, which he sarcastically
brought up against me on many future occasions. I was angry,
too—with myself, chiefly ; as I was manœuvred, step by step,
into an absurdly false position. I found myself actually defending the Poshocracy against Chalmers' attacks; and finally,
against the very charges I had brought against them, only an
hour earlier, myself. Next morning, peace was tacitly declared.
From that day onwards, my flirtations with the "nice" world
became fewer and fewer. I still attended occasional coffee
parties and play-readings, but always guiltily and with humorous apologies to Chalmers. "Oh yes," he would say, "I'm
well aware I've wrecked your social chances."

The college tutor had sent a very courteous reasonable
reply to my letter. He understood perfectly my position, he
appreciated my frankness, he welcomed the opportunity of
discussing my difficulties. At the same time, he was sorry not
to be able to agree with me. The change I proposed—from
the Historical to the English Tripos—appeared to him to be
not in my own best interests. Further, I must remember that,
as a scholar of the college, mine was a special case; if I had
certain privileges, I had also certain responsibilities. The tradition of the college was against such changes, and he found
himself, unfortunately, unable to decide that the occasion
had come to break with that tradition. After I had taken the
first part of the Tripos, we might, of course, discuss the matter

further. In the meanwhile, he relied upon me not to disappoint the very considerable expectations which my papers in the scholarship examination had aroused.

So that was that. The decision of the college authorities hadn't upset me unduly at the time; for Cambridge was then still remote on the horizon, nearly nine months ahead. But now here I was gowned, seated uneasily on the edge of the chair, reading my first essay aloud to my history tutor, the dreaded Mr. Gorse. The subject of the essay was: "Better England Free than England Sober." I had finished it with some pride: it exactly suited my idea of Mr. Gorse's requirements—snappy, epigrammatic, a bit daring in its language, sprinkled with witticisms borrowed unacknowledged from Mr. Holmes. Only now, for some reason, all my effects seemed to have gone wrong: the verbal fireworks were damp; the epigrams weren't epigrams but platitudes, pompous, painfully naïve, inept and priggish. It was positive misery to have to utter them. I writhed with embarrassment, coughed, made spoonerisms, gabbled through the worst bits with my face averted: "Apart from this consideration, there is no doubt that our own liquor restrictions are demoralizing. . . . The places where it is sold are unpleasant, and the upper classes, disdaining them, repair to their own homes, where they are no longer under the restraining eye of the world, and often fare badly in consequence. . . ." (Heavens, did I really write that? The sweat began to break out on my forehead.) "The French café, with its refinement, its high social status and its atmosphere of harmless gaiety" (Phew) "is as far removed from the English pub as the hotel is from the brothel. . . ."

"How do *you* know," snapped Mr. Gorse, "how far an hotel is removed from a brothel? Very often it *is* a brothel. Go on."

I grinned nervously, and faltered through to the end. The last paragraph was particularly heavy going, because Mr. Gorse had begun to drum with his fingers on the mantelpiece. "Yes, yes . . ." he kept muttering: "Yes, yes . . ." as though his impatience were increasing with every word. "Well," he told me, when, at last, I had finished: "I'll say this for you—it's not the work of an entirely uneducated fool." He paused. I grinned hopelessly; regarding him like a poodle which is going to be kicked. "Look here, Isherwood," he appealed to me abruptly, "don't you yourself agree that it's all tripe?"

Alarming as it was, there was something very attractive

about Mr. Gorse's manner; he was so fidgety, so impetuous, so direct. Pale and fair-haired, his handsome, aggressively intelligent face was like the edge of a very sharp tool. He was still under thirty; and his violent abruptness made him seem younger, less sure of himself, than the smooth-voiced sophisticated undergraduates of the post-war generation, who accepted his lurid comments on their work with polite unruffled mock humility and ever so slightly raised eyebrows. If Mr. Gorse, in his own ferocious way, seemed to like me, it was perhaps chiefly because he was glad to find somebody whom he could so easily reduce to a state of jelly. Oddly enough, he sometimes strongly reminded me of Chalmers.

We both agreed that we liked Gorse the best of the college dons. You could speak openly to him—if you dared; he was a human being. Once, he had said to Chalmers: "Does the history school seem worse to you than working in a bank?" He didn't expect an answer to such questions, they were his form of expressing sympathy. He had been in the trenches as an infantry officer, then joined the Air Force and nearly got himself killed in a crash. He said of the War: "It was bloody, but I'd do it again to-morrow"—a statement one seldom heard in 1923. He was a bad but stimulating lecturer; bad because he over-estimated the knowledge of his audience, and was continually making apologetic references to facts we had never heard of, as "all that stuff they tell you in the little books" or "the things you learnt in the Lower Fourth"; stimulating, because constitutional history was obviously, for himself, a subject of vital and absorbing interest. When he lectured, he was terribly nervous.

I had not been in Cambridge a fortnight before I began to feel with alarm that I was badly out of my depth. The truth, as I now discovered for the first time, was that I was a hopelessly inefficient lecturee. I couldn't attend, couldn't concentrate, couldn't take proper notes. In the great hall of the college, where many of our lectures were held, I could hardly keep my attention down to the subject for thirty seconds at a time; away it drifted, idly, like a child's balloon, around the ring of bent studious faces, then rising, to the enormous windows, to the Holbein over the dais, to the portraits of former Masters and dead notables—a salmon-pink, sneering Orpen, a suave tailored Sargent, a de Laszlo, a Watts—then higher still, to the carved beams and rich-coloured shadows of the famous sixteenth-century roof. And all the while, the clear dry legal voice of the third greatest authority in Europe was explaining to us the exact shade of significance to be attached to a Latin word or phrase in the passage under discussion—page one hundred and forty-seven of Stubbs' *Select Charters*. For me, it was a voice in a nightmare—the perfectly distinct voice speaking a known language which is nevertheless, because of some mysterious curse, totally unintelligible. Here were the precious minutes going by and with them my academic career, my whole future; it was twenty-five minutes to eleven already, and I alone among all my busily scribbling fellow students had not written a single word.

It was now that I truly discovered how much I owed to Mr. Holmes. How adroitly, how tactfully he had hammered knowledge into our dreamy heads. How appetizingly he had served up the driest and stodgiest facts! He had always known which of us had not been following his explanations—a single trained glance at our faces was enough; and at once, tirelessly, without reproaches, he would begin again at the beginning, but from a slightly different angle, with fresh jokes, new epigrams and all sorts of minor variations, lest anybody should be bored. He seldom, if ever, dictated notes directly; yet everything he said was a subtle kind of dictation; his lessons were so well-planned, proceeding so logically from step to step, that note-taking was painlessly easy. The difference between a Holmes lesson and a Cambridge lecture was the difference between an intimate cabaret performance in a Paris *boîte* and a Salzburg festival production by Reinhardt; grave, magnificent, remote. The Reinhardt production was wonderfully impressive, but I missed the back-chat, the encores and the catchy tunes. Questions, of course, were allowed, but to raise one's voice in that majestic room was to claim a part in the whole solemn performance, and nothing I could ever find to say seemed worthy of such a setting. So I just sat there, dull, moony and silent drawing meaningless pictures on an empty page.

During those first few weeks, I worried a good deal about the future. I even made some feverish attempts to pull myself together, to cover the lost ground in my spare time, to copy out other people's notes. Then, by degrees, I ceased to bother at all. Nobody else bothered, why should I? The first part of the Tripos exam. wasn't till 1925; by that time, most likely, we should all be dead. As for the Mays, which was next summer, everyone agreed that it didn't matter, anyhow. And in Cambridge there was so much to distract you from the sordid subject of work. There were the bookshops, where you could read for hours without being disturbed; the curiosity shops which no undergraduate can resist; the tea-shops full of sickly but delicious cakes. There were comic games of squash with a boy from my old preparatory school, and wild night-rides in Sargent's car. There were the flicks with the films which were, even in those days, not silent, because the audience supplied the popping of champagne corks, the puffing of trains, the sound of horses' hooves and the kisses. Above all, there was the private world which Chalmers and I had deliberately created for ourselves, a world which was continually expanding, becoming more absorbing, more elaborate, sharper and richer in detail and atmosphere, to the gradual exclusion of the history school, the Poshocracy, the dons, the rags, the tea-parties, the poker, the play-reading; the whole network, in fact, of personalities, social and moral obligations, codes of behaviour and public amusements which formed the outward structure of our undergraduate lives.

People frequently said to me: "I saw you and Chalmers in the street this morning. What on earth was the joke?" For, when we were together, we were always laughing. The mere tones of Chalmers' voice would start me giggling in anticipation, and I had only to pronounce some quite ordinary word with special emphasis in order to send him into fits. We were each other's ideal audience; nothing, not the slightest innuendo or the subtlest shade of meaning, was lost between us. A joke which, if I had been speaking to a stranger, would have taken five minutes to lead up to and elaborate and explain, could be conveyed to Chalmers by the faintest hint. In fact, there existed between us that semi-telepathic relationship which connects a crossword puzzle-setter with his most expert solvers. Our conversation would have been hardly intelligible to anyone who had happened to overhear it; it was a rigmarole of private slang, deliberate misquotations, bad puns, bits of parody and preparatory school smut:

"Ashmeade's giving a political tea-party to six puss-dragoons from the Union."

"Let's go in and *j'en appelle* it."

"No good. They'd only namby us off. It'd just be quisb."

"What *are* Ashmeade's politics, anyway?"

"He's a lava-Tory."

"I met him, just now. He told me he's reading *The Living Corpse.*"

"*The Living Corpse.* . . . I suppose that was a man who *smoked*?"

Our jokes were usually connected in some way with the college, the Poshocracy and the dons. The dons were, for us, utterly remote and unreal figures, like the bogies in a child's book ; indeed, we were careful to avoid contact with them (excepting Gorse) altogether, in order to maintain more completely our vision of the "two sides," "the combine" directed expressly against ourselves. And, in addition to the actual living dons, we had invented an ideal, imaginary don, the representative of all his kind, to be our special enemy and butt. We named him Laily (which means "loathly")—a word taken from a ballad in the Oxford Book.

> And she has made me the laily worm
> That lies at the fit o' the tree

Laily, or The Worm, soon became a figure as important to our lives as The Watcher in Spanish himself. We referred to him in terms of disgust which were almost affectionate. He was the typical swotter, the book-worm, the academic pot-hunter ; but, at the same time, being eager to succeed with and be accepted by the Poshocracy he was careful to pretend an enthusiasm for athletics and the team spirit. In fact, we contradicted ourselves a good deal in describing him—our own standards and prejudices being, at this time, in a highly confused and contradictory state.

Our conception of "the Combine" and our burlesque cult of the Sinister coloured the most trivial incidents of our everyday life. We were psychic tourists, setting out to discover a metaphysical University City. Everywhere, we encountered enemy agents. We recognized them instantly, by the discreetly threatening tones of their voices. One afternoon, I was buying some clothes at a draper's. "This tie's rather nicer," I said. And the shopman, with what we later described as a "reptilian sneer," answered smilingly: "Yes—they're *all* rather nicer. . . ." There was a college waiter who murmured into one's ear, as he took the order: "Most *certainly,* sir." This man seemed positively fiend-like: he must surely be an important spy. Our enemies, we liked to imagine, were perfectly well aware of our activities ; they knew that we alone, of all the undergraduates in Cambridge, had seen through their tremendous and imposing bluff. Therefore, in due time, we should be dealt with. But there was no hurry. For the present, they contented themselves with warning us, through the mouths of their myriad underlings, that we had better be careful, we were observed, we were only here on sufferance. Chalmers swore that he had seen a servant leave a pair of cleaned shoes on the steps of the college chapel: "That's their headquarters." One evening, as we were strolling along Silver Street, we happened to turn off into an unfamiliar alley, where there was a strange-looking, rusty-hinged little old door in a high blank wall. Chalmers said: "It's the doorway into the Other Town."

This idea of "The Other Town" appealed to us greatly; for it offered a way of escape from Cambridge altogether. It was much more exciting than our attempts to dramatize the prosaic figures of the dons. Here was a world which the dons didn't even dream existed, although, we said, it was right in their very midst. "The Other Town" began as an extremely vague, mystical conception, emanating from a few romantic-sinister phrases. Exactly like two children, we pretended to each other to know far more about it than we actually said; each new improvisation was tacitly accepted as a statement of existing fact. To admit that we were merely playing a sophisticated kind of nursery game would, of course, have made the game itself impossible. So we capped each other's fantastic inventions—drawing, for the furniture of our private fairy-story world, on memories of *Alice in Wonderland*, Beatrix Potter and Grimm, and on the imagery of Sir Thomas Browne, Poe and the ballads. We examined, with new interest, the three Dürer engravings in Chalmers' room. *Melencolia* specially excited us. We speculated endlessly as to the significance of the ladder, the bell, the tablet with its curious signs and figures, the sinister-looking instrument sticking out from beneath the angel's skirts, in the right-hand bottom corner. What was the meaning of the enormous star or sun, blazing with immense beams under the rainbow, in a black sky? How should one understand the inscription on the wings of the small flying dragon? Was it "Melencolia One" or "Melencolia, I"? Needless to say, we disdained the standard works of art criticism which could, no doubt, have answered all these questions. How could such books tell you anything worth knowing? They had been written by dons.

"The Other Town" could best be visited by night. So every evening, after supper, we wandered the cold foggy streets, away from the lights and the shops, down back alleys to the water's edge. We leant over clammy stone parapets, in a state of trance-like fascination, auto-hypnotized by the tones of our own voices and the ink-black movement of the stream. Sometimes, we dropped pennies into the water. One evening, I happened to read aloud the name under a fluttering gas-lamp: "Garret Hostel Bridge." "The Rats' Hostel!" Chalmers suddenly exclaimed. We often conversed in surrealist phrases of this kind. Now we both became abnormally excited: it seemed to us that an all-important statement had been made. At last, by pure accident, we had stumbled upon the key-words which expressed the inmost nature of the Other Town. "The Rats' Hostel," we kept repeating to each other, as we hurried back to our rooms to discuss this astonishing revelation.

During the days that followed, "The Rats' Hostel" became gradually defined in our minds as a name for a certain atmosphere, a genre: the special brand of medieval surrealism which we had made our own. (I use the term "surrealism" simply for the purpose of explanation: we had, of course, no idea that a surrealist movement already existed on the Continent. Had we known this—such was our indiscriminate horror of all "movements"—we should most probably have abandoned the Rats' Hostel altogether.) Soon we began to describe as "rats" any object, animal, scene, place or phrase which seemed connected, however obscurely, with our general conception of the "Rats' Hostel," "Rats" were, of course, the entire menagerie of Dürer—the skinny greyhound, the fat pussy-like lion, the serpents entwined in Death's crown, the lizard, the horned and snouted Devil, the gentle-eyed, crafty-looking horse—and all his emblems—the hour-glass, the suspended pumpkin, the scales, the lodestone, the compasses and the skull. Graveyards were "rats" and very old gnarled trees, and cave mouths overhung with ivy, and certain Latin phrases, like: "*Rursus ad astra feror.*" In fact, we used the new word more and more loosely and indiscriminately, until it came to mean, simply, "romantic" or "quaint."

At the height of our "Rats' Hostel" phase, Chalmers wrote a poem which contains some typical examples of our private vocabulary:

> You who must ponder cause and act
> Historian, from the quag of fact
> Search out, propound a cause for this—

The cross of life we bear who miss
Life's truth, and grope with baffled hands
About a stage none understands.

It is an old word how the door
Has closed on other mimes before,
And how time counterchecks man's jest,
And stops the jolly lips with pest,
And how the blague of splendid state
Is hushed beyond the wormhouse gate;
Death is a saw men comprehend,
A truth no history can mend.
But for our pain propound a cause.
We should be glad of nature's laws,
And take, unquestioning, this crust
Of various life, this freak of dust.
We should have mind to mark the gleam
In the strong chaos of time's stream,
And in this hubbub and this night
Glimpse the unapparent light. . . .

It is an old word how clowns pass
To a green bridewell under grass.
Search out, propound a cause for this—
The cross of life we bear who miss
Life's truth, and grope with baffled hands
About a stage none understands.

As the "Rats' Hostel" was our own discovery and property,
so it followed that its denizens were our natural allies. Our
enemies were their enemies. If we pretended to believe that
Laily and his colleagues were plotting day and night against
us, we said also that, very soon, the powers of the Hostel
would counter-attack. Chalmers made a ballad which began:

About the middle of night, a Thing with fins
Came to reprove the Tutor for his sins . . .

(The rest, unfortunately, is not printable. And it wasn't merely a gang of medieval bogies that was on our side ; we claimed
the support of the ghosts of our favourite writers, particularly
of Wilfred Owen, Katherine Mansfield and Emily Brontë.
These three ("Wilfred, Kathy and Emmy," as we called them)
seemed in some way specially connected with our idea of the
Rats' Hostel. We talked about them as if they were personal

44

friends, wondered what they would have said on certain occasions, how they would have behaved, what advice they would have given us. One thing we never for a moment doubted: that they would have loathed Cambridge and all its works.

Looking back, I think that those first two University terms have been amongst the most enjoyable parts of my whole life. I had sufficient money, and no worries and as long as I could be together with Chalmers, which was all day and most of the night, the word boredom didn't exist. I was in a continuous state of extreme mental excitement. Every idea we discussed seemed startling and brilliantly new. My official education was, it is true, at a standstill: but Chalmers was educating me all the time. Under his influence, I began to read the poetry I had been pretending for years to admire. I also started to take, mildly and gingerly, to alcohol. The icy layers of my puritan priggishness, which were thicker far than he ever suspected, had begun, very slowly, to thaw.

It seems odd now to think of the two of us, so excited, so passionately self-absorbed in that little fog-bound room, thirteen years ago—declaiming poetry, jumping on the table, shouting *"J'en appelle!"* appealing to Wilfred or the Watcher in Spanish, keeping a journal of our imaginary lives called *The Diary of Two Shapes,* leaving on each other's breakfast-tables a series of indecent stories about Laily and the dons, in which we, the narrators, figured as "Mr. Hynd" and "Mr. Starn"—odd, when one remembers that this was the winter of Hitler's Munich *Putsch,* of Mussolini's final campaign against the democrats, of the first English Labour Government, of Lenin's death. Hitler's name was, I suppose, then hardly known to a dozen people in all Cambridge. Mussolini was enjoying a certain popularity: rugger and rowing men, at this epoch, frequently named their terriers "Musso." The Labour Government and all its works were, for ourselves, comprehended in the withering word "politics" and therefore automatically dismissed as boring and vile. As for Lenin, he was a vaguely exotic figure, labelled, along with Trotsky, in our hazy minds as an "anarchist," and therefore worthy of mild benevolence. I think that, if we had seen his photograph, with the short stabbing beard and the Mongolian eyes, we might even have patronizingly pronounced him "rats."

All this time, by fits and starts, I had been writing away at a novel—"*the* novel," I might almost call it ; for it was much less a work of art than a symptom—of a certain stage of pubic development in a member of a certain class, living in a certain country, and subjected to a certain system of education. *Lions and Shadows* was, in fact, a very typical specimen of the "cradle-to-coming-of-age" narrative which young men like myself were producing in thousands of variations, not merely in England, but all over Europe and the United States. It was based, of course, upon a day-dream about my Youth— *le vert paradis,* from which I felt myself, as did my great army of colleagues, to be hopelessly and bitterly excluded. Such novels were written in equally large numbers prior to 1914, but with this difference: we young writers of the middle 'twenties were all suffering, more or less subconsciously, from a feeling of shame that we hadn't been old enough to take part in the European war. The shame, I have said, was subconscious: in my case, at any rate, it was suppressed by the strictest possible censorship. Had I become aware of it and dared to bring it up to the light, to discuss it, to make it the avowed motif of my story, *Lions and Shadows* would have ceased to be a curiosity for the psycho-analyst and become, instead, a genuine, perhaps a valuable, work of art. But I didn't. And thousands of others didn't, either.

The title was taken from a passage in *Fiery Particles,* by C. E. Montague (himself pre-eminently a writer of war stories): "arrant lovers of living, mighty hunters of lions or shadows . . ." So far as I know, it has never been used on the cover of a published book: I hit upon it with a lot of pride. Actually, it would have been hard to discover a less suitable name for my novel. It was simply an emotional, romantic phrase which pleased me, without my consciously knowing why, because of its private reference to something buried deep within myself, something which made me feel excited and obscurely ashamed.

This feeling of guilty excitement, now I come to think about it, can also be explained. (I am only speaking for myself now. It may be that my readers, even those whose locked study drawers or lumber-rooms contain similar manuscripts, may find what follows quite meaningless or remote from their own experience.) Like most of my generation, I was obsessed by a complex of terrors and longings connected with the idea "War." "War," in this purely neurotic sense, meant The Test. The Test of your courage, of your maturity, of your sexual prowess: "Are you really a Man?" Subconsciously, I believe, I longed to be subjected to this test; but I also dreaded failure.

I dreaded failure so much—indeed, I was so certain that I *should* fail—that, consciously, I denied my longing to be tested, altogether. I denied my all-consuming morbid interest in the idea of "war." I pretended indifference. The War, I said, was obscene, not even thrilling, a nuisance, a bore.

In *Lions and Shadows* the War is hardly mentioned. Some of the older characters get involved in it, but their experiences are dismissed in a couple of paragraphs. The hero, Leonard Merrows, is still a preparatory schoolboy when the Armistice is signed. He is due to enter his public school, "Rugtonstead," in 1919. Then, quite suddenly, he gets rheumatic fever and is ill for several months. The doctor says his heart has been strained. "Rugtonstead" is out of the question. Leonard must stay at home and have a private tutor. His disappointment and despair know no bounds. He becomes quite hysterical. Several chapters are devoted to describing his visions of the paradise he has missed. Boys whom he meets during the holidays ask him which school he is at: he lies, then admits the truth, and is "bitterly ashamed." Later (and these are depicted as his worst, basest moments) he even comes to have a sneaking feeling of relief that he didn't go to "Rugtonstead" after all: it is so comfortable at home, and then—perhaps he would have been a failure!

Thus it was that "War" dodged the censor and insinuated itself into my book, disguised as "Rugtonstead," an English public school. But here we enter upon further complications. I myself had been to a public school. I knew, or had known while I was there, that public-school life wasn't, in my heroic sense, a "test." It was a test, if you like, of social flexibility, of a capacity for "getting on" with one's contemporaries, of slyness, animal cunning, criminal resource—but certainly not of your fundamental "Manhood" or the reverse. I *had* known all this: did I know it now?

No, I did not. I was rapidly forgetting the inconveniently prosaic truth about my old school. I was deliberately forgetting, because "war," which could never under any circumstances be allowed to appear in its own shape, needed a symbol—a symbol round which I could build up my daydreams about "The Test." Gradually, in the most utter secrecy, I began to evolve a cult of the public-school system. It was no good, of course, pretending that my own school career had been in any sense romantic, heroic, dangerous, epic—that wasn't necessary. I built up the daydream of an heroic school career in which the central figure, the dream I, was an austere young prefect, called upon unexpectedly to captain a "bad" house, surrounded by sneering critics and open enemies, fighting slackness, moral rottenness, grimly repressing his own romantic feelings towards a younger boy, and finally triumphing over all his obstacles, passing the test, emerging—a Man. Need I confess any more? How, in dark corners of bookshops, I furtively turned the pages of adventure stories designed for boys of twelve years old? No illustration was too crudely coloured, no yarn too steep for my consuming guilty appetite. How, behind locked doors, I exercised with a chest expander, bought after nightfall, with precautions such as a murderer might observe in purchasing his weapon? I went out of my way to tell the shopman that it was for my younger brother.

Soon, the dream was vivid enough to risk comparison with the reality. I joined a party which was to visit my old school in Sargent's car. We arrived late on a grey spring afternoon and left again at midnight. I did not see Mr. Holmes. As we rushed towards Cambridge through the early hours before dawn along deserted roads, I remembered, with voluptuous excitement, the narrow dingy little studies, the bare wash-room, the iron stairs, and certain lamplit faces. The transformation was now complete. The reality was lost in the dream. It is so very easy, in the mature calm of a library, to sneer at all this homosexual romanticism. But the rulers of Fascist states do not sneer—they profoundly understand and make use of just these phantasies and longings. I wonder how, at this period, I should have reacted to the preaching of an English Fascist leader clever enough to serve up his "message" in a suitably disguised and palatable form? He would have converted me, I think, inside half an hour—provided always that Chalmers hadn't been there to interfere.

Needless to say, I avoided the whole subject in our conversations together. Chalmers had a way of smiling, faintly but acidly, puffing at his pipe and saying nothing. I hated this smile: it deflated my most extravagant enthusiasms in a moment. Even if I had tried to explain, I don't think he would have understood. The idea of "The Test" would have seemed to him amusingly neurotic or just meaningless. In these matters, he was much more adult than myself.

I had shown him the manuscript of *Lions and Shadows* two or three times; and he had seemed impressed, even excited by it. What impressed him was really, I think, not the literary merit but the extreme slickness of some of the passages; for *Lions and Shadows* is, as I look through it again, astonishingly slick. Chalmers envied my fatal facility for pastiche—of which he himself was luckily incapable: pastiche of Hugh Walpole, of Compton Mackenzie, of E. F. Benson. I churned it out, as smooth as butter—arch, pretty, competent, quaint.

When Leonard Merrows reviewed his childhood he seemed to turn over the pages of an antique book whose legend was often incomprehensible and whose pictures, though brightly coloured, were few.

Therein he saw his home—a long white house over which the elms tossed their spangled shadows. A house surrounded by its wild garden, where the paths were greener than the lawns, and flowers and weeds grew side by side. Tiles had fallen from the coach-house roof, into a paved yard where dandelions filled the crevices. Rats infested the hay-barn and the ruined pig-sties. Down by the river, where there was a gap in the garden wall, the meadow had flowed through like a tide, in wave after wave of poppies. And, beyond, the river itself slipped by, plucked idly at the spinning weed and glided on, under the bridge, past the mill, past the island where the cripples went to be cured, over the foaming rapids and farther yet, past a thousand mysterious places, into the West. . . .

The house itself was old and rambling. In the front hall and on the staircase which mounted in easy flights under a glass dome, the faded portraits of ancestors, cracked and darkened, were hung. One in particular had impressed itself deeply on Leonard's imagination. When very young, he had first noticed that strange proud lady with her white face and dark staring eyes, and thereafter he had often paused before her frame of tarnished gilt to stare seriously back. . . .

A couple of years later, when Chalmers used to visit me in London, we seldom passed the day without reading from one or other of the four thick typescript files of *Lions and Shadows*. Such readings were, for myself, orgies of sheer masochism. At each fresh "quisb" (a standard word in our vocabulary, correspondingly roughly to the terms "shy-making," and "shaming" later employed by the Mayfair society world) we writhed in our chairs, prodded each other in the ribs or jumped up and danced about the room. Then the "quisb" would be mercilessly pounced upon, vivisected, analysed:

" 'To stare *seriously* back' . . . Why is that so disgustingly sham?"

"Yes, let's get to the bottom of this . . . Why is it?"

"Well, I think what makes me want to vomit is the suggestion that children are *serious*. . . ."

"No, no, old boy, you're on the wrong track . . . I see it now: it's something far worse. . . . The whole point is: why *shouldn't* children be serious? Why does it have to be mentioned at all?"

"My God, I believe you're right. . . ."

"You see, it's the Grown-up speaking—that's what's so vile . . . He's standing there and interpreting all Leonard's sensations for us—like some bitch of a woman at a children's party . . . He's saying: 'The dear little fellow's *so serious*!' "

"Faugh. . . ."

And so on. Often, no doubt, our criticisms were captious, far-fetched and unjust; but for myself, at any rate, as the squirming author, they were as brutally stimulating as a Russian bath. However, all that was still in the future. At present, *Lions and Shadows* was only three-quarters finished; and the passages I have quoted seemed to me, privately, so beautiful that, in re-reading them, I sometimes found my eyes were full of tears.

During my third term at Cambridge, Chalmers and I saw less of each other. There were several reasons for this. Chalmers was now extremely busy. He had the first part of the Tripos examination before him; and he was working on a poem for the Chancellor's Medal. The authorities (with Mr. Holmes, probably, behind them), had persuaded him to enter for this prize. In fact, the persuasion had been very nearly an order: Chalmers was expected to do something to justify his reputation as a literary man. The subject of 1924 was "Buddha." Chalmers set to work with every possible ironic reservation and the Watcher stationed permanently at his elbow; but soon, I think he began to enjoy himself. When I praised certain passages, he admitted that he'd put them in "just to show those swine." Meanwhile, we prepared our minds for all eventualities. If Chalmers won the Medal—well, it was a disgrace he shared with Tennyson: if he failed to win it, there was always the precedent of Rupert Brooke, who had been defeated by an embryo don. As for the "Combine," their methods of intrigue were so tortuous and obscure that nobody could say in advance whether it would best serve their purposes to snub Chalmers or to honour him.

Meanwhile, our interest in our private world had somewhat lapsed. "The Other Town" was essentially a winter fantasy. It was invisible by daylight; and now the evenings were drawing out. The Rats' Hostel tourist season was over for the summer. But I think my chief motive for seeing less of Chalmers was a feeling of guilt. Wasn't I betraying him, hourly, in my thoughts?

Wasn't all my dallying with *Lions and Shadows* and these public-school daydreams an act of high treason to Wilfred, to Kathy, to Emmy, to the Rats' Hostel and everything it meant to us both? Not that I ever admitted this, even to myself. Whenever we met, we conversed in the same slang and made the familiar jokes; only the words seemed to have lost some of their power and flavour.

My "war" complex now brought me to a sensational decision: I would buy a motor-bicycle. Chalmers, when he heard of it, made no comment: he lit his pipe with an acid smile. The Poshocracy were much intrigued: Isherwood becomes a hearty—here was a quaint new pose. I could have killed them all. I felt dreadfully silly. But there was no backing out, now. With the expert assistance of Sargent and Queensbridge, I chose the machine, a 1924 model A.J.S. The college tutor, to whom I had to go for permission, remarked: "Don't let it keep you from your work for the Mays." He, at any rate, didn't seem to find anything comic or neurotic in my purchase. I felt quite a wave of gratitude towards him as I left the room.

"The Test" had now transformed itself into a visible metal contraption of wheels, valves, cogs, chains and tubes, smartly painted black. There was no avoiding it any more. It was legally and morally mine. I was obliged to visit it at least once daily in its garage and take it out for a ride. How I loathed and enjoyed those rides! The street outside the garage was narrow and full of traffic. My departure was always a moment of sheer terror: no sooner had I released the grip of the clutch than I seemed to shoot forward like a bullet, cleaving my way through wavering crowds of push-cyclists. Three or four experiences of this kind were enough for my nerves; I basely took to walking the A.J.S. as far as the corner of the nearest turning, a broad unfrequented side-road leading right out of the town, where I had plenty of room to mount and wobble. I thus began to fail the Test almost before it had begun.

Out on the long arrow-straight stretches of the Newmarket Road it was glorious. I shouted and sang to myself and rode quite fast, at more than three-quarter throttle. Then the exhilaration of the spring air would overcome my caution; I would open her flat out. I don't suppose, even then, that the bike did more than fifty-five; but it was more than enough for me. I clung on, horribly scared, with the wind screaming in my ears: I wasn't allowed to reduce speed until I had counted up to a hundred, at least. Once I went into a bad wobble and very nearly crashed. I was so shaken that, when I got back into the town, I dismounted and wheeled the machine nearly a quarter of a mile, bending, every few yards, to peer and frown at the engine, so that passers-by should think it was out of order.

My "social side" was, again, under cultivation. But this time it wasn't the Poshocracy. I had got to know a man from another college, named East. He had straw-coloured hair, horn-rimmed spectacles, a receding chin and a mild, diffident, attractive voice. Together with a couple of other undergraduates, he had just founded a Cambridge Film Club. I became a member. I had always been fascinated by films—ever since the pre-war days in Ireland when, at the town's first tiny cinema, I had never missed a single "Western" or one instalment of the enormous serial about a lady detective who wore a mask and black tights and lived in a house where, at the touch of a lever, all the doors and windows automatically opened and shut, and the staircase folded up like a concertina when the master criminal and his gang were half-way to the top. I was a born film fan. Chalmers was inclined to laugh at my indiscriminate appetite for anything and everything shown on a screen. He pointed out, quite truly, that as soon as I was inside a cinema I seemed to lose all critical sense: if we went together, I was perpetually on the defensive, excusing the film's absurdities, eagerly praising its slightest merits. The reason for this had, I think, very little to do with "Art" at all; I was, and still am, endlessly interested in the outward appearance of people—their facial expressions, their gestures, their walk, their nervous tricks, their infinitely various ways of eating a sausage, opening a paper parcel, lighting a cigarette. The cinema puts people under a microscope: you can stare at them, you can examine them as though they were insects. True, the behaviour you see on the screen isn't natural behaviour; it is acting, and often very bad acting, too. But the acting has always a certain relation to ordinary life; and, after a short while, to an *habitué* like myself, it is as little of an annoyance as Elizabethan handwriting is to the expert in old documents. Viewed from this standpoint, the stupidest film may be full of astonishing revelations about the tempo and dynamics of everyday life: you see how actions look in relation to each other; how much space they occupy and how much time. Just as it is easier to remember a face if you imagine its two-dimensional reflection in a mirror; so, if you are a novelist and want to watch your scene taking place visibly before you, it is simplest to project it on to an imaginary screen. A practised cinema-goer will be able to do this quite easily.

One of our first lecturers at the new Film Club was the producer, George Pearson. He invited us all to visit him at the Lasky Studios in Islington, where he was making a film called *Reveille*. I went, during the Easter Vac., with another member of the Club named Pembroke Stephens. Arriving early, we were hurried along passages and up and down staircases into a large and wildly disordered dressing-room. "You'll have to look sharp," said our guide. "The crowd's been on the set half an hour already." With this, he left us. "Good God!" I said to Stephens, "does he mean we've got to *act*?" Already a wardrobe man had appeared with two bundles: "Get into these and look slippy!" There was no time for coy hesitations. Within three minutes I was a midshipman; Stephens wore the uniform of a Canadian officer. He was much more collected than myself; methodically, he began to make himself up from a box which lay open in front of the mirror. Wildly and vaguely, I applied some colour to my cheekbones, smearing it over with tan powder: my face, when I had finished, looked like a burst poached egg. While I was still unhappily examining the effect, another man appeared, seized us both by the elbows and rushed us down more stairs, into the studio itself.

The studio was the Savoy Hotel on Armistice Night, 1918. This was all any of our fellow-guests could tell us. They were very friendly and chatty, laughed at my make-up, complained of their corns, wondered if coffee would be brought round before lunch. The ladies were all in evening dress, the men mostly in uniform: Christian names were general and everybody was addressed "dearie" or "darling". Somebody had heard that we were going to work late. Somebody else said no; Bill had told him they'd knock off at five—there were half a dozen close-ups on the evening schedule. Meanwhile, high above our heads, the electricians went to and fro, balancing dangerously on their narrow plank gangways, shouting to each other: "A bit more round with number four . . . kill that spot . . ." The carpenters were hammering away in the background and the painters were putting the finishing touches to the hollow wooden pillars, turning them, with expert dabs of the brush, into veined marble. There was more noise than in a big railway station.

Noise was my chief impression of the day. It ceased only for a few moments at a time, when the assistant director blew his whistle for silence and Pearson, looking ill and exhausted, in a great-coat, told us what he wanted us to do. Mostly we had to dance, while the people seated at the surrounding tables pelted us with balloons and streamers. Round and round we went. As we passed close to the platform on which the camera was mounted, our faces jerked into smiles of joy which became more and more mechanical as the day wore on. The assistant director bawled through his megaphone; the orchestra, with superhuman endurance, repeated its fox-trot tune. By lunch, which we ate standing crowded round the canteen counter, my feet were like lead; by six o'clock in the afternoon they were aching and flat as fish. I had one big moment: together with a dozen others, I was told to descend a flight of steps, drunkenly, my arms round two girls' necks. This was a close shot: I must have been clearly recognizable. Needless to say, it was cut out of the finished picture.

Our day ended at 10 p.m. With the others, I limped to the pay-desk and was given twenty-four shillings. It was the first money I had ever earned in my life, and certainly the last I shall ever earn as a film actor. Pembroke Stephens fared very differently. His tall handsome figure had been noticed by the sharp eyes of the casting director. A few months later Pearson made a film called *Satan's Sister* in which the hero is an English undergraduate who goes out to the tropics. Very sensibly, Pearson decided to get a real undergraduate to play the part: to the envy of us all, he took Stephens with him to the West Indies. The film was duly shot and released. Pearson's choice was justified: Stephens was excellent. In fact, he is probably the most convincing undergraduate who has ever appeared on the screen.

June came, and with it the Mays examinations. My artificially sustained sang-froid didn't desert me until the very end. I had twenty-four hours of panic, and read constitutional history all the afternoon in a punt. When I went into the examination room I had nothing in my head but a few fading memories of Mr. Holmes' lessons. Piously invoking his aid, I sat down and unscrewed my pen.

I got a Two I—a feat which I have always regarded as remarkable, almost miraculous. The college authorities could not, of course, be expected to see it in this light: the tutor's letter, though lenient, was mildly pained. How was he to know that, throughout the academic year, I had barely opened a book?

In the Tripos, Chalmers and Black both got Thirds. It was the end of poor Black: his scholarship was taken away. Chalmers was forgiven. He had won the Chancellor's Medal. At a special ceremony, soon after the beginning of the Long Vac. he was obliged to return to Cambridge and read his poem aloud. I wanted to be present. Chalmers forbade me, on pain of losing his friendship for ever. But the Watcher, no doubt, occupied a front seat.

CHAPTER III

PHILIP LINSLEY lived in North Kensington, away out at the far end of Ladbroke Grove: my home was on the Kensington Road, only a few hundred yards from the bridge which crosses the railway to Olympia. We visited each other regularly, during the Long Vacation, two or three times a week.

I liked being with Philip. He was chronically unhappy, and always ready to talk endlessly and amusingly about his troubles. He made me feel wealthy, lucky and successful, as indeed, in comparison with him, I was. Philip was at a crammer's, preparatory to entering the medical school of a big London hospital. He loathed the crammer's, loathed chemistry and physics, didn't want to become a doctor. What he did want was to become a brilliantly successful society novelist and man-about-town, perpetually in full evening dress, surrounded by beautiful and expensive mistresses. Symptoms of these ambitions had been already apparent in his school library opus, *Donald Stanton*. But *Donald Stanton* had been abandoned long ago. Philip was already three-quarters of the way through a much larger and more ambitious novel of society life. He wrote with astonishing ease and speed, very neatly, on enormous ruled sheets of paper like the pages of a ledger, hardly ever erasing a word. He would usually be writing as I entered his gloomy basement room, which was hung with pictures of favourite film stars. But he would rise at once, never in the least put out, delighted to see me—short, pale, stout, dapper, with faultlessly brushed hair, dazzling white teeth, spotless cuffs and hands. The cigarettes would be produced: usually from some new patent box or specially designed case—Philip had a mania for gadgets; especially if

56

the shopman could contrive to hint that this particular novelty was in favour with the Bright Young People—and the invariable question and answer would be exchanged:

"Well, boy—how's life?"

"Life? You call this *Life*? Ha . . . my God! You may well ask——!"

Philip could be very funny when he described the crammer's. He was a first-rate mimic. He imitated his fellow pupils and treated me to samples of their conversation. The height of their sexual daring was, he said, to ask a strange girl at the Palais for a tango. If one of them had performed this feat, he boasted about it afterwards for days. "It's not," said Philip, "that I grudge them their simple pleasures, God knows. . . . But it's the ghastly *sordidness* of it all. . . . One could simply lie down and weep. . . ." Philip's own amours were hardly more enterprising, it is true; but his intentions, at any rate, were of the worst. At the moment, there was a girl named Eva whom he'd kissed once in a taxi, coming home from a dance. Nothing particular had followed the kiss, but, when next they met, Philip had looked at her "in a certain way," and she had looked back: an understanding, he felt certain, had been established between them. (He demonstrated this special glance for my benefit: it was a sideway squint delivered almost in profile, followed by a slight movement of the left eyebrow.) For several weeks we both waited, in almost equal suspense, for Eva to give "the sign." Meanwhile, Philip made all possible preparations—from buying a patent scented mouth-wash to sending me on a delicate errand to a shop in Soho, whose window prominently displayed *The Works of Aristotle*. But the only sign Eva did finally give was to become engaged to a bank clerk. Philip took his defeat like the popular novelist he was one day to become: "Poor fools," he murmured, "one can't even be angry. . . . I suppose I'm born to be a cuckold. . . ."

With Philip, I felt always perfectly at home. His endless succession of little chills, twinges of rheumatism, worries about his health (twice, already, he had been seriously ill with rheumatic fever) were, somehow, very endearing. He understood perfectly my complex about "War" and "The Test." He himself did exercises night and morning: he was terribly concerned at the prospect of becoming fat. He wanted, of course, to be tall, lean, angular, saturnine, and struggled desperately against the plumpness which was his essential good-nature, his saving, endearingly vulgar touch. He was generous and absurdly extravagant with his small allowance—and quite rightly, for the least whiff of luxury gave him pleasure out of all proportion to its cost: a stall at a theatre or a cup of tea in a really smart café would compensate him for a whole penniless week. One of our favourite amusements was pretending to be very rich. Wearing our best clothes, we would saunter down Bond Street, pausing at every second shop, entering a watchmaker's to enquire the price of a gold waterproof wrist-watch, turning up our noses at a selection of seven-and-sixpenny ties, choosing the most expensive tobacconist's to buy a small packet of cheap cigarettes.

Two tastes we had in common—a passion for cinema-going and an endless pleasure in walking about the London streets. Particularly, we were fascinated by the great lost decaying districts, where the fly-blown respectability of the lower middle class clings to its dreary outposts against the slums: Pimlico, Camden Town, West Kensington, Notting Dale. Then there were the areas dedicated to favourite novels: *Sinister Street* shed a glamour over Sinclair Road, *Riceyman Steps* lent atmosphere to Mount Pleasant; Wapping and Limehouse, at first glance so disappointing, achieved mystery and danger when seen through the Chinese spectacles of Thomas Burke. But for myself, at this time London was much more than a sociological pageant or a complex of literary associations. It was the only big city I really knew, and so it was a synthesis of all big cities; it fed my place-romanticism and my boundless dreams of travel. From the shapes of familiar buildings my fancy caught hints of Moscow, Budapest, Vienna; glancing down side streets, I had glimpses of Rio, Venice, New York. Chance meetings, faces seen for an instant from the top of a bus, a voice calling at night from a darkened house, could pigment the whole neighbourhood: henceforward, that square was indelibly evil; always, when I walked along this crescent, I should experience a slight but delicious nausea of sexual desire. Needless to say, I had initiated Philip into the cult of the "Other Town." On our walks, we found plenty of examples of the sinister and the "rats"—a notice: "Work done with cart and horses"; an illuminated sign over a Salvation Army meeting house down by the river: "Blood and Fire"; a strangely ecclesiastical-looking building standing among the railway lines on the way to Wembley, which we named "The Engines' Chapel." This was the summer of the Wembley Exhibition. Whenever we had enough money, we visited the amusement park; preferably in the evenings, for darkness and the coloured lights made the switchbacks seem doubly thrilling. One of our games was to try and read aloud to each other from a newspaper while tearing up and down the slopes and whizzing round the curves of the Giant Racer: to do this continuously was almost impossible, because the speed took away your breath.

Towards the end of the Long Vac., I sold my motor-bicycle. In London traffic, it was merely dangerous; and I had ceased to get a neurotic pleasure out of being afraid of it. Once, skidding on a wet road, I had fallen off a few yards in front of a lorry (I remember the look of its starting-handle to this day) and had narrowly escaped the wheels. And, before this, there had been a humiliating trip to the New Forest, with two motor-cycling school friends and their girl cousins. One of the girls had insisted on riding pillion behind me along a bumpy forest track; we had crashed, and she, not I, had been hurt. Everybody was very nice about the accident, but I noticed, or imagined, contemptuously pitying glances; and, two days later, received, at my own request, an urgent telegram from London, recalling me home. Philip did much to soothe my damaged self-esteem by assuring me that he, personally, wouldn't dare to mount the A.J.S. for all the money you could offer; much less ride it through the streets. But I no longer needed his consolation. "War," for the moment, was at a discount. I had failed the Test, and knew it, and was, for the time being, comfortably and ignobly resigned.

So the motor-bicycle was succeeded by a small thick, strongly bound manuscript book: I had decided to keep a journal. It was to be modelled upon Barbellion's *Diary of a Disappointed Man*. My chief difficulty was that, unlike Barbellion, I wasn't dying of an obscure kind of paralysis—though, in reading some of my more desperate entries, you would hardly suspect it: "Too miserable to write any more . . ." "All the same symptoms . . ." "This is the end . . ." By these outbursts, I meant, as a rule, simply that I was bored (a perfectly legitimate complaint, too often and too easily sneered at by elders, in the young), or that I couldn't get on with *Lions and Shadows*. The private excitement which had inspired the earlier scenes was dying down. I was losing interest in my huge straggling narrative; already well over a hundred thousand words long. But somehow, it had got to be finished. I had talked about it so often and so endlessly to my family and friends: my prestige, my whole claim to be "a writer," was at stake. So I plodded on— encouraging myself by daily additions to the journal; all of which went to build up the new day-dream self-portrait—Isherwood the Artist.

Isherwood the artist was an austere ascetic, cut off from the outside world, in voluntary exile, a recluse. Even his best friends did not altogether understand. He stood apart from and above "The Test"—because the Test was something for the common herd, it applied only to the world of everyday life. Isherwood refused the Test—not out of weakness, not out of cowardice, but because he was subjected, daily, hourly, to a "Test" of his own: the self-imposed Test of his integrity as a writer. This Test was much harder and more agonizing than the other, because it had to be kept absolutely secret: if you succeeded, there was no applause; if you failed, there was nobody to console.

Now that Isherwood had taken the vow of abstinence from the world (by which I meant, vaguely, that I should never again risk making a fool of myself socially, in public; as on that dreadful New Forest tour) it became natural to think of him as being a kind of invalid. And indeed this invalid role was only too fatally attractive. Hadn't Kathy and Emmy been invalids? Didn't Baudelaire die of a frightful disease? Had I ever been seriously ill, I should no doubt have been scared out of my mental bath-chair soon enough; but my health—apart from constipation and occasional touches of flu—was excellent. So it was quite easy for me to imagine myself subtly and incurably infirm. I remained so, off and on, for the next five years.

When October came, I was quite glad to be going back to Cambridge. The fag-end of the Long Vac. had been depressing enough. Wembley was closed, Philip, who had started work at the hospital, had less time to see me, and I was getting heartily bored with Isherwood and his journal of lonely struggle and suffering. I wanted to be amongst people again, to go to tea with the Poshocracy, to enjoy the comfort of my new and much nicer rooms. Chalmers, who had been up to visit me once or twice, was in high spirits. He had finished with History for good. This year, he was being allowed to read English for the second part of the Tripos. He was full of ideas for developing the "Hynd and Starn" stories and breathing new life into the Other Town. We were going to open a monster offensive against the dons. Laily was to be persecuted, denounced, exposed; very soon, said Chalmers, he would find the University too hot to hold him.

Chalmers looked in on me an hour or two after my arrival at the college, while I was still unpacking. Nervously rubbing his hands together, smiling his conspirator's smile, he told me: "Something very very *nasty* has happened."

"What?"

"They've given me the haunted rooms."

I laughed; but it was perfectly true. The rooms to which Chalmers had been moved in the Old Court, were the recognized property of the college ghost. I hurried along to inspect them. The sitting-room with its deep window-seats was light and even cheerful, for the wooden panelling had been covered with white paint. I was rather disappointed. I asked: "Where's the bedroom?" Chalmers opened the small narrow door of what I had supposed to be a built-in cupboard and showed me a flight of steps, tiny and very steep, leading up into pitch darkness: I mounted, bumping my head, and found myself in an attic bedroom, adjoining which was a minute empty boxroom or closet, already christened by Chalmers "the Oubliette." It was only the staircase, we were later told, that was haunted: sometimes heavy footsteps had been heard, climbing the stairs and stopping suddenly inside "the Oubliette"; sometimes the stairs were descended and there would be a sharp knock on the sitting-room door. Nothing had ever actually been seen. I need hardly add that, although Chalmers and I were frequently together in his sitting-room until midnight or even two o'clock in the morning, we never once heard any kind of sound which even our only-too-willing fancy could interpret as supernatural. Perhaps the Watcher in Spanish was too jealous to allow any rivals in his domain.

Chalmers at once began to tell me his latest discoveries and ideas about the Rats' Hostel and the Other Town: "The whole conception's disgustingly quisb. . . . We were on the wrong track, altogether. The Other Town has nothing whatever to do with Cambridge. That's where we made our fatal mistake—trying to pretend that Cambridge was somehow romantic. You see, Cambridge isn't romantic in the least: it's loathsomely real and sordid. It's absolutely solid—every stupid brick of it. No, no. . . . I saw it all so marvellously clearly, last Vac.: I was walking in the public park on a Sunday morning, just before lunch, and a voice said quite distinctly: "Nor was I indeed ignorant of the flowers and the vine. . . ." The Other Town is miles and miles away from Cambridge; in fact, it couldn't possibly be farther. . . . Another thing: it isn't a town at all—it's a village, somewhere among the enormous downs, on the edge of the Atlantic Ocean. . . ."

We wondered what the village should be called: "Rats' Hall. . . . Stoat Grange. . . . Grangemere. . . . Moatpool. . . . Mortpool—sounds too much like Blackpool. . . . What a pity Mortlake's a real place. . . . I've got it! Mortmere!"

Mortmere it was; Mortmere it remained. A few days later, Chalmers began writing an account of the village which struck a mystical, almost religious note:

It has been said that Mortmere rectory does not seem to be the work of an architect, but to have grown as an oak grows, from the soil of the fields. There is scarcely a colour throughout the surrounding land that has not its counterpart in the garden and the rectory walls. In sunlight the blue-grey slates of the roof seem almost to reflect the leaves of the garden trees, much as the muddy village pond dimly reflects the elm-leaves that lift and dip above it. The red creepers obscuring the dull red walls, the lemon verbena that cloaks the trellised supports of the veranda, even the grey cowls and the chimneys, have an appearance of continuity with the surrounding country. Not only the rectory, but the smaller houses and cottages of the village have this strange likeness to living growths of the soil. The Rector of Mortmere once said that, if every building were to be transplanted during the night, he would scarcely notice the change when he woke in the morning. . . .

The Rector, the Reverend Welken, was our first Mortmere character. Tall, very thin, with lank hair parted in the middle, he was once described as resembling a diseased goat. His beliefs were Anglican, and very high: he had, in fact, indulged his taste for ritual to a point bordering on magic, and his brain, in consequence, was a little turned. He had been guilty of moral offences with a choirboy and had later suffered severe pangs of conscience, persuading himself, at length, that, as a punishment for his crime, his dead wife was appearing to him in the form of a succubus. Welken was so much afraid that some of the other inhabitants of Mortmere might see the succubus that he deliberately spread a rumour that he was engaged in breeding angels in the belfry of Mortmere church. Finally, he actually began to perform a ritual of angel-manufacture, at which the choirboy assisted; and the original offence, incorporated in this ritual, became a mechanical and even distasteful duty. In ordinary life, the Rector was the mildest and most affable of men; particularly apt with classical quotations to suit every imaginable occasion. He was also a rather horrifyingly skilful amateur conjuror.

Welken's most intimate friend was Ronald Gunball, a frank unashamed vulgarian, a keen fisherman, a drunkard and a grotesque liar. Gunball's world was the world of delirium tremens: he saw wonders and horrors all about him, his everyday life was lived amidst two-headed monsters, ghouls, downpours of human blood and eclipses of the sun—and everything he saw he accepted with the most absolute and placid calm. His favourite comment in telling one of his own preposterous stories, was: "Of course, it didn't surprise me in the least."

Here is a typical fragment of a scenario (written much later) for a tea-party in the garden of Mortmere rectory. The "Hearn" referred to is simply an observer from the outside world: "Hynd" and "Starn" fused into a single character:

(*The maid hands the Reverend Welken a pot of shrimp paste which she has been unable to open. Welken opens it without effort—ostentatiously, Hearn thinks.*)

GUNBALL (*aside to Hearn*): You might not think it, but the Rector's one of the strongest men I've known. (*Leaning forward with an expression that suggests the pleased grimness of the story-teller.*) They say that once on the pier at Bognor . . . You've seen those try-your-grip machines? (*Smiling tentatively, as though wishing to assure Hearn in anticipation that the story is not intended as an insult to his intelligence.*) He not only rang the bell but got half a crown back, into the bargain.

HEARN: Ha . . . (*Then he notices certain facts about Gunball's expression of face. It indicates* (a) *that Gunball realizes that his story will be taken as a joke, and* (b) *that he half hopes that Hearn will* pretend *to take it seriously.*)

GUNBALL (*With sudden zest, and a renewal of the ghost-story tone*): You see what that would mean if it were true?

HEARN (*amiably*): I must confess I don't——

GUNBALL (*very suggestively*): It would mean that he must have put half a crown *into* the machine. . . .

Gunball also featured in a story by Chalmers called *The Little Hotel.* Reynard Moxon chose him as the ideal manager for his hotel, which was really a brothel for necrophiles. Gunball, never in the least inquisitive, remained quite insensitive to the ludicrously sinister atmosphere of the establishment and the unpleasant appearance of the guests: he found nothing strange in the behaviour of Mr. Aneurin, who paid for his room by handing the porter a diamond ring. Indeed, Hynd himself (who had been duped by Moxon into taking the job of reception clerk) might not have discovered the true purpose of the hotel until it was too late, had he not happened to catch a glimpse of a kind of sedan-chair being carried through the fog towards the tradesmen's entrance, and, running back to the museum of which he was supposed to be curator, found that the Egyptian mummies were missing from their case.

The Little Hotel had nothing to do with Mortmere; and Reynard Moxon wasn't, originally, a Mortmere character. We invented him for the benefit of a friend named Percival. Percival was an enthusiastic person, always gushing over some newly discovered teacher or master. This term, it was a Dutchman. The Dutchman, whom we never saw, was a rather sinister figure: he read philosophy, was an anthroposophist, and kept white mice. Percival quoted his every word with the utmost admiration and awe: we got very tired of hearing about him. The climax was reached when, one day, Percival informed us, not without malice, that he had just told the Dutchman about our Watcher in Spanish, and that the Dutchman had dismissed the whole idea as "childish and silly." Naturally we were furious—with ourselves, chiefly, for having ever confided our "blagues" to a third person: we decided that Percival must be taught a lesson. We, too, would have a sinister, omniscient friend. A few days later we began describing to Percival the first encounter with our new acquaintance, Reynard Moxon. No, he wasn't exactly an undergraduate, or a don; he had nothing, officially, to do with the University at all; but he preferred to live near Cambridge—for certain reasons. We had met him walking along the river bank, rapidly, looking deadly pale, in an opera hat and a light overcoat with black silk facings. Touching Chalmers abruptly on the wrist with his gloved forefinger, he had asked, in the tone of a man who is accustomed to being obeyed, for the exact time, and, on hearing that we neither of us possessed a watch, had nodded and seemed pleased. Later, we said, he had invited us to his house, to drink sherry and inspect his collection of diamonds. The gullible Percival believed all this and was deeply impressed; but when Chalmers, carried away by his own improvisation, went on to describe how Moxon kept a cat in a birdcage and a canary flying free about the room, and when I added that he owned a large black serpent which accompanied him on rambles after dark, Percival began to smile reproachfully and murmured, in his deep musical tones: "Do you know, I believe you're ragging me?"

Henceforward, we kept Moxom to ourselves. He appeared in two new Hynd and Starn stories—*The Javanese Sapphires* and *The Garage in Drover's Hollow*. The Javanese sapphires have come into Gunball's possession in a typically "Starnese" manner:

That they really had been given him on the jetty at Portsmouth by an elderly man who, scarcely a minute later, boarded the paddle-steamer for the Isle of Wight, I didn't for an instant doubt. Such things frequently happen to my friend, who, by his bland and robust exterior, appears to awaken some species of temporary mania in many of those who encounter him, especially while travelling. The desire to startle him has led a number of total strangers to present Gunball with gold watches, cheques, handbags, clockwork bombs, paralytic babies or live ferrets. But never, on any occasion, have these extravagancies achieved their object. . . .

C

Gunball, of course, has talked about the gems to everybody in the town, and Starn is nervous for their safety. His worst fears are confirmed when, a few days later, he thinks he catches a glimpse of Moxon sauntering past the house:

I knew that my instincts could not have so deceived me. Nor should I easily forget that nonchalant yet rapid stride, the scarcely visible limp, the wooden action of the pointed shoulders, the inert hand carelessly flashing with its five diamond rings. . . .

Henceforward, Starn barricades the house every evening like a fortress and goes to sleep with a six-shooter under his pillow. For a week, nothing unusual happens; then he begins to notice the peculiar appearance of a baby in a perambulator which a nursemaid has taken to wheeling, several times a day, up and down the street. One morning, when he and Gunball are out walking, they meet the perambulator and the nursemaid face to face. Starn engages the woman in conversation. Her behaviour is guilty and highly suspicious. Gunball becomes impatient:

"Why did you stop and yarn with those two? I can't say I thought there was anything so very wonderful about the kid, either."

"No," I retorted, "I can well believe that, to you, there is nothing out of the common in a baby whose jacket is stuffed with straw and who wears a cardboard mask."

"Well—what if he does?" said Gunball mildly. "I dare say the poor little beggar's feeling the cold."

The "baby" is, of course, Moxon's black serpent in disguise. Moxom is training it for the proposed burglary. In due course, his plan is put successfully into execution; the serpent enters Gunball's house through the bathroom pipe, swallows the sapphires one by one, and escapes, taking with it Gunball's old green felt hat. But Moxon is foiled, nevertheless. Try as it will, the obedient reptile cannot vomit up the stolen jewels, and when at last Moxon in desperation tries to recover them with an umbrella and a fishing-line, it becomes angry, sends him flying with a stroke of its tail and disappears. Some time afterwards, it is captured while asleep in the pulpit of a village church and presented to the London Zoo. Starn and Gunball, hoping against hope, travel up to town and visit the Reptile House:

66

A small crowd was usually gathered there, gazing in wonder at the newly acquired monster, as it moved languidly amidst a miniature forest of artificial greenery—its skin oiled and sleek from the keeper's toiler, its jaws rouged, the markings on its forehead made yet more striking with touches of paint. Foppishly, the pampered reptile swayed and lolled beneath violet and orange lights. It snarled, showing scrubbed and carefully sharpened fangs. The crowd drew back, murmuring with fear and admiration.

But Gunball and I regarded the brute's elegant slimness sadly:

"No good," said Gunball, in a broken voice: "It has digested them."

"Drover's Hollow" is a long straight stretch of Roman road, somewhere in the depths of the country, crossing an expanse of almost uninhabited plain. Starn and Dr. Mears are motoring along it when they meet with a rather curious accident: the wheel of their car is punctured by a number of small spiked metal objects which lie scattered over the otherwise smooth surface. They are therefore particularly surprised and pleased to discover, only a few hundred yards farther on, a large and well-equipped garage—an astonishingly large establishment for so lonely a place. Naturally, they expect that the puncture will be repaired in an hour, but the foreman assures them that the damage is far more serious than they imagine—the back axle is broken, the cylinder cracked, the accumulator leaking, the piston rings bent—in short, the car will be ready, thanks to a special quick-repair service, in three days. Dr. Mears is furious, where on earth are they to stay? But here they get another surprise. The hotel at the tiny neighbouring hamlet of Martock St. Bavin turns out to be most luxurious; the manageress tells them she has plenty of custom; all gentlemen whose cars have broken down.

Next morning they find the garage staff in a state of great excitement. The manager, Mr. Castor, is expected—a very particular gentleman, he likes to see everything in perfect order. His temper is reported to be frightful, all the mechanics are afraid of him. Scarcely have they finished scrubbing, when the scream of an approaching car is heard. It is an enormous limousine, painted all over a gleaming black:

Already, the black car was within a quarter of a mile of where we stood. The menace of its tremendous speed made us instinctively draw back a little into the shelter of the doorway. It was within a hundred, within fifty yards of the garage. Then, suddenly, and with a prolonged hiss, its driver applied the brakes. The huge machine spun round like a top through two complete revolutions in the middle of the road; then, before I could have cried out, it shot through the archway and came to rest within an inch of the garage wall.

A mechanic ran to hold open the door and Mr. Castor descended. He was short and very thin, with a pale angular face and bearing of almost fiendlike nonchalance. He wore a black double-breasted suit of the best cloth and a black tie. His voice was languid but peremptory: "Tea in the office at once."

The foreman approached him: "These gentlemen are staying at Martock during some repairs to their car, sir."

"Indeed?" Mr. Castor looked at us for a moment with half-closed eyes:

"Very deeply privileged," he said, and turned to enter the office. . . .

Castor, needless to say, is Moxon. In this out-of-the-way part of the country, he is doing profitable business as a car-wrecker. Nor does he always confine himself to causing punctures. If any word or action of his clients happens to annoy him, he orders the unlucky victims of his displeasure to be supplied with the "Superfine Mixture"—a special kind of high explosive petrol which will blow their car to atoms. I forget now how I had planned the story to end; like so many of the Hynd and Starn series, it remained unfinished.

Dr. Mears was the Mortmere physician. His most remarkable achievement was his cure of Gunball, who was suffering from a Rats' Hostel disease known as Suffolk Ulcers, by the application of a species of inland seaweed only to be found in the crypt of Mortmere church. He was the author of a book called *Awards and Miseries of Astronomy*. And he was at work upon a new method of classifying the human race. He had divided man into two main groups—"Dragoons" and "Dorys": Dragoons were subdivided into "Puss-dragoons," "Cogs-dragoons" and "Imperials"; Dorys into "Itchers," "Repellers" and "Consumers"—and each of these three sub-divisions could be further classed as "Pouters," "Poupees," "Buttocks" or "Throstles." (I leave the recognition of all these types to the reader's imagination and personal taste.)

Then there was Sergeant Claptree, who kept the Skull and Trumpet Inn. And Mr. Wherry, the architect and engineer, who, years before, had built a railway tunnel under the downs. This tunnel collapsed—owing to an infinitesimal error in Wherry's trigonometry—just as the first Mortmere express was passing through it, burying the passengers so deep that they could never be dug out; all that now remained was the solitary railway signal in the grounds of Henry Belmare's estate. Henry Belmare, the Mortmere landowner, had a sister, Miss Belmare, the artist. She was a formidable, mannish figure with a loud commanding voice who wore starched blouses and a small steel padlock inside her stiff collar. She spent most of her time bullying Welken and setting her fierce tomcat on Gunball's dog Griever. She had painted the frescoes of the Mortmere village hall.

Such were the leading Mortmere worthies. Minor characters included Gustave Shreeve, the Headmaster of Frisbald College for boys (the Frisbald Cellar Game was quite unlike any known football code); Harold Wrygrave, Welken's curate, who also taught at the college; Boy Radnor, the choirboy who assisted at Welken's ritual of angel manufacture; Anthony, Henry Belmare's son whose extraordinary beauty was a source of perpetual jealousy between Shreeve and Mr. Wherry; Alison Kemp, the village whore; Ensign Battersea, who helped Sergeant Claptree at the Skull and Trumpet; and Gaspard Farfox, the private detective, who was called down to Mortmere in connection with the Mystery of the Dead Wasp. All these people were assembled gradually, casually, without plan. It was only later that we thought of writing *Mortmere* as a connected dramatic story.

If *Mortmere* was to have a plot, what was to be our central theme? Obviously, the eternal conflict between the Rats' Hostel and the University system. Laily must be brought to Mortmere, as a destroyer. So we created Mr. Chardes, a more dynamic and dangerous reincarnation of the Worm: he is a young archæologist, engaged in excavating some Roman remains on Belstreet Down. From the first, he hates and fears the anarchic, eccentric freedom of Mortmere life; and soon his hatred becomes concentrated and directed against Gunball. We thought that Mr. Chardes might actually murder Gunball—or perhaps that wouldn't be necessary. It might be sufficient if Chardes, in some semi-mystical manner, could discredit and thereby shatter Gunball's marvellous delirium world: if he did this, it followed that Gunball would die a natural death—and, possibly, with Gunball's death, Mortmere itself would dissolve and fade away.

Mortmere would certainly have to be a tragedy; but we couldn't bear the thought of Chardes' triumph. He, too, must be destroyed. The Rats' Hostel must be avenged. This was where Reynard Moxon would come in useful. In the last chapter, Moxon, by some peculiarly horrible method, kills Chardes.

We discussed all this at great length, but I don't think we had ever any serious intention of literally sitting down to write the book. Quite apart from mere laziness, it hardly seemed necessary: indeed, it would have spoilt all our pleasure. As long as *Mortmere* remained unwritten, its alternative possibilities were infinite; we could continue, every evening, to improvise fresh situations, different climaxes. We preferred to stick to the Hynd and Starn stories, and to make utterly fantastic plans for the edition-de-luxe: it was to be illustrated, we said, with real oil paintings, brasses, carvings in ivory or wood; fireworks would explode to emphasize important points in the narrative; a tiny gramophone sewn into the cover would accompany the descriptive passages with emotional airs; all the dialogue would be actually spoken; the different pages would smell appropriately, according to their subject-matter, of grave-clothes, manure, delicious food, burning hair, chloroform or expensive scent. All copies would be distributed free. Our friends would find attached to the last page, a pocket containing banknotes and jewels; our enemies, on reaching the end of the book, would be shot dead by a revolver concealed in the binding.

At the end of that term, there was a college feast. Chalmers and I had looked forward to this ceremony for some time: it promised to be a suitable opportunity for an overt act of hostility to the "Other Side." Exactly what we were going to do, we didn't know. Perhaps Chalmers would simply jump on to the table and shout: *"J'en appelle!"*—whereupon, we said, the earth would open, and the dons, the silver heirloom plate and the college buildings themselves would be immediately engulfed. The phrase *"J'en appelle!"*, which occurs in a poem by Villon, meant, in our private slang, a kind of metaphysical challenge. Just as when, in poker, one says:

"I'll see you!" we challenged the "Other Side" to show us their cards. They dreaded this challenge because, of course, they had been bluffing. Once the bluff had been called, we liked to imagine, the entire academic "blague" became bankrupt and would automatically collapse.

Needless to say, what really happened was that we had an excellent dinner and that I got drunk. The drunker I became, the more amiable I felt. The Poshocracy were really too nice for words. I slapped their backs; they slapped mine. I talked a great deal: I wanted them to share every nuance of my exquisite sensations on drinking Scotch whisky for the first time in my life. I could have murdered the college tutor smilingly, in purest love: I could have lighted the cigar he offered me, unabashed, with a page from our twelfth-century illuminated missal. I tried to tell them about Mortmere as, arm in arm, we all bounded down the steps and out into the freezing intoxicating midnight air.

We were in Chalmers' sitting-room: it was so full of people that you could hardly turn round. And there was Chalmers himself, whom I hadn't seen all the evening, writing with a fountain-pen on Ashmeade's shirt-front: "A la très-chère, à la très-belle. . . ." Ashmeade leant against the wall, smiling dreamily. When Chalmers had finished writing, he opened the cupboard, took out a hammer and tapped Ashmeade several times smartly on the head. Then a butter-fight began. Chalmers was in the middle of it: he and one of the largest members of the Poshocracy were smearing butter into each other's hair. Soon there was butter everywhere—on the pictures, on the walls, on the ceiling, all over the lapels of the beautiful silk dinner-jackets. Several people wore great yellow pats of it stuck to their buttonholes like diplomatic decorations. The lights went out, went on again. Chalmers was shouting and waving a knife. Everyone laughed uproariously and someone said: "That's enough." Half a dozen Poshocrats saw me to bed.

Next morning I woke early. I was feeling wonderful: not a trace of sickness. Dressing quickly, I hurried round to Chalmers' room and entered friskily to find him dozing in an armchair. He had stayed up all night, packing: my reception was extremely cool. "Do you seriously mean to tell me you didn't realize that it was all a plot?" he indignantly demanded. "Obviously the whole thing was a put-up job: they were out to wreck the whole place." The butter-fight, it seemed, had been in deadly earnest: Chalmers had done his best to stab his adversary through the heart: "And, instead of helping me," he added bitterly, "you just sat in the corner and grinned." He then told me that, in the first flush of resentment, he had written me a drunken note, saying that I had betrayed him, we must part for ever. I was rather hurt; but soon we were laughing together over the whole affair. As for the alleged "conspiracy," I have never quite made up my mind whether to believe in it or not. That the Poshocracy should all have assembled, without invitation, in the rooms of such socially insignificant people as ourselves, was certainly rather queer. Ashmeade, no doubt, was at the bottom of it.

I spent that Christmas Vac. in London, roller-skating and writing *Lions and Shadows*. At this time, there was still a large skating rink in Holland Park: Philip and I were there nearly every day. Skating, like ballroom dancing, belonged to the list of accomplishments essential to the Mayfair literary Don Juan: both on wheels and on the ice, Philip was quite an expert. Natty, absurdly graceful, with poised arms which reminded you of a penguin's wings, he circled, curved, described threes and eights, waltzed with the most attractive instructress, and finally, approaching the barrier at enormous speed, stopped himself within a couple of inches and murmured: "No good, boy . . . Can't do a thing to-day. . . . Shall we have some tea?"

At the rink Philip was in his element. Indeed, on a crowded Saturday afternoon, he came near to fulfilling his own wish-dream. Everybody admired him. Pretty schoolgirls, home for the holidays, giggled self-consciously whenever he shot by: schoolboys wondered how he did those backward turns. Even the lady in black velvet, with a bunch of violets at her bosom and a little veil, whom we supposed, for some insufficient reason, to be a Russian Princess, didn't refuse when he asked her for a dance. At one period, Philip even seriously considered leaving the medical school altogether and becoming a skating instructor. He pictured a romantic bohemian existence, under the pseudonym of "Mr. Philips," which would lead, in due course, to a liaison, perhaps even a marriage, with one of his pupils—alternatively an "Honourable" or the daughter of an American millionaire. And what a novel he would later be able to write about it all!

On the seventh of January I finished *Lions and Shadows*—

and about time, too. I had been writing at it, on and off, since the July of 1923. Even as I toiled my way through the last chapter to the last page, I knew, in my heart, that it was no good. But it was a satisfaction, at any rate, to have done the job; and of course, I still cherished desperate hopes. It seemed to me then that to have published a book—any kind of book— would be the greatest possible happiness I could ask from life. A lady novelist who was an old friend of our family had promised to read the completed manuscript, and, if she liked it, to put in a word for me with her own publisher. Seated in her chintz drawing-room with a tea-cup on my knee I heard her verdict—a death-sentence charmingly pronounced in the phraseology of Henry James: "In a book like this, one expects the material to be more—how shall I say?—its own *justification*, than yours, for the most part, is . . ." I nodded brightly and tried to smile. Yes, she was perfectly right. I hated her, at that moment, for her perceptiveness: but I was grateful to her, at least, that she had told me the truth. I know now how easily she might have got rid of me with a couple of dishonest compliments and a lazy suggestion that I should "rewrite certain passages." Instead, she advised me frankly to put my year and a half's work away in a drawer and forget it. It was nice in places, of course, but it wouldn't do—and that was that. As we were saying good-bye, she told me. "If you really *have* talent, you know, you'll go on writing—whatever people say to you." This was exactly the kind of unsentimental encouragement I so badly needed. As I walked away from her house, I felt much more cheerful, almost exhilarated: my head was full of fresh plans.

That Lent Term was an unsatisfactory time, both for Chalmers and for myself. We were restless and unhappy, and we jarred on each other's nerves. We seemed to have lost, temporarily, that telepathic thread of communication: it often happened, now, that one of us said something which the other found meaningless, or forced, or even antipathetic.

Chalmers, a year older than myself and in his eighth University term, was beginning to find Cambridge absolutely intolerable. He was disappointed, as Mr. Holmes predicted, in the English school: its necessarily academic approach reduced all literature to the status of "texts." He was sexually unsatisfied and lonely: he wanted a woman with whom he could fall in love and go to bed—not any more of these shopgirl teasers and amateur punt-cuddling whores. And he was deeply depressed about his own writing. He felt, now, that he would never be a poet. Everything he had done or would do, he said bitterly, was ornamental: his thought was tied up in bizarre adjectives, deliberately obscure phrases, conceits. Rats'-Hostelism, so fatally attractive to his temperament, dangerously easy to his pen, had been his final undoing. "And now," he exclaimed in desperation, "I can't write a single line which isn't *strange*."

I was unhappy, too; but less consciously so because, being in a much more complex psychological mess than Chalmers himself, I had evolved a fairly efficient system of censorships and compensations. Unnaturally lively, I acted in Poshocracy charades, helped to found a literary society, sat up late arguing with the members of the Film Club, threw cushions in people's rooms after tea. Then came days of depression, when I huddled in my arm-chair, empty as a burst paper-bag —turning the leaves of *The Constant Nymph* or *The Boy in the Bush*, dreaming miserably of the Tirol, of Australia, hating my life, knowing I should never escape, and then comforting myself by ordering a double portion of buttered toast. I wrote nothing; didn't work. It was easy enough to banish from my conscious mind the steadily approaching spectre of the Tripos. Lectures I now cut in increasing quantities. As for my new tutor, he was less exacting than Gorse; and he set the essay subjects of the previous year—but even copying out Chalmers' old essays with suitable variations became at length such an exhausting duty to one in my pathological state of laziness that I found I could only get through it when the room was full of people and a gramophone was playing.

For both of us, the great event of that term was the series of lectures on modern poetry given by Mr. I. A. Richards. Here, at last, was the prophet we had been waiting for—this pale, mild, muscular, curly-headed young man who announced in his plaintive baa-lamb voice: "According to me, it's quite possible that, in fifty years' time, people will have stopped writing poetry altogether. . . ." The substance of those lectures has since become famous through Mr. Richards' books. But, to us, he was infinitely more than a brilliant new literary critic: he was our guide, our evangelist, who revealed to us, in a succession of astounding lightning flashes, the entire expanse of the Modern World. Up to this moment, we had been a pair of romantic conservatives, devil-worshippers, votaries of "Beauty" and "Vice," Manicheans, would-be Kropotkin anarchists, who refused to read T. S. Eliot (because of his vogue amongst the Poshocracy), or the newspapers, or Freud. Now, in a moment, all was changed. Poets, ordered Mr. Richards, were to reflect aspects of the World-Picture. Poetry wasn't a holy flame, a fire-bird from the moon ; it was a group of interrelated stimuli acting upon the ocular nerves, the semi-circular canals, the brain, the solar plexus, the digestive and sexual organs. It did you medically demonstrable good, like a dose of strychnine or salts. We became behaviourists, materialists, atheists. In our conversation, we substituted the word "emotive" for the word beautiful; we learnt to condemn inferior work as a "failure in communication," or more crushing still, as "a private poem." We talked excitedly about "the phantom æsthetic state."

But if Mr. Richards enormously stimulated us, he plunged us, also, into the profoundest gloom. It seemed to us that everything we had valued would have to be scrapped. We had reactions, of course, in favour of genre, of strangeness, of the Rats' Hostel—now regretfully stowed away in the lumber room of "private poetry." But it was no good: we were banished from that world forever: we could only pay it short occasional visits, as mourners visit a cemetery, and then return.

About the middle of February, I had sufficiently pulled myself together to be able to start a new novel: it was to be called *Christopher Garland*. Here is the synopsis, exactly as I wrote it, on the first page of a clean exercise book (my handwriting, at this period, had shrunk into strings of tiny hooks and dots—because, as an expert explained to me several years later, I hated myself so much that I was trying to disappear altogether):

A young man's first year after leaving school. The action takes place in London, Sussex and Cambridge. Roughly speaking, it is to show how the young man is, through a series of experiences and incidents, gradually committed to art—to the art which he had, at first, not taken very seriously.

The story opens with the arrival of the young man after his last term at school; goes on to his first great period of inspiration, while staying in Sussex. Then comes Cambridge, with its terrible stupefying effect on the brain and spirit. In the vacation, the young man, cut off from his friends by his perceptions but not yet fully initiate, drifts into a dismal struggle with the personality of the aunt with whom he lives. A love affair with a friend's fiancée brings him to himself, and, with its renunciation, he enters upon a period, if not of peace, at least of courage and assurance for the future.

It will be noticed at once that "Isherwood the Artist" was now in full temporary ascendancy over "War." The mood of *Christopher Garland* was to be monastic renunciation of all life's pleasures— and of all life's difficulties as well. But Garland, like most of his kind, was only a pseudo-monk; and so this was only a pseudo-subject for a novel—doomed as unworkable from the start. The key-phrase—"cut off from his friends by his perceptions"—touching in its adolescent arrogance, comes strangely from an admirer of Katherine Mansfield ("To be rooted in Life—that is what I want, that is what I must try for.") It hadn't yet occurred to me that the artist, just because he has these "perceptions," is thereby under an obligation to communicate them to "his friends." Christopher Garland might, in fact, be described as a "Life-snob." Note the snobbish-religious flavour of "gradually committed to art" and "not yet fully initiate." But I mustn't be too hard on poor Christopher. With all his faults, he was an advance on Leonard Merrows (who would undoubtedly have developed into a full-blown Poshocrat): he did care, in deadly earnest, for the cultural values—had he lived in these less complex days, he might even have found himself defending an art gallery with a machine-gun. I suppose that what I, in my muddled way, was trying to do was to define the artist's position in society—a legitimate and interesting theme. But as "society," for me, still meant the peerage; and as I still imagined that "being an artist" was a kind of neurotic alternative to being an ordinary human man, it is hardly surprising that my ideas got a little mixed.

My sixth term began—the term of the Tripos examination. Now, at last, I had to look my bogy in the face. What on earth was I going to do? I wasn't dead. I saw no prospect of becoming seriously ill. Certain legendary heroes had jumped out of windows or thrown themselves downstairs, deliberately breaking an arm: I hadn't the nerve. Of course, there was work. Even now, with desperate cramming, I might scrape a Second, make sure of a Third. I did try, after a fashion, to cover some of the lost ground: it was like starting to walk across Siberia. After a couple of days I gave it up. The absurd truth was that my vanity sided with my laziness: I was still secretly rather proud of being a scholar. I knew I could never get a First; a Second I scorned. I didn't want to be ignominiously degraded. Rather than that, I would fail altogether.

Next autumn, no doubt, I should at length be allowed to read English. But I had lost my enthusiasm for the English school. And, next autumn, Chalmers would be gone. That was the blackest part of the whole prospect. I simply couldn't imagine how I should be able to bear Cambridge without him.

Suppose I stayed on and did, somehow, get a degree: what would become of me? I should have to be a school-master. But I didn't want to be a schoolmaster—I wanted, at least, to escape from that world. I wanted to learn to direct films. Roger East was going to try for a job in the Stoll studios; and he'd said, already, that it was a pity I couldn't join him. How I longed to be independent, to earn money of my own! And I had got to wait another whole year!

Chalmers and I were walking round the college court together, one evening late in April. I said: "You know, there's a perfectly simple way out of this. I shall have to get myself sent down."

I hadn't really meant it; and yet, as I spoke the words, I felt suddenly that this was an unalterable decision. Chalmers was delighted. We at once began discussing ways and means. A public scandal with a woman—too difficult to arrange. Damage to a University monument—too expensive. Assault on a don—risk of prison or a lunatic asylum. (Besides which, all these offences *might,* conceivably, be forgiven.) No, my crime must be strictly academic; and, as such, unpardonable. What about a lampoon pinned to the college notice-board? An attractive idea; but probably a tactful servant would whisk it out of the way before the harm was done: it would never get to the eyes or ears of the authorities. And a single lampoon, however insulting, would be far too little: I should have to open a regular campaign—banners, leaflets, notes thrown in at the tutor's window, manifestos on lavatory paper: the technical problems would be enormous. None of these schemes would do. My gesture must be in connection with the Tripos itself. That was it! I must actually go into the examination-room and write my insults as answers to the questions. The examining body itself would see them: they couldn't possibly be ignored. And, when the sealed packets were opened—imagine the examiners' faces! Imagine what they would say to each other! Chalmers laughed riotously. He hadn't, as yet, the least suspicion that this wasn't just one more of a thousand fantastic anti-Cambridge plots. And I was glad that he didn't suspect. As long as I could keep my intentions to myself, they remained a little unreal. I had more than a month to get through, before the examinations. I mustn't, on any account, allow myself to get rattled. Meanwhile, I took the precaution of stopping any possible funk-holes or emergency exits—I burnt all my history note-books (most of them three-quarters empty) and sold my history text-books—all except Bishop Stubbs. Him I dropped ceremonially into the River Cam. On the title page I had written a quotation from *Julius Cæsar*, Act III, Scene 2: "Which, pardon me, I do not mean to read. . . ."

Beethoven and Schubert helped to fill the interval. We took them up the Backs in a punt, on Chalmers' portable gramophone, and lay listening for hours under the willows to the *Eroika*, the "C Sharp Minor Quartette" and the "Trio in B Flat." The slow movement of the "Trio" reminded me, for some reason, of *The Boy in the Bush*: indeed, my whole pleasure in music was literary-romantic. When I told Chalmers about this, he immediately discovered that the violin was singing: "Oh, Mister *Law*-rence! Oh, Mister *Law*-rence. . . ." The opening of the *Eroika* symphony he described as: "*Already* the crowds prepare. . . ." The first movement of the "C Sharp Minor" we called "The Angels."

The middle of May was glorious and very hot. Now that I was irrevocably doomed to leave Cambridge, I began to enjoy University life as never before. I spent whole afternoons on the river, in punts and canoes. I made several new friends—neither Poshocrats nor hearties but nice ordinary intelligent people whom I'd said good morning to every day for six terms, without ever getting to know. One of them even asked me to share digs with him next autumn, when, according to custom, I should be living outside college. I felt inclined to reply that I should be living a very long way outside College; but I only thanked him, and said my plans were vague.

Philip paid us a visit, at our joint invitation. He and Chalmers got on well together. It was amusing to stand Philip against our academic background. He was so entirely the Londoner: his smart slick suit looked comic amidst the fashionable dilettante untidiness of the Poshocrats. He read us passages from his latest opus, *The Deverels*. It was wonderfully sordid—eighty thousand words of sheer middle-class gloom: for Philip, on my advice, had temporarily abandoned Mayfair and was writing about North Kensington. How he gloated over it! By the time he had finished with the district, there wasn't a window left unbroken; every pair of lace curtains was faded, every aspidistra was dusty, every venetian blind was falling to pieces; not a single door-bell or lavatory chain was in working order; all coal fires smoked, all gas leaked; the electric light glared, ruining your eyesight, the rooms were draughty, stuffy, freezing, far too hot; the baths dripped, the clocks chimed incorrectly, the telephone was shrill; the smells were quite indescribable—though Philip certainly did his best; no back garden was without its rubbish heap, composed of rusty sardine-tins, smashed beer-bottles, hair-combings, odd shoes and at least one dead cat. And the people who inhabited this wilderness! All were hideous, diseased, underdeveloped, sly, lecherous, hypocritical, stingy, pot-bellied, cancerous, deaf—with the exception of a few girls, grudgingly admitted to be "cheaply pretty," who, of course, left home at the age of seventeen for a life of vice, ending in the clinic or the river. Philip had still three more chapters to write: he hadn't yet killed off all his principal characters.

The Tripos began on June the first. There were no portents; no signs in the heavens. Nothing happened to disturb the illusion of absolute matter-of-factness with which I filled my fountain-pen, put on my gown, and set out, in plenty of time, for the examination hall. You would have noticed nothing strange about me as I followed the other candidates obediently through the doorway, and took my place. The paper was before me on the desk, the ink was in its bottle, and there lay the printed question-sheet. And now, at length, I had to ask myself: what exactly was I going to do?

Deliberately, I had avoided making any plans. I would leave everything to the inspiration of the moment. I had vaguely expected that my excitement and desperation would, when the time came, provide me with some daring, amazing idea. But now, confronted with a paper on mediæval history, I felt neither excited nor desperate nor, in the very least, daring. The task before me no longer appeared as a sensational act of defiance, but rather as a kind of literary puzzle; I had got to write something which would ensure my being sent down from Cambridge. That was all. But—what?

I hear the reader exclaim: "How can you ask?" Wasn't this the opportunity of a lifetime—for a communist manifesto, a scalding satire, a magnificent passage of obscene libel, a frank reasonable open letter to the authorities on education and the inalienable rights of youth? Of course it was. And I missed it. Alas, I was no Shelly. I felt, that morning, no warmth of generous indignation against the examiners: indeed, my attitude towards them had become timid, almost respectful. I wanted to achieve my object without unnecessarily hurting anybody's feelings. After all, this act of mine was a strictly private affair: it had nothing to do with them, personally. I merely asked them to record a certain decision. Insults were out of the question. So also was the terse retort, the brief ironical lampoon: whatever happened, I had got to sit here three hours—and three more this afternoon, and all day to-morrow, and the next, as well. If I left early or cut altogether, I should only make myself conspicuous. And I didn't want to be conspicuous; I wanted things to take their course, automatically, without my further intervention. I wished, if possible, to avoid any kind of a scene. In the meanwhile, somehow, I must make use of my time.

Tentatively, gingerly, I began to experiment. Concealed verses seemed a possibility, for a start (we had been asked to discuss the political problems of the Doges in connection with the Crusades):

But these considerations were outweighed by others. The Venetians thought of trade. Their friendly converse with the Moslem king must cease if Christian Powers were threatening to declare war on him and to attack Jerusalem. And always, at their back, the Papal sanction menaced the unwilling; they, too, would have to lend a hand at killing. Therefore, they leased their ships at heavy prices and told the warriors to bring back spices.

But this was really too easy. Next I tried some mild silliness, in the style of *Punch*:

One cannot be a missionary nowadays—as a class, they have been too much exposed; and, indeed, the demoralizing effect of having to wear boots in the tropics must be very serious. But the missionary monks did not wear boots; they wore sandals and fuzzy smocks that itched, and leather wallets. . . .

A rather unfortunately worded question ("Innocent the Third's policy with regard to South Italy sowed a fatal crop for his successors." Examine this statement) gave me the chance to be impudent:

1. It is difficult to say whether a "policy" can sow a crop. Perhaps "sow" is a dead metaphor, but "a fatal crop"—referring, of course, to that favourite myth of hack journalists, the Dragon's Teeth—assuredly is not.
2. The warriors who sprang from the Dragon's Teeth killed each other, not the onlookers. Therefore the metaphor fails utterly to apply to any conceivable combination of facts.
3. The statement is not true.

When I had finished, I copied out my answers for the benefit of Chalmers, touching them up as much as possible in the process. He, of course, was delighted. As I read them to him, he danced gleefully about the room, exclaiming that Mortmere was avenged. I didn't feel so sure; but his enthusiasm silenced my doubts. I resolved, at any rate, to try to be a little funnier that afternoon.

Most of what I wrote during those three days was dreadfully stupid, however. When I read through all that nonsense now, I feel really ashamed. Perhaps my sonnet on the causes of the Restoration is just worth quoting:

When Charles the Second had, at length, returned, most Englishmen received him with relief rather than real affection. Bonfires burned to welcome back the Stuarts; and no grief was then expressed for Puritanical customs and fasts and sabbaths. Men were tired of martial law and major-general. A monarchy was all that they desired.

81

And, besides this, now Oliver was dead and Richard had been tried with ill-success as Lord Protector; now that all the slow tide of opinion, gathering to a head, demanded Charles; now they were leaderless—the Roundheads were resigned to lying low.

And here is my last answer to the last question (on Usury and the Jews) in the last Tripos paper, Economic History:

The Jews are all very well in their way and usury is all very well in *its* way; but how can I think of either when, for the last two days, I have been wondering, almost to the point of agony, whatever can be the use of those long strips of dirty cloth which are hung, like washing, from the ceiling of this room? If the authorities have any human sympathy, they should have them taken down before the next Tripos, or else put up a notice describing the function they perform. And, while we are on the subject of this place, may I add that, in my opinion, the portrait of Albert the Good which hangs over the magic-lantern emplacement is an act of *lèse-majesté*—no less?

My first impulse, when it was all over, was to go straight to the college tutor and tell him what I had done. Chalmers dissuaded me. Such a move, he insisted, would be tactically fatal. I should be putting myself in the position of a penitent. I should have to make some kind of apology; I might, even risk being forgiven. He was quite right, of course. My real motive had been cowardice: I wanted to get the whole business over and done with as soon as possible.

The Term came quietly to an end. Several of the dons, in saying good-bye to me, asked if I thought I had got a First. I replied modestly that I was afraid I hadn't.

A week later, the tutor's expected telegram arrived: "Essential I should see you as soon as possible please return."

I travelled back to Cambridge that afternoon. The interview which followed wasn't, in any sense of the word, a success. The tutor spoke his language: I had shown ingratitude to the college and to those who had taught me, I had betrayed my responsibilities as a scholar, I had told a deliberate lie. I sat silent. What was there to say? My act now seemed more than ever unreal to me: failing the Tripos had merely been a kind of extension of dream-action on to the plane of reality. How was I to tell the tutor that we had often plotted to blow him sky-high with a bomb? How was I to tell him anything? The tutor wasn't the tutor: he was a kindly but aggrieved middle-aged gentleman with whom I now sat face to face for the first time in my life. How could I talk to this perfect stranger about Mortmere and Hynd and Starn and the Dürers and Laily and the willows by Garret Hostel Bridge? He was asking me whether the trouble had been money. Oh, no, sir. Had it anything to do with a woman? No, sir. Nothing. Was it—any other kind of trouble? No, Sir. No trouble at all.

Very well. . . . All possible allowances had been made. The tutor sighed as he relit his pipe. I felt very apologetic. I should hardly have blamed him if he had given me a good smacking. Admirably controlling his temper, he told me that I might be required to leave—he couldn't tell what the authorities would decide—but that, if I voluntarily withdrew my name from the college books before next Monday: well, he made no promises, but he'd see what could be done. In other words, I wasn't to be disgraced. I thanked him. He wished me luck. We shook hands (I omitted to tell Chalmers this, in describing the scene to him later). It was all over. The door shut. I hurried downstairs, across the court, out at the gate. I called a taxi. I was free.

Years afterwards, someone told me that Mr. Holmes had got possession, by intrigue or theft, of my Tripos papers; and kept them, ever since, in a locked drawer. I hope this is true. It would be just like him.

CHAPTER IV

ON my twenty-first birthday, I found that a hundred and fifty pounds had accumulated to my account at the Post Office Savings Bank. I decided, at once, to buy a second-hand car.

My choice, expertly guided by two brilliantly talkative gentlemen from a neighbouring garage landed upon an enormous old olive-green Renault—a five-seater which could hold seven—with great brass headlamps, a gate-change gear and black leather upholstery like a cab. Driven downhill, at top speed, she was capable of doing close to forty.

Unlike my motor-bicycle, the Renault had no connection whatever with "The Test." She represented, indeed, a mood of complete irresponsibility: I could hardly have found a more absurd way of spending my money. I had no use whatever for any kind of car—much less this miniature motor-bus. On my tiny allowance, I could barely afford the ordinary running costs; as for the garage and any large repairs, they would have to be paid for out of the remaining forty pounds—the car had cost a hundred and ten. So my days as a motorist were obviously numbered. But, for the moment, I didn't care. I was extraordinarily happy. Cambridge was over for ever. And I had returned from a romantic holiday by the sea. Something wonderful, I felt certain, was just about to happen. That I hadn't written a word for months; that my film prospects, after a discouraging interview with Stolls, had disappeared, didn't worry me in the least.

A moral millionaire, I was lavish with my invitations: the Renault was kept going from morning to night. I had no longer any reason to be afraid of the London traffic. My enormous vehicle was certain to get the better of any collision, short of an omnibus or a tram. I bent several mud-guards, buffers and wings: twice I had to pay. The Renault, much dinted, began to look her age. But Philip, always chivalrous, still declared her to be the most comfortable car in town.

Philip loved motoring. Seated beside me, in his smart blue overcoat, with the silk handkerchief just showing from the breast pocket, he fairly beamed with satisfaction and pro-prietory pleasure. His presence invested the Renault with a certain air of careless, if faded, luxury: I felt as though I were his chauffeur and the car a Rolls-Royce.

One afternoon in the middle of September, a friend who had come to lunch with me talked enthusiastically about the charming Anglo-Belgian family he had met on holiday in a Breton village. The husband, Monsieur Cheuret, was a well-known violinist, the leader of a string quartette. He had been living in London for the last fifteen years. His wife was an Englishwoman. They had two boys. One of the boys, Edou-ard, had cut his knee very badly and had been laid up, now, for several weeks. We might go and visit them that afternoon, my friend suggested; and wouldn't I, perhaps, offer to take Edouard out in the car to Richmond Park? Needless to say, this was exactly what he himself had already proposed to the Cheurets; so I could only agree.

They lived in Chelsea, in a mews just off the King's Road. As we drove up, all the doors and windows were standing open, so that you could see right into the downstair room; and the whole place with its gay check curtains and steep miniature staircase looked like a big doll's house. In the bright sunshine its appearance was so disarmingly cheerful that I felt myself, after the first glance, already quite charmed. And now the doll's house effect was heightened by the ap-pearance, on a tiny balcony above the front door, of a real live Dutch doll, with plump, red dimpled cheeks, who shouted to my friend: "Hullo, Eric! Quite a stranger, aren't you?" and disappeared. "That's Rose," my friend explained. "She's their cook."

Next, M. Cheuret himself looked out, leaning on the half-door which opened directly into the ground-floor. He was a thin youthful-looking man of about forty, with plentiful grey-ish hair brushed back from his lined sunburnt face, and a pleasant rather sleepy smile: "So it's you, Eric," he said.

"Please come inside." He spoke gently, with a slight foreign accent, and seemed tired.

Later, I was introduced to the rest of the family. Edouard, with his bandaged knee, lay on the sofa; a pale dark-haired boy of eleven. Jean, his elder brother, was a year older: he seemed livelier, less intelligent, more English. Madame Cheuret herself, dark and elegant, a cigarette between her sharply-coloured lips, was rather my idea of a Russian woman out of a Tchekhov story. This is how real human people live, I thought, as my eyes wandered over the comfortable untidiness of the large room; the music stacked on the grand piano; the pencil, pipe, orange and block of resin beside the keyboard; the violin on the chair next to the tennis-racket; the fishing-rods in the corner; the photographs with scrawled inscriptions; the Japanese prints on the whitewashed brick walls; the Breton cupboard crammed with music-stands, pictures, books, clothes. People living together, busy, friendly, intent upon their work, had created the atmosphere in this house: nothing was planned, forced, formal, consciously quaint. Mentally, I compared it with my own, with Philip's home: it was difficult to realize, even, that we were all inhabiting the same city. This was another world.

During tea, Cheuret himself began to talk to me. He asked me about myself. His curiously soft, direct approach, his almost feminine air of attentiveness, broke down the last of my shyness in a moment: I began telling him about Cambridge and the Tripos. He nodded. He seemed to find what I had done perfectly natural: there was no need whatever for the semi-defensive explanations I had so often rehearsed. Here was a man old enough to be my father, to whom I could talk openly as if to a friend of my own age:

"Yes," he repeated, "I understand, of course. . . . It was impossible for you to remain any longer." He passed his hand, with a tired, soothing gesture, through his hair: "And what shall you do now?"

"Well—I want to get on with my writing, of course. And I'm looking out for a job."

"Aha!" Cheuret seemed amused. He smiled his sleepy, rather sardonic smile. "What kind of job, may I ask?"

"I thought perhaps I could get work as somebody's secretary. I can't do shorthand, though. I can type a little; I'd soon learn that. I know I wouldn't be much good in an office. . . ."

"Vous parlez Français?"

"Un peu. Mais je peux comprendre très bien."

"Splendid!" Cheuret laughed. "Now let me tell you something. Since some time, I have been looking for a person like yourself. Will you be my secretary, Mr. Isherwood?"

"Yes . . . Of course . . . Thank you very much. . . ."

And so it was settled.

At first, I could hardly believe in my astounding good luck. That I should be allowed to come to this house every day ; to have a part, however insignificant, in the life of the Cheuret family, seemed too wonderful to be true. All my friends, when they heard of the new job, were consumed with envy ; Philip was so excited and upset that he nearly ran away from the medical school, there and then. Even my relatives were intrigued—though they didn't fail to point out that this was probably only an interim occupation, that it "led" nowhere, that it wasn't very well paid. (For the first fortnight I was to come on trial free ; after that, Cheuret promised me a pound a week.) Officially, I worked only in the mornings, from ten to twelve: but it was understood that I would sometimes stay on longer, if necessary, subject to our mutual convenience.

Two days later, I presented myself for duty at the mews, carrying the brand new portable typewriter which, in the first flush of enthusiasm, I had insisted on buying—despite Cheuret's assurance that a machine could easily be borrowed. Rose, the cook, opened the door to me. "Oh, it's you, is it?" was her welcome. "Thought it was the butcher." She grinned, showing her absurd dimples, and shouted upstairs: "Secretary's here!"

Cheuret hadn't exaggerated when he told me that he needed a secretary. Indeed, he could have done with two, and a book-keeper as well. For the last five years he had dealt with all his own correspondence, both business and private, in both languages—and this despite the fact that he had to rehearse, play at concerts, transpose music, make researches at the British Museum, run a music society and spend two days a week out of town altogether, giving violin lessons to the pupils of various large schools. He wrote English easily but incorrectly ; while Madame Cheuret, who helped him a great deal, was incapable of spelling any but the simplest words. We laughed a lot while they told me all this. Cheuret dragged out an immense suitcase from beneath one of the beds: it was full of letters. "These," he told me, "are extremely urgent." He opened a cupboard: letters poured out in an avalanche: "These are not so urgent: we ought to answer them by Christmas."

But letter-answering was to be only a part of my duties. Cheuret had great, almost visionary schemes for the future. So far, he said, the quartette had worked without method: they had given concerts here and there, where they were already known or had happened to be invited. That was all wrong. Often, they had had to take an isolated engagement in a distant town, and their travelling expenses had, in consequence, been very high. What they needed was someone to plan for them. Tours must be worked out; schools and provincial music societies must be written to in advance; alternative dates must be offered and alternative programmes; a book ought to be prepared stating exactly which items had been performed at which concerts, to avoid unnecessary repetition. (Here Cheuret casually indicated a large washing-basket, stuffed full of old concert programmes: "You'll find all details in there," he added.) And then there was the B.B.C. And the question of gramophone-recording. "When you have spare time, you may look through some catalogues and try to think of some suggestions for new records." I nodded, trying to be as brisk and businesslike as possible; but I couldn't help thinking that that "spare time" would be long in coming.

Certainly, Cheuret could scarcely have found a less efficient employee than myself; and yet I doubt if anyone, however highly trained, could have done much better. The ideal secretary-manager of whom he dreamed would have been compelled to keep away from the house altogether; otherwise, Cheuret would never have left him alone. The truth was that, like most very energetic men, he couldn't bear to see anybody else working. And although he was for ever complaining that he hadn't enough time to give to his music because of these wretched letters, letter-writing seemed to have a fatal fascination for him. Suppose a lady had written to ask whether the quartette would be free to come down to her club and give a concert during the month of January; Cheuret would never merely tell me to write "Yes" or "No." He would compose a complete answer, half-French, half-English, in pencil, on the back of the original letter. This answer I would translate, correct, type out and bring to him to sign. He would read it through, smile encouragingly, murmur: "Good . . . Good . . . Very good . . . Excellent. . . ." and then began to scribble further notes in the margin. Another, revised copy would be typed. And there would be more approbation, more notes. I was lucky if this didn't happen three or four times in succession.

Letters, and copies of answers, had, of course, to be filed. We had bought a very handsome file, dull grey in colour, which opened like a concertina—it was known, always, as "The Mud-Coloured File." This file gave me more trouble than any other inanimate object I have ever encountered, before or since. How often, on arrival, I would be greeted by Rose or Jean or Edouard from the top of the staircase with the news: "The Mud-Coloured File's lost again! Have you seen it? The Governor's been hunting for hours!" And then, at last, it would be discovered, lying innocently unnoticed on a chair, toning perfectly with dull grey shadows of a late autumn morning and, from the distance of a few yards, nearly invisible. Not only could the mud-coloured file uncannily disappear: its roomy pockets seemed to swallow letters like a conjurer's vanishing-box. Cheuret's conception of filing differed radically from my own: if he put a paper away under the letter P, then I was sure to hunt for it in M, N, O, Q and R—and vice versa. At last, by tacit consent, we stopped using the file altogether; except for correspondence which was no longer important. Urgent letters were popped into the suitcase, slipped between sheets of music or left lying on the sitting-room mantelpiece, as in the days before my arrival.

But, if our interior organization still left a good deal to be desired, we became, outwardly, at least, very official. Cheuret had some new business notepaper printed which was headed not only with the address, telephone number and names of the quartette, but also with my own name. "Secretary: Christopher Isherwood"—with what furtive pride I read and reread those three words! They were my passport to the great outer world, the world beyond the schoolroom windows, which I had waited so long and so impatiently to enter. Never again should I blush or stammer or feel awkward when ladies at tea-parties asked me what I "did." I had my answer ready.

And not merely was I now a humble member of the enormous musical community; I had my colleagues, my equals. Over the telephone, at any rate, one secretary was as good as another. We knew each other's names; we said good morning and chatted politely for a few moments before stating our business. True, I could hardly echo the words of Miss Gibson, of the B.B.C., whose invariable formula was: "I'll just call down to the porter's lodge and find out if Mr. So-and-So's still in the building." But I did try to convey the illusion that Cheuret had to be hunted for through a whole suite of rooms; and, even when he was sitting in the opposite chair, I liked to keep the enquirer waiting for at least a couple of minutes. My particular friend was Mr. Hardy, of the Gramophone Society. We had never met, but our politeness was excessive. Picturing a dynamic middle-aged man seated amidst a subservient staff of stenographers, I was, nevertheless, determined not to be outdone. "Very well, Mr. Hardy," I would rattle briskly into the mouthpiece, "I'll have that typed out and sent round to you to-night . . . oh, splendid, thanks . . . Rather busy, you know . . . Yes, certainly, Mr. Hardy; I'll take the matter up with Monsieur Cheuret at once . . . *Good* morning. . . ." Nearly a year later, we met at a concert and were introduced. Mr. Hardy proved to be a mild, agreeable, literary young man of my own age. He told me that he had always supposed me to be forty, at least.

Although Cheuret had lived in England for so long, had married an English wife, wore English clothes, played English games, he remained a Belgian to the marrow; I think this was really the secret of his great personal charm. He made none of those ridiculous, touching and irritating attempts, so common to expatriates, to ape the manners and peculiarities of his adopted country. Amongst Englishmen, he was frankly a foreigner, and therefore perfectly natural. An artist, born in a country where art has a respected social status, he nevertheless contrived to adapt himself to a way of life founded upon a denial that the artist (unless commercially successful) has any right to exist. I never heard him say a word against England. And, indeed, it might be argued that England had made him the man he was. Had he remained in Paris or Brussels—like one or two of his now famous fellow students whom I was later to meet—he would still, no doubt, have been charming, considerate, kind; but he would also have been inescapably *"le maître."* In London, he wasn't *"le maître"*—except to a small clique of society snobs; and they, even, didn't pay him half the homage they reserved for a stranger of inferior talent from Amsterdam, Barcelona or Berlin. In London, he was Mister Shuray, who played tennis and the violin, both well. Many of Cheuret's best friends— sincere lovers of music in their way—valued him chiefly as a keen fisherman.

Cheuret's career was a salutary object-lesson to "Isherwood the Artist." Here was a man who had spent the best years of his life performing other people's music—and trying to perform it, not according to some showy personal interpretation, but as the composer himself would have liked to hear it played. This was his whole aim as a musician: a faithful anonymous performance. To this aim he had sacrificed all prospects of stardom and big material success—had sacrificed them as a matter of course, without any complaint, or posing, or fuss. He wasn't jealous of the great solo musicians ; on the contrary, he admired them, both personally and collectively—provided that they could really play. He recognized their importance and the function they performed. He laughed, of course, at the hysterical demonstrations they provoked from pseudo-admirers ; never at the men themselves. Talent, in others, excused every affection and oddity. He was quite shocked when I hinted that oddity had helped to earn that seventy-guinea fee for an evening's concert, at which Cheuret himself had received five.

Music, as far as he personally was concerned, meant chamber music, performed by a string quartette. The quartette, he was never tired of saying, consisted of four equal instrumental voices, and *not* a solo violin accompanied by three subsidiary instruments. His only bitter criticisms were reserved for first violins who "led" their quartettes egotistically, dictatorially, to the overthrow of balance in the music. Cheuret wanted a musical democracy of four persons. I remember his jokes about a celebrated central European quartette in which, he said, the leader had absolute power over his three colleagues ; even their wives had to obey him ! So strong, indeed, was his antipathy to any form of imposed authority that he refused absolutely to call his quartette "The Cheuret," even when its three other members wished him to do so.

And yet, for all his self-dedication, his material sacrifice, his quality of unworldly simplicity, Cheuret wasn't and didn't in the least feel himself to be "exiled" from the world. My conception of "Isherwood the Artist," the lonely, excluded,

monastic figure, was something he could never have understood. He never asked for or expected any kind of preferen-
tial treatment—either from strangers or members of his own
family—on the strength of his "perceptions" or "temperament" or "nerves." If he wanted to be alone, to concentrate
on some difficult piece of work, he didn't ask us to leave the
room: he retired, as a matter of course, to the bathroom or
the coal-hole under the stairs. He seemed to be able to start
and stop working instantly, at will: when we were all together, he took his full share of the conversation—there were
no moody self-conscious creative silences. To think private
thoughts in public he would probably have considered rude—
as, indeed, it is. Once, when I was trying to write a poem in
my head during a party, Cheuret said mockingly: "Christopher, you look like some deep thing that hasn't got its instrument."

He and Madame Cheuret were admirable parents: their
relations with Jean and Edouard astonished me—they were
so easy, so natural, so entirely unlike anything I had ever
seen before. There was something very youthful about
Cheuret, despite his grey hair and thin, lined face; one saw
it most clearly when he was talking to Edouard about fishing
or arguing with Jean as to who should take the better tennis-
racket. Sometimes he got angry, and shouted; he was never
cold and biting, and he didn't try and trap his sons into
promises, obligations, confessions. If somebody said something subtle and cutting, he was curiously helpless: he
couldn't speak that language. There were moments when the
two boys seemed infinitely more sophisticated, more adroit,
more canny than their father.

Yet they were charming, too, in their different ways: Jean,
already at his preparatory school, so very much the English
schoolboy, yet a bit unsure of himself, conscious of a difference, his foreign blood showing itself in the way he moved
his head, laughed, told a funny story: Edouard, dark, pale,
squarely built, like the child of a warmer climate, riper and
more self-possessed than his age, clever at making little draw-
ings and writing verses. Cheuret gave both of them violin
lessons during the holidays, but neither had any special musical talent. This must have been a great disappointment to
him, yet he never twisted it into a reproach against them,
even when he had lost his temper.

I made friends with Madame Cheuret more slowly. At

first, I was shy of her: she seemed so elegant, so collected, and always, though she was kindness itself, just a little aloof. Later, she told me that I had embarrased her dreadfully, during my first weeks at the house, by my politeness, always jumping to my feet when she came into the room and hurrying to hold the door open as she went out. These Kensington manners had, it seemed, also seriously worried Cheuret himself: he had begun to try to live up to them—though I must say that I never noticed this. When the shyness had worn off, I discovered that Madame Cheuret was one of the most placid people I had ever known. She had a genius for making herself comfortable: if there were five minutes to spare after lunch or before a concert, she would sink, with a sigh of pleasure, into the nearest chair, and, if possible, put her feet up. If Cheuret lived perpetually wound up, like a spring, she was always uncoiling, gently relaxing—and we all, to some extent, relaxed with her. In that agitated household, with its continual coming and going, its flurry and excitement, she radiated ease and calm—and contrived, nevertheless, to get through as much work as any two of us put together.

Last of all, after a long period of probation, I was accepted by Rose. Rose, despite her dimples and plump smiles, was a merciless critic: if she didn't like you, she didn't. Nobody's recommendation counted with her. She came from Suffolk. She had been with the Cheurets for ten years, and had given them notice at least a hundred times during that period. Cheuret she called "The Governor" or "The Boss"; Madame Cheuret was "Madam"; Edouard was "Tiggy"; Jean was "His Lordship"—this last a term of disapprobation. Jean had "got in wrong" with her shortly before my arrival, and she didn't really forgive him for two and a half years. Edouard she squabbled with intermittently; usually because he had interfered in the cooking (he himself was already an accomplished cook): "Get out of my kitchen, will you?" she would suddenly exclaim. "I'm all bloody behind, this morning, as it is!" Edouard loved these rows. He danced round her, slapping her ample bottom, embracing her, pinching her, shouting: "Rose is all behind! Rose is all behind!" until she picked up the soup-ladle or the rolling-pin and chased him downstairs.

Rose called me "Christopher," and spoke of me to the others as "Secretary." "Hullo, Christopher," she would greet me. "How's life?" If I spoke first, and said, "Hullo, Rose,"

93

she would answer: "Hullo yourself"—but this only if she happened to be in a particularly good humour. When something had annoyed her, which was about three times a week, she would only give me a very curt, "Hullo," and disappear at once into the music-room, because, on that tiny staircase, it was otherwise quite impossible for me to get past. If I followed her and asked what was the matter, she snorted, "Fed up—that's what I am," or merely didn't reply. But generally, in this case, as I was going up the stairs, I would hear a loud, instantly suppressed snigger. One evening I invited her to come with me to the cinema. *The Four Horsemen of the Apocalypse* was being shown. I had seen it, long before, three or four times already, and, towards the end, I fell asleep. Rose was delighted. And, when the bombardment began and I woke up with a violent start, her fat hearty laugh rang out, louder than all the guns. Afterwards, she told Madame Cheuret that Secretary was "ever so nice to go out with."

As for myself, I had long since fallen in love with the entire family. My attitude towards them became violently possessive. I was jealous of their friends. Looking enviously through old photograph albums of past holidays and concert tours, I hated to think of all the years of their company I had missed. I wanted, in some vague daydream manner, to help and protect them against the outside world that seemed to menace their gaiety and their curious quality of innocence: and I wanted also, contradictorily, to be taken under their wing, to be acknowledged by them as elder brother and son. On weekdays, I invented work, so as to be able to return to the house in the afternoons: often I stayed on until ten or eleven o'clock at night. On Sundays, when I had no excuse whatever for seeing them, I felt lonely and terribly bored.

Kurella, the second violin, was of Polish extraction. He was a pale, heavy-lidded young man, with arched sensitive nostrils and big, well-formed sensual lips. He was always well dressed, in smart city suits, with silk handkerchief, gloves and spats: he might have been an exceptionally intelligent stockbroker, if you hadn't noticed his hands. When he played, he leaned forward persuasively in his chair, his shoulders hunched together, as though he were dancing; his whole attitude diffident, persuasive, discreetly erotic. If a string quartette can be regarded as a kind of conversation, Kurella seemed to me to be stating a case for the smooth discreet life of the world; hinting, in his playing, that everything is all right, is perfect, so long as you're careful, so long as you aren't found out. But all this with a certain wistfulness, a certain nostalgia for romance. Yes, he was really very romantic, in his up-to-date, understated fashion: he represented romance in 1925—a wistful little half-question, refined away to the faintest innuendo. He had a sensitive profile, fine-drawn, melancholy, impassive, which ladies in the audience often admired.

Tommy Braddock was the baby of the quartette, not yet twenty years old. He was large and hefty and nice-looking, with black eyes and hair and dazzlingly white teeth. Later, he would run to fat. Everybody liked Tommy—including Rose. He used to clown about in the kitchen, stuffing himself with anything sweet he could lay his hands on, and giving her wet, smacking kisses. He could play almost every known instrument including the saxophone and the ukulele; and already he had had offers from one of the most successful jazz-bands in London. Cheuret wouldn't be able to keep him much longer. They both realized this: Tommy was apologetic and rather guilty; Cheuret reasonable but secretly pained—in his heart of hearts, he couldn't understand how anybody of Tommy's talent could abandon classical music. Tommy, himself, didn't look at things in that way at all. If he felt guilty it was only because he was fond of the Cheurets: Beethoven and Mozart claimed no more and no less of his loyalty than the composer of the latest "hot" rhythm. At the moment, he was playing jazz in his spare time: once he confessed to me that he had sat up most of the night with his saxophone: "You see, Chris," he added, very seriously, "Jazz isn't like classical music. It needs a lot of rehearsing." He wore horn-rimmed spectacles, double-breasted waistcoats, bell-bottomed trousers, gaudy ties. When he played the viola, he was deadly serious. The tip of his tongue appeared between his lips as he worked his way through a tricky passage; then, when the difficulty was safely past, his big mouth opened into a broad grin, deeply satisfied and a trifle surprised, as though he had unexpectedly won some money at cards.

Forno, the 'cellist, was Anglo-Italian. He was small, dapper and dark, with lustrous passionate eyes and a short prominent imperious nose—very much the musician, in his choice of broad-brimmed black hats and floppy ties: his temperament was consciously operatic, he burlesqued it to conceal a charming, touching shyness—every woman was to him, secretly, a princess. He held the 'cello as though a very beautiful young girl had fainted in his arms. When he played his eyes were closed; he seemed to swoon, to drown in a sombre passionate dream. Certain notes vibrated visibly through his whole body, making him shudder in the very marrow of his bones; his eyelids clenched more tightly and his lips parted, as if in extreme pain. But he could be jolly, also, when the quartette rehearsed its lighter pieces, the arrangement of Scotch airs and Goossens' *Jack o' Lantern*: then his 'cello ceased to be a girl and became an Italian barrel-organ, to which he sang, at rehearsals, with a pipe in the corner of his mouth.

Early in October, Cheuret had arranged four concerts, at schools and music societies in Kent and Sussex. He suggested that we should take the Renault and combine business with a three days' motoring trip.

My memories of this remarkable journey are vivid but confused. There was a girls' school in the middle of a forest—an immense Georgian house with terraced gardens, circular flower-beds, fountains and box hedges, at which King Edward the Seventh had once stayed: we arrived there very late at night. Tea was brought while the quartette tuned up in front of a roaring fire. Forno lay flat on his back on a couch, plucking his 'cello-strings. Cheuret wandered restlessly round the room scraping out improvised airs. All four of them played like this during the intervals: if I wanted to say anything to them, I had to go up close and shout into their ears. I remember the faintly tittering hush as the quartette took their places; the moment's pause of silence: then the sudden vivid shock of sound, as the opening bars of the Haydn B Flat poured out into the stillness of the crowded room. The four ringing voices of the instruments, so clear, so fearless, so alive, were like a challenge—from the four men on the platform to the three hundred girls and women seated below. Their plain, vibrant statement seemed, at that moment, so absurd in its frankness that I began to smile. Surely, this wouldn't be allowed? Surely, in that first instant, something had been exploded for ever; blown into millions of pieces which could never again be collected and put together—the elegant demure vase-like form of artificially virginal life in that palatial cloistered house? Surely some girl would jump to her feet and scream the *J'en appelle*? But no, apparently not. Perhaps I was merely a trifle drunk: we had all had whiskies at the pub to keep out the cold. The faces around me were pleased, appreciative, quite placid: this was evidently just another concert—classical, Haydn, most suitable. As the quartette continued to explore the variations of the air, my own senses dulled into normality: the audience was quite right; this, after all, was only chamber music: before the end of the last movement, I had nearly fallen asleep.

The big school near Brighton was built chiefly of glass. Windswept, ruthlessly modern, it seemed to receive us into an atmosphere of Amazonian mockery: only the highest efficiency could excuse our male presence here. The concert was held in a vast magnificent hall. Told by Cheuret to arrange the music on the stands, I emerged timidly from a small door on to what seemed to be a full-sized theatrical stage. We were already rather late and the audience was restless: my appearance was greeted by half-ironical, half-genuinely mistaken applause. Thoroughly rattled, I distributed the parts at random, amidst just inaudible comments. A mistress showed me my seat, in the front row, between two girls. I glanced furtively at one of them: she turned her head away and gave a loud scornful snigger. Then the quartette appeared and took their places. There was clapping and an expectant hush; but the music didn't begin—Cheuret and Kurella were hastily exchanging sheets, Tommy's were in the wrong order and Forno's were upside down. More sniggering. Cheuret wagged his finger at me in comic reproof. I wished the earth would swallow me whole. But worse was to follow. During the Ravel, I became gradually aware that I was the centre of some kind of violent disturbance: the girls on either side of me made nervous movements, the air was full of suppressed giggling and, just behind me, someone was having hysterics into a handkerchief. Presently the excitement spread to the quartette itself. Cheuret couldn't see me, but Tommy, who could, was broadly grinning, and Kurella kept making signs with his eyebrows and head. I felt my cheeks burning like hot coals, but I didn't dare look round. When it was all over, and I could rejoin the others, I found them nearly as hysterical as the girls themselves. "You mean to say you didn't know?" gasped Tommy: "Why, there was a mouse—sitting right under your chair!"

That evening, we started back towards London. It was fearfully cold, and the Downs were wrapped in fog. The farther we went, the thicker it got, until, at last, we decided

97

D

to muffle the headlamps. We stopped, at the bottom of a little hill: this was the highest and loneliest part of the road. Cheuret, who was sitting next to me, got out of the car with a couple of scarves. As he did so, five men suddenly appeared out of the surrounding fog. It was difficult to say where they had come from; but they certainly seemed to have been waiting for us. They stood round the car in a casual, vaguely threatening semi-circle, without speaking. Kurella and Tommy, in the back, were alarmed. Forno called to Cheuret to hurry up. Only Cheuret himself, bending over the lamp, seemed quite unconcerned. I saw one of the men turn to another, as if asking a question. The other shrugged his shoulders slightly. Then, without a word, they all turned and disappeared; dispersing, apparently, along the sides of the road. Nothing happened. We drove on.

The lights began to fail. I had had trouble with them before: something was wrong with the battery. Now they slowly faded out altogether. We followed the tail-lights of other cars or simply crawled along in the dark, as best I could, going now and then into the ditch but never actually colliding with anything or getting stuck. It was long after midnight when we drove up to the door of Cheuret's house.

This was the Renault's last and longest voyage. I sold her soon afterwards. I only got forty pounds; and she had ruined me for many months to come. I never want to own a car again. But I bore her no ill-will. She had served her purpose. She had got me my job.

On Sundays, I used sometimes to take the train from Liverpool Street Station to the little suburban Essex town where Chalmers lived. I always enjoyed these journeys. They were deeply tinged, in my imagination, with the pigments of the Hynd and Starn stories. First came the glimpses of the river, at the bottom of slum streets; the gas-works; the funnels of steamers; then the rows of little houses, with their close-drawn curtains and sharp-leaved shrubs, jealously guarding the secrets of a sinister provincialism. Murders were committed here, with coal-hammer or weed-killer, to obtain small amounts of petty cash or a few shares in a South American company, discovered, too late, to be already bankrupt. And there was the Little Hotel itself, standing at the verge of the sooty fields, amidst a litter of building materials.

Moxon's delicate white hand drew down the blind as my train rolled past.

Even one's fellow passengers on this line seemed often unusual; intriguingly criminal or suggestively odd. One Sunday in December, some card-sharpers got into my carriage. Their leader, a scarlet-faced man in a check cap, opened the conversation by exclaiming heartily: "Well, Christmas is here!" He offered all of us his cigarettes; stretched himself, gave a large theatrical yawn: "Been at the club, all night," he told his two friends, "playing with a Yankee." "What were you playing?" one of the friends asked. The red-faced man didn't answer directly; he smiled round at us, knowingly, tantalizingly: "We played for a turkey a point." "What were you playing—cards?" "*Cards?*" (with great scorn). "*No!* We were playing—and I beat him every round." "You were boxing, perhaps?" the accomplice suggested; winking at us, as if to say that this was a lunatic who must be humoured. The man in the check cap laughed out loud: "*Boxing? That's good! No!* We played two into four, four into six, six into eight, eight into ten, ten into nothing. . . ." "Come on, now," interrupted the other accomplice, "we don't want to hear all that. We want to know what you were playing. Was it billiards?" "*Billiards? Ha, ha!*" Deliberately, timing his effect, check-cap produced from his pocket three greasy cards, and laid them, as carefully as if they had been banknotes, on a piece of newspaper unfolded on his lap: "Just take a look at these." We all stared, unwillingly fascinated—an elderly farmer in leggings, with his wife, a bullet-headed young man and his girl, a mild gold-spectacled bank clerk in the corner, who had been reading *Our Mutual Friend*. "This morning there's a match between the Bakers and the Butchers: who do you say'll win, sir?" The red-faced man addressed me: "The Butchers have got more beef, but the Bakers have got more dough." He began to run the cards through his fingers, picking them up, showing them, throwing them down, over and over again, with a mechanical regularity which was, perhaps intentionally, hypnotic. At first, only the two accomplices betted. Three or four times, they lost. Then one of them, winking at the company, turned up the corner of a card. After this, he won, again and again. Check-cap kept trying to draw us into the game: we were all shy, except the bank clerk, who said that he didn't want to bet, but he thought he could spot the ace. He did spot it, needless to say; and check-cap tried to force him to accept a shilling. Within five minutes, the bank clerk was betting; within ten, he had lost five shillings. He was indignant. The two accomplices soothed him by taking his side; and check-cap, as he pocketed the money, said kindly but reproachfully: "You're not a cry-baby, are you, sir?" They all three got out at Maryland Point. Check-cap shook hands with the farmer and his wife: "Always shake hands with the old folks," he told us. "Good morning, ladies, and gentlemen. Happy Christmas!" When he had gone, there was a general outburst of conversation and mutual sympathy in the carriage. We all congratulated ourselves on our shrewdness and consoled the bank clerk for his loss. "We thought you was one of them, see?" the bullet-headed young man explained; and his girl confided: "We'd been warned, you know—only last night. Just fancy!" "Ah well," sighed the bank clerk, philosophically, "they say it takes all sorts to make a world." He adjusted his spectacles and reopened *Our Mutual Friend.* The farmer and his wife said nothing. They just sat there, with their oblique sparkling little eyes, smiling fatly and seeming pleased.

In the afternoons, we were again much occupied with the idea excursion to Canvey Island, or Southend. Arriving after dark, we had tea in a shop and hurried down to the pier. Almost always, there would be a thick fog over the sea, and the lowing of invisible sirens would sound from ships lost in the estuary. Out at the pier-head, the great pavilion was locked up for the winter; we tried the slot machines and peered down over the railing at the ornate iron columns which supported the framework; Chalmers found an adjective to describe them—"necropolitan." *Le mot juste* still seemed to be the solution of most of our problems.

At this time, we were again much occupied with the idea of writing *Mortmere* as a book. But the technical difficulties, when we really began to examine them, were very serious. The trouble was that *Mortmere* must somehow be rationalized: we were both agreed about this. Mere Arabian Nights fantasy didn't, any longer, satisfy us: we should never be able to keep up a sufficiently high level of surprise throughout the book. No—the exploits of Welken and Gunball must have *some* relation to everyday reality. And it wasn't interesting enough to say, merely, that all the characters were mad. So it was that we came round to the idea of an Observer. Hynd and Starn should be introduced into *Mortmere* as a single observer-character, Hearn. Hearn is a somewhat fantastically minded young man who has had a nervous breakdown and goes to this remote village for a rest. The book opens as Hearn is on his way to a tea-party in the rectory garden. As he walks, he imagines himself writing an amusingly fanciful letter to a friend in London ; noticing a few wisps of straw dangling from the louvre-boards of the church tower, he mentally begins: "Dear Christopher, The Rector keeps some large animal stabled in the belfry . . ." This private game, once started, continues and develops, until Hearn has *imposed* imaginary characteristics, freak vices and miraculous attributes upon his mildly eccentric but really quite normal village neighbours. He thus creates *Mortmere* for his own amusement: it exists only as long as he wills it to exist. When he is tired of it, it disappears.

At first, this scheme seemed workable ; but it had one fatal disadvantage—it concentrated all the reader's interest upon Hearn himself. And who is Hearn? A fanciful invalid. Why does he create *Mortmere*? To escape from the boredom of a townee exiled into provincial life. No, it wouldn't do. It wasn't sufficiently interesting. But wait—suppose Hearn isn't merely a bored neurotic: suppose he's a dangerous madman? Suppose, at the end of the book, he has a violent attack, burns down the church, blows up the parish hall and kills everybody in the village? Wouldn't this make him more significant, more exciting? No, not really. For Hearn represented nothing—beyond our own reasons for wanting to write *Mortmere*. He wasn't and could never be a tragic figure. Well, never mind, then: Hearn needn't be tragic ; he needn't be anything. He need hardly appear at all. Having introduced the letter trick at the beginning, we could drop it altogether . . . But, if we did that, we abandoned all attempt to rationalize *Mortmere* ; we were thrown back on strangeness and fantasy . . . And there we stuck.

Thinking this all over again to-day, I still believe that our problem really was insoluble—provided that we were determined to retain the entire museum of *Mortmere* freaks and oddities. But a modified, less extraordinary version of the story could certainly have been written ; if only we had seen that the vital clue to the action was contained in Hearn's relations with the village characters *as ordinary people*. A young writer, neither mad nor ill, comes to live in a village inhabited by a normal rector and a typical collection of country parishioners. These parishioners are bound together by a complex of the usual relationships, based on love, jealousy, ambition, avarice, snobbery, pride and fear. The writer, being a writer, is deeply interested in these relationships, acquaints himself with all their intricacies, and starts constructing a novel, in which his neighbours are distorted into the characters of an extravagant and lurid fable, and their mild impulses, lukewarm emotions and timid half-intentions are developed into fantastically violent acts. For a time, the two worlds exist side by side—the Cranfordesque world of the real village and the Starnese world of the young man's novel. Then comes the moment when the novelist can no longer resist the temptation to introduce his fabulous characters to their originals. Perhaps he reads the opening chapters aloud at a garden party ; perhaps he only confides in "Gunball" or "Welken"—in either case, the entire village soon gets to hear about the book. They are horrified, of course ; scandalized, indignant—but also profoundly, guiltily excited. The writer continues to write ; his audience wait eagerly for each fresh instalment. *Mortmere* begins to exercise a fatal fascination upon each member of the community : he or she begins to feel that the Mortmere personality is stronger, more vital, the Mortmere existence infinitely more vivid and alluring than anything they have ever experienced on the plane of everyday life. And so, gradually, every man and woman in the village starts thinking and behaving, more or less consciously, in imitation of his or her Mortmere counterpart. The village becomes Mortmere. Every day, its inhabitants speak and act with increasing wildness : crime is usual, vice is commonplace, murder is in the air. And now it is the novelist's turn to feel horrified. He makes a desperate effort to bring these madmen to their senses by deliberately altering the shape of his novel ; he tones down characters and situations, invents anti-climaxes, tries to drag Mortmere back to normality. But it is too late. The original plot of *Mortmere* continues to work itself out among the mad villagers ; it is only the novel which returns to what is sane and real. At length, when the full tragedy has been enacted, the novelist escapes from the village he has unwittingly destroyed. He alone has remained, from first to last, a quiet undistinguished ordinary young man.

This idea is largely cribbed—as many of my readers will recognize—from Gide's *Les Faux-Monnayeurs,* which we both read about a year later. The plot of this novel, as described, so thrillingly, suggestively and misleadingly, by E. M. Forsters in his *Aspects*, excited our imagination beyond all bounds; indeed, the novel itself came as something of an anti-climax. In our impatience, we both bought copies and began reading simultaneously. We even reported our progress to each other on a series of postcards. Chalmers wrote: "Have just finished chapter seven. The idiot has ruined everything." But later: "Page 359. Gide is the greatest. Whatever he does, he can't spoil it now." What our final verdict was I forget. In fact, I have almost entirely forgotten what *Les Faux-Monnayeurs* was actually about. What remains, immense, vague, profoundly exciting, is my conception of Forster's conception of Gide's original idea. One day, I shall attempt the nearly hopeless task of fixing it and writing it down.

About the middle of January, Chalmers went down to Cornwall, to start work as a tutor at the house of some people who lived near St. Ives. And soon his letters began to arrive:

A very steep road leads up from the station to the front gate of the house. From the summit of the hill one can see the entire bay. A white-funnelled tug has the appearance of a lighthouse on a rock. Every morning one glimpses Colonel Shagpennon at his red baize table, slightly elongated, like a shape seen beyond a screen of falling water. His long flax-coloured moustaches seem to wave vaguely towards me through the dimness—like the feelers of a lobster imprisoned in an aquarium. . . .

I am a shape in a stained yellow mackintosh and a new plus-four suit. It is always raining here, not continuously but four or five times a day. My view of the surrounding country is blurred by occasional Schoolboy's Apprehension. The unreal world of evening preparation for next day's Latin and mathematics.

I teach the children in a small hut or summer-house at the bottom of the garden. Close to this hut is another and larger one into which they disappear for a quarter of an hour every morning. They live in a peculiar Mortmere of constructing model ships. Or so I imagine. I haven't yet been into the larger hut.

I work in the mornings only.

The front door of this lodging house opens above the bay.

The food is good and seldom adulterated either with frog's viscera or prunes. Several old men live in a room which is separated from mine by a mere lath partition. They are all scholars and readers of the *Times Literary Supplement*. I met one in the hall to-day. He apologized for having cataract in both his eyes.

The lath partition acts as a kind of amplifier of all conversation. One of the old men is Ibsen. He said at lunch: "Well, we are half-way through another day."

I have travelled by bus to St. Ives and Penzance. Fortunately, I saw no artists at St. Ives. Seagulls drop their dung on a church tower whose top is level with the top of the hill which leads down to it. There is a stone jetty, and the pilchard-fishing fleet is drawn up on a semicircle of white beach. I noticed some clay-coloured and bluish rocks slashed with scars at all angles. The scars were always straight lines and had the effect of making the shapes of individual rocks seem doubtful, like changing forms seen through a slight mist. This is the true cubism.

But Penzance is better. It has the supreme provincial flavour—with white-faced bank clerks comfortably smoking pipes in the street after tea and trees spraying the air vaguely above the Corinthian pillars of banks. Also there is an unusually large esplanade, and this is appropriately invisible from the high central part of the town. . . .

Just back from St. Ives quay. Two hours' sun to-day. It drops from the sky in cubes and almost tangible rectangles. Like the rocks I mentioned. Brightness falls from the air. . . . At Penzance the esplanade lashes the sea to tall boiling plumes like white cypress trees. At low tide when there is a wind the sand streams towards my feet like writhing mist or like innumerable snakes gliding at sixty miles an hour. The sun changes the land utterly. I know now quite definitely that I am sentimental to the bone. Let me admit once and for all that I prefer a wall with ivy on it to a wall without ivy. I prefer purple to grey and sun to rain. I prefer downs to crags. . . .

The St. Ives Art Club: the Poshocracy over again, but with a certain ratsness due to the fact that they are most of them old. Death always assists at their charades. I have collected from among them six new characters for *Mortmere*. But this eternal blazon may not be in a single letter. I'll content you with naming the chief of them—

Mr. Corner, a potter who works on a hill above St. Ives. He has spent most of his life in Japan. His pottery unites the English ballad with Japanese folk-lore. He has designed and built a gate in this style which—from what I saw of it—opens directly on to the edge of a cliff. . . .

The most suggestive of all technical terms: "The Theory of Tensors." Like a symphony in the iron tunnel of a colossal telescope. And the opening bars of course are: "*Genus humanum ingenio superavit.*" But I have left out a few illuminating words: ". . . for this purpose we employ an instrument of higher mathematics commonly known as the Theory of Tensors." This is accidental beauty and reminds me chiefly of the almost sinister geometrical atmosphere of Dürer's *Melencolia*. "A mathematical hint seldom known as the lustreless compasses and aqueous horizon. . . ."

In the yellow-papered room with its fretworked piano, obscene curtains, torn theological books, vases and communicative historic smell—*soupçon* of rancid ova, whisper of metallic-voiced prayers in double beds, ooze of self-pitying tears—I put on my slippers for the night. The cold maddening drone of an indistinct prayer penetrates from the room above. In the armchair opposite me an invisible paralytic sits wearing my outdoor shoes: the corkscrew watcher who, every night, puts on the clothes that one has thrown off in disgust. A shadow crosses the clock's face. "*No, I will never let you in! Not to-night.*" Madness like a mandarin is standing outside the pane in the slanting moonlight, foot-firm on the drenched, quiet forget-me-nots. His brittle hand lifts from beneath the waving kimono and perishes briefly in a sickly dust. The wind begins to come up from the sea. I bite my thumbnail to the quick. . . .

Day by day, the coiled obsession grows: I must write *The Market Town*. The plot is utterly changed and most of the characters have gone, but it is the same town. *It is always the same town.* Whether they wear surplices or corduroy breeches or black velvet coats, whether they live in Kensington, Cambridge or Cornwall—the same boiling fraud hangs like an exhalation on tile and tree. O boy, I have the vision at last. I see the enormous calm disaster and the pouring tears. I stand by the matchwood scoring board in the sun and watch the awed fielders as they carry away the dead boy from the wicket. Ninety-nine runs. His white flannel trousers have grass stains at the knee. . . . Far away a paddle-steamer is stuck in the afternoon sea. . . .

I am standing on a white heap of sand above Tallwater Estuary. Dusk rises like a grey sweat from the hills and the shore. Two moorhens vanish wildly beyond the granite paw of a jutting cliff. From the depths of the land the windows of a golf club-house throw out feelers of light against a spinney of naked birches. It is too late to go home. I try to pass unnoticed by the black entrance of the cave. But the overhanging grasses stir with a dry hushing sound, and a grey mammoth-like shape protrudes its trunk from the dark hole. It is going down to bathe in the estuary. I notice its hideous lobster eyes and its puffed dewlaps soggy in the sand. The trunk lifts slowly and I peer down the aperture. Men are moving about inside, some in bowler hats, others in bathing dresses, and one, I particularly notice, in complete polo kit. It turns sadly and wallows onward into the increasing darkness. . . .

At Easter, I travelled down to visit him. In my suitcase were the first six chapters of a new novel called, provisionally *The Summer at the House*. It was a curious by-product of Romer Wilson's *The Death of Society*, stiffened with undigested chunks of Henry James: it was inspired, vaguely, by my vision of the life of the Cheuret family. I didn't show it to Chalmers: I wanted, I said, to write more of it first. Actually, I was ashamed. I knew already that it wasn't much good.

Cornwall was exactly as he had described—except that he had forgotten to mention St. Michael's Mount and the shafts of the abandoned tin-mines. The bare hillside was pitted with them ; they looked like shell-craters, surrounded with barbed wire. We walked over the moors to Zennor, because D. H. Lawrence had lived there ; and Chalmers told me about the novel he wanted to write—*The Market Town*. His description of the plot seemed to me, at the time, to promise an obvious masterpiece: to-day, I have forgotten it almost down to the last detail—deliberately, perhaps ; since I was later to steal several of the best scenes for myself.

But more exciting, even, than Chalmers' schemes for *The Market Town* were his new theories about novel-writing in general: "I saw it all suddenly while I was reading *Howards End* . . . Forster's the only one who understands what the modern novel ought to be . . . Our frightful mistake was that we believed in tragedy: the point is, tragedy's quite impossible nowadays . . . We ought to aim at being essentially comic writers . . . The whole of Forster's technique is based on the tea-table: instead of trying to screw all his scenes up to the highest possible pitch, he tones them down until they sound like mothers'-meeting gossip . . . In fact, there's actually *less* emphasis laid on the big scenes than on the unimportant ones: that's what's so utterly terrific. It's the completely new kind of accentuation—like a person talking a different language. . . ."

As we had arranged, we took the steamer to the Scilly Isles and stayed there a week. At Hugh Town there was a good hotel, with excellent beer and a waiter with discreet Mortmere tones, who murmured: "Plenty of young *ladies* on this island, sir." In the visitors' book were the names of people who had stayed at the hotel after their ships had been wrecked on the surrounding rocks. Looking out of my bedroom window, one morning, across the harbour to the peaks of Tresco and Bryher, I knew, with exquisite relief, that I needn't go on trying to write *The Summer at the House*. It was sham all through. Walking down deep grassy lanes between wallflower fields, sheltered from the Atlantic breeze, we began, at once, to plan my new book. It was to open, of course, on Scilly. Two young men, one of them a would-be painter and writer, the other a medical student, are staying at the Hugh Town hotel. The painter has defied his family and run away from an office job in the city: the medical student has egged him on to do this. Also staying at the hotel is a Cambridge Poshocrat-athlete, whom the medical student loathes. And there is a girl of fourteen, in whom both the student and the Poshocrat are romantically interested.

"And then," said Chalmers, "I think there's some kind of accident . . . Yes, my God, that's it! The Poshocrat insists on taking her out climbing, and she gets killed."

The accident was to be in the best Forster tradition, "tea-tabled," slightly absurd. The girl slips from a rock a couple of feet high, breaks her neck and dies instantly. At the enquiry which follows, the student publicly blames the Poshocrat and there is a violent scene. Later, they all go back to London. The painter returns to his office. The student and

107

the Poshocrat are rivals: they both want the painter's sister. The Poshocrat gets her, chiefly by using his cash and social position to dazzle the painter's mother and aunt. In his status as fiancé he begins to boss the household (resembling, more and more strongly, his original in *Howards End*): he also tries to pack his future brother-in-law, the painter, off to a job in an African colony. The painter, in desperation, runs away for the second time. The Poshocrat, feeling sure that the student is at the bottom of it, goes round to see him: there is an argument, a jealous scene about the sister, and finally, a fight—in which the student kills the Poshocrat with a poker: this last episode, said Chalmers, would have to be written as almost pure farce.

In the intervals of discussing all this, we wandered about the island, went out in a launch to see the seals, talked to the boatmen about wrecks. Enough dollar bills had been washed ashore to build a whole terrace of houses; also several ladies in full evening dress with diamonds, and a whole cargo of lead pencils. We landed on Tresco, where the Abbey stands, in the middle of a sub-tropical garden: a flamingo-like bird came out to meet us, threateningly, from beneath the cedars. Chalmers quoted: "This castle hath a pleasant seat." The days passed only too quickly, in the excitement of literary composition and the pleasant haze of beer. When the time came for our return to the mainland, I had already started on the first chapter of the novel: I had decided to call it *Seascape with Figures*.

The General Strike, which everybody in Cheuret's circle of friends said was impossible and sure to be called off at the last moment, began without any visible fuss at midnight, after a concert at which Forno had realized his ambition to conduct a small string orchestra. They had played Bach, Vivaldi, Purcell. Forno himself, immaculate as a bridegroom, with his white carnation and brand-new evening tails, had struck out powerfully through the Vivaldi, like a swimmer breasting a strong sea. When it was over, he had received the squeaky congratulations of Arnold Bennett. As I took my ticket home on the bus, the conductor said: "'Fraid you'll have to drive this thing yourself, to-morrow, sir."

And, sure enough, next morning, the tremendous upper-middle-class lark began: by lunch-time, the Poshocrats were down from Oxford and Cambridge in their hundreds—out

108

for all the fun that was going. And the medical students—
"spoiling for a fight," as elderly Kensington ladies admiringly
said of them—paraded the streets in their special constables'
armlets, licensed to punch at sight. Every bus and underground train was a ragtime family party: goodness knew
where you were going or how long it would take. If you
fussed because they took you to Mornington Crescent instead
of Hyde Park Corner you were a spoil-sport, an obstruction-
ist, even a trifle unpatriotic. Not that anybody talked about
patriotism—this wasn't 1914. Everything was perfectly all
right, really. The strikers were all right—except for a few paid
agitators controlled by Moscow, and some gangs of professional roughs. The great mass of working class entered "into
the spirit of the thing." Why, wasn't there the case of Sandy
Ross, the son of a friend of the Cheurets, captain of his college first fifteen? Sandy had volunteered to bring supplies
every day from the north of London in his racing sports car:
he had to go through a "bad" district, in the neighbourhood
of Paddington: the first day a crowd wouldn't let him pass.
Sandy had hopped out of the car with a spanner in his hand.
Things had begun to look ugly ; and then Sandy had shouted,
with his best accent: "Are there no Scotsmen here?" And, at
once, a dozen voices had answered: "Aye, laddie, we're with
ye." And every day, the story concluded, these compatriots
had formed a bodyguard for Sandy's car, till he was safely
through the district. Such anecdotes, people agreed, were very
reassuring. They showed that the Englishman's heart was still
in the right place.

Philip, swept along in the crowd from his medical school,
had volunteered for national service on the first day of the
strike: they made him conductor on an underground train at
four pounds ten a week. My friend Eric became a docker.
Most of the young men I knew were special constables: the
girls worked in canteens. Those who had cars drove round
the streets, offering interesting-looking men "a lift." The professional prostitutes, like the rest of the working classes,
found themselves being blacklegged on their own beats. That
special kind of hysteria known as "Business as usual" mani-
fested itself in the least unexpected places: a comic actress,
one of the Cheurets' oldest friends, went tragic about the
danger to the British Constitution and denounced all those
who had failed to "do their bit." Only the Cheurets themselves remained calm, regarding, with civilized amusement,

the antics of their circle. "Oh, dear," sighed Madame, sinking comfortably on to the divan after washing up the lunch plates, and reaching for a cigarette; "Why *do* they have to do this sort of thing? It's *so* un-cosy." (She would have been considerably surprised if she could have seen herself, exactly ten years later, addressing a co-operative women's meeting on the necessity for helping the Government in Spain.)

But, despite her example, I couldn't laugh at the strike. From the first moment, I loathed it and longed for it to end. It wasn't that I seriously expected street fighting or civil war. But "war" was in the air: one heard it in the boisterous defiant laughter of the amateur bus drivers, one glimpsed it in the alert sexual glances of the women. This was a dress rehearsal of "The Test"; and it found me utterly unprepared. I wanted to lock myself away in a corner and pretend that nothing was happening. For the first time, I knew that I detested my own class: so sure of themselves, so confident that they were in the right, so grandly indifferent to the strikers' case. Most of us didn't even know why the men had struck. I didn't know, myself. I couldn't think about such things: I could only shudder with fear and hatred; hating both parties: my female relative announcing briskly at breakfast: "But *of course* I take sides!"—looking fresher and more alive than she'd looked for years; and Rose, gloating over the bus-wrecking in Hammersmith Broadway: "That'll teach the bloody, damn blacklegs!" I hated myself, too, for being neutral. I tried to get on with my novel; instead, I found myself opening Wilfred. He, at least, had understood what I was feeling: "Waving good-bye, doubtless they'd told the lad. . . ." But Wilfred hadn't buried his disgust in the cushions of a Kensington drawing-room: or tried vainly to pretend that as an intellectual he belonged to some mystical Third Estate, isolated above the battle. If I had known a single person connected with the Labour Movement; if Chalmers, even, had been with me—I might have been able to get my ideas into some kind of order. But Chalmers was back at his job in Cornwall, unreachable even by letter. There was nobody I could talk to. After a miserable week of doubts and self-reproaches, I sneaked round shamefacedly to the Chelsea Town Hall and volunteered for duty. "What kind of work would you like?" my lady recruiting officer asked me brightly. "Which kind do you get least application for?" I said. "Well . . ." she made a little grimace: "I suppose . . .

help on a sewage farm." "All right," I said, reflecting that this, at any rate, had a sort of spurious Mortmere flavour: as so often, I had an instantaneous picture of myself writing about it to Chalmers: "Please put me down for that."

However, before I could be called up, the strike had ended. The Poshocracy had won, as it always did win, in a thoroughly gentlemanly manner. And, just as on the college feast evening in Chalmers' rooms, so now it was quite prepared magnanimously to pretend that nothing more serious had taken place than, so to speak, a jolly sham fight with pats of butter.

CHAPTER V

AT my preparatory school, during the last two years of the War, there had been a boy named Hugh Weston. Weston—nicknamed "Dodo Minor" because of the solemn and somewhat birdlike appearance of his bespectacled elder brother—was a sturdy, podgy little boy, whose normal expression was the misleadingly ferocious frown common to people with very short sight. Both the brothers had hair like bleached straw and thick coarse-looking, curiously white flesh, as though every drop of blood had been pumped out of their bodies—their family was of Icelandic descent.

Although Weston was three years younger than myself, he had reached the top form before I left the school. He was precociously clever, untidy, lazy and, with the masters, inclined to be insolent. His ambition was to become a mining engineer; and his playbox was full of thick scientific books on geology and metals and machines, borrowed from his father's library. His father was a doctor: Weston had discovered, very early in life, the key to the bookcase which contained anatomical manuals with coloured German plates. To several of us, including myself, he confided the first naughty stupendous breath-taking hints about the facts of sex. I remember him chiefly for his naughtiness, his insolence, his smirking tantalizing air of knowing disreputable and exciting secrets. With his hinted forbidden knowledge and stock of mispronounced scientific words, portentously uttered, he enjoyed among us, his semi-savage credulous schoolfellows, the status of a kind of witch-doctor. I see him drawing an indecent picture on the upper fourth form blackboard, his stumpy fingers, with their blunt bitten nails, covered in ink: I see him boxing, with his ferocious frown, against a boy twice his size; I see him frowning as he sings opposite me in the choir, sur-

pliced, in an enormous Eton collar, above which his great
red flaps of ears stand out, on either side of his narrow
scowling pudding-white face. In our dormitory religious arguments, which were frequent, I hear him heatedly exclaiming
against churches in which the cross was merely painted on the
wall behind the altar: they ought, he said, to be burnt down
and their vicars put into prison. His people, we gathered,
were high Anglican. As a descendant of a Roundhead judge,
I felt bound in honour to disagree with him, and sometimes
said so: but I could never work up much enthusiasm, even
in those argumentative days, for ritualistic questions.

Weston and I met again, by purest chance, seven years
later. Just before Christmas, 1925, a mutual acquaintance
brought him in to tea. I found him very little changed. True,
he had grown enormously; but his small pale yellow eyes
were still screwed painfully together in the same short-sighted
scowl and his stumpy immature fingers were still nail-bitten
and stained—nicotine was now mixed with the ink. He was
expensively but untidily dressed in a chocolate-brown suit
which needed pressing, complete with one of the new fashionable double-breasted waistcoats. His coarse woollen socks
were tumbled, all anyhow, around his babyishly shapeless
naked ankles. One of the laces was broken in his elegant
brown shoes. While I and his introducer talked he sat silent,
aggressively smoking a large pipe with a severe childish
frown. Clumsy and severe, he hooked a blunt dirty finger
round the tops of several of the books in my shelves, over-
balancing them on to his lap and then, when his casual
curiosity was satisfied, dropping them face downwards open
on the floor—serenely unconscious of my outraged glances.

But when my acquaintance, who had another engagement,
had gone, Weston dropped some of his aggressive academic
gaucherie: we began to chatter and gossip: the preparatory
school atmosphere reasserted itself. We revived the old jokes;
we imitated Pillar cutting bread at supper: ("Here you are!
Here you are! Help coming, Waters! Pang-slayers coming!
Only one more moment before that terrible hunger is satisfied! Fight it down, Waters! Fight it down!") We remember how Spem used to pinch our arms for not knowing the
irregular verbs and punish us with compulsory fir-cone gathering. We tried to reconstruct the big scene from Reggy's drama,
The Waves, in which the villain is confronted by the ghost
of the murdered boy, seated in the opposite chair: ("The

waves . . . the waves . . . can't you hear them calling? Get down, *carrse* you, get down! Ha, ha—I'm not afraid! Who says I'm afraid? Don't stare at me, *carrse* you, with those great eyes of yours. . . . I never feared you living; and I'm demned if I fear you now you're—*dead*! Ha, ha! Ha, ha! Ha ha ha ha ha ha ha!") Weston was brilliant at doing one of Pa's sermons: how he wiped his glasses, how he coughed, how he clicked his fingers when somebody in chapel fell asleep: ("Sn Edmund's Day. . . . Sn Edmund's Day. . . . Whur ders it *mean*? Nert—whur did it mean to *them, then, theah*? Bert—whur ders it mean to *ers, heah, nerw*?") We laughed so much that I had to lend Weston a handkerchief to dry his eyes.

Just as he was going, we started to talk about writing. Weston told me that he wrote poetry nowadays: he was deliberately a little over-casual in making this announcement. I was very much surprised, even rather disconcerted. That a person like Weston (as I pictured him) should write poems upset my notions of the fitness of things. Deeper than all I. A. Richards' newly implanted theories lay the inveterate prejudices of the classical- against the modern-sider. People who understood machinery, I still secretly felt, were doomed illiterates: I had an instantaneous mental picture of some childish, touchingly crude verses, waveringly inscribed, with frequent blots and spelling mistakes, on a sheet of smudgy graph-paper. A bit patronizingly, I asked if I might see some of them. Weston was pleased, I thought. But he agreed ungraciously—"Right you are, if you really want to"—his bad manners returning at once with his shyness. We parted hastily and curtly, quite as though we might never bother to see each other again.

A big envelope full of manuscript arrived, a few mornings later, by post. The handwriting, certainly, was all I had expected, and worse. Indeed, there were whole lines which I have never been able to decipher, to this day. But the surprise which awaited me was in the poems themselves: they were neither startlingly good nor startlingly bad; they were something much odder—efficient, imitative and extremely competent. Competence was the last quality I had been prepared for in Weston's work: he had struck me as being an essentially slap-dash person. As for the imitation, it needed no expert to detect two major influences: Hardy and

Edward Thomas. I might have found Frost there, too ; but, in those days, I hadn't read him.

Here are four which I now think the best—chiefly because they most successfully resemble their originals :

The Traction Engine

Its days are over now ; no farmyard airs
Will quiver hot above its chimney-stack ; the fairs
It dragged from green to green are not what they have
    been
        In previous years.

Here now it lies, unsheltered, undesired,
Its engine rusted fast, its boiler mossed, unfired,
Companioned by a boot-heel and an old cart-wheel,
        In thistles attired,

Unfeeling, uncaring : imaginings
Mar not the future ; no past sick memory clings,
Yet it seems well to deserve the love we reserve
        For animate things.

The Engine House

It was quiet in there after the crushing
Mill ; the only sounds were the clacking belt
And the steady throb of waters rushing
That told of the wild joy those waters felt
In falling. The quiet gave us room to talk :
"How many horse-power is the large turbine?"
"Seventy. The beck is dammed at Greenearth Fork :
Three hundred feet of head. The new pipe-line
Will give another hundred though, at least ;
The mill wants power badly." He turned a wheel ;
The flapping of the driving-belt increased
And the hum grew shriller. He wiped a steel
Rail with a lump of waste. "And now," he said,
"I'll show you the slimes-house and the vanning
        shed—
This way." He opened a small wooden door
And the machinery leaped into a roar.

RAIN

This peace can last no longer than the storm
Which started it, this shower wet and warm,
This careless striding through the clinging grass
Perceiving nothing; these will surely pass
When heart and ear-drums are no longer dinned
By shouting air: as surely as the wind
Will bring a lark-song from the clouds, not rain,
Shall I know the meaning of lust again;
Nor sunshine on the weir's dull dreamless roar
Can change me from the thing I was before,
Imperfect body and imperfect mind
Unknowing what it is I seek to find.
I know it: yet for this brief hour or so
I am content, unthinking and aglow,
Made one with horses and with workmen, all
Who seek for shelter by a dripping wall
Or labour in the fields with mist and cloud
And slant rain hiding them as in a shroud.

THE ROOKERY

When we were half asleep we thought it seemed
Stiller than usual; but no one dreamed
That aught was wrong until we came downstairs
And looked, as we had done these many years,
At the huge wall of elms that flanked the lawn
And shouted every time a wind was born.
Someone cried "Look!": we crowded to the pane:
Their tops still glittering from last night's rain,
They swayed a little, and upon their boughs
Swung to and fro each black untidy house
The rooks had made in some past century,
And mended every springtime. But no rook
Showed dark against the early sky, or shook
Down twigs, or cawed; a hungry fledgling's cry,
Waiting a breakfast that would never come,
Was all we heard; the world seemed stricken dumb.
"The rooks have gone, have gone. . . ." We said no word;
But in the silence each one's thought was heard.

Six months later—this was July 1926—Weston came down
to stay with me at the seaside. I see him striding towards me,

along Yarmouth Pier, a tall figure with loose violent impatient movements, dressed in dirty grey flannels and a black evening bow-tie. On his straw-coloured head was planted a very broad-brimmed black felt hat.

This hat I disliked from the start. It represented, I felt, something self-conscious and sham, something that Oxford had superimposed upon Weston's personality; something which he, in his turn, was trying to impose upon me. He wore it with a certain guilty defiance: he wasn't quite comfortable in it; he wanted me to accept it, with all its implications—and I wouldn't. I will never, as long as I live, accept any of Weston's hats. Since that day, he has tried me with several. There was an opera hat—belonging to the period when he decided that poets ought to dress like bank directors, in morning cut-aways and striped trousers or evening swallow-tails. There was a workman's cap, with a shiny black peak, which he bought while he was living in Berlin, and which had, in the end, to be burnt, because he was sick into it one evening in a cinema. There was, and occasionally still is, a panama with a black ribbon—representing, I think, Weston's conception of himself as a lunatic clergyman; always a favourite role. Also, most insidious of all, there exists, somewhere in the background, a schoolmaster's mortar-board. He has never actually dared to show me this: but I have seen him wearing it in several photographs.

The black hat caused a considerable sensation in the village where I was staying. The village boys and girls, grouped along the inn wall by the bus stop, sniggered loudly as we got out of the bus. Weston was pleased: "Laughter," he announced, "is the first sign of sexual attraction." Throughout the journey, he had entertained our fellow passengers and embarrassed me furiously by holding forth, in resonant Oxonian tones: "Of course, intellect's the only thing that matters at *all*. . . . Apart from Nature, geometry's all there *is*. . . . Geometry belongs to man. Man's got to assert himself against Nature, all the *time*. . . . Of course, I've absolutely no use for colour. Only form. The only really exciting things are volumes and *shapes*. . . . Poetry's got to be made up of images of form. I hate sunsets and flowers. And I loathe the *sea*. The sea is formless . . ."

But however embarrassing such statements might be to me, when uttered in public vehicles, they never for a moment made me feel—as I should have felt if a Poshocrat had been speaking—that Weston himself was a sham. He was merely experimenting aloud; saying over the latest things he had read in books, to hear how they sounded. Also they were a kind of substitute for small talk: for Weston, in his own peculiar way, made strenuous attempts to be the model guest. He really wanted every minute of the visit to be a success—on the highest intellectual plane. I was touched and flattered to discover, bit by bit, that he admired me; looked up to me, indeed, as a sort of literary elder brother. My own vanity and inexperience propelled me into this role easily enough: nowadays I should think twice about assuming such a responsibility—for Weston, who was as lazy as he was prolific, agreed without hesitation to any suggestion I cared to make; never stopping to ask himself whether my judgment was right or wrong. If I wanted an adjective altered, it was altered then and there. But if I suggested that a passage should be rewritten, Weston would say: "Much better scrap the whole thing," and throw the poem, without a murmur, into the waste-paper basket. If, on the other hand, I had praised a line in a poem otherwise condemned, then that line would reappear in a new poem. And if I didn't like this poem, either, but admired a second line, then both the lines would appear in a third poem, and so on—until a poem had been evolved which was a little anthology of my favourite lines, strung together without even an attempt to make connected sense. For this reason, most of Weston's work at that period was extraordinarily obscure.

Over, in any case, were the days of his pastoral simplicity. Since our meetings at Christmas, Weston's literary tastes had undergone a violent revolution. Hardy and Edward Thomas were forgotten. Eliot was now the master. Quotations and misquotations were allowed, together with bits of foreign languages, proper names and private jokes. Weston was peculiarly well equipped for playing the *Waste Land* game. For Eliot's Dante-quotations and classical learning, he substituted oddments of scientific, medical and psycho-analytical jargon: his magpie brain was a hoard of curious and suggestive phrases from Jung, Rivers, Kretschmer and Freud. He peppered his work liberally with such terms as "eutectic," "sigmoid curve," "Arch-Monad," "ligature," "gastropod"; seeking thereby to produce what he himself described as a "clinical" effect. To be "clinically minded" was, he said, the first duty of a poet. Love wasn't exciting or romantic or even disgusting; it was funny. The poet must handle it and similar themes with a wry, bitter smile and a pair of rubber surgical gloves. Poetry must be classic, clinical and austere.

I got very tired of the word "austere" in the course of the next few days: I began to wonder whether it didn't, as a rule, mean simply "pompous" or "priggish." At this time, Weston was a warm admirer of the works of Edwin Arlington Robinson: Robinson, it appeared, was very austere indeed. We nearly had a serious quarrel over:

> The forehead and the little ears
> Have gone where Saturn keeps the years

a couplet which he particularly liked, but which I thought, and still think, unintentionally very funny.

"Austerity" was also mixed up with Weston's feelings about the heroic Norse literature—his own personal variety of "War"-fixation. Naturally enough, he had been brought up on the Icelandic sagas; for they were the background of his family history. On his recommendation, I now began, for the first time, to read *Grettir* and *Burnt Njal*, which he had with him in his suitcase. These warriors, with their feuds, their practical jokes, their dark threats conveyed in puns and riddles and deliberate understatements ("I think this day will end unluckily for some, but chiefly for those who least expect harm"): they seemed so familiar—where had I met them before? Yes, I recognized them now: they were the boys at our preparatory school. Weston was pleased with the idea: we discussed it a good deal, wondering which of our schoolfellows best corresponded to the saga characters. In time, the school-saga world became for us a kind of Mortmere—a Mortmere founded upon our preparatory-school lives, just as the original Mortmere had been founded upon my life with Chalmers at Cambridge. About a year later, I actually tried the experiment of writing a school story in what was a kind of hybrid language composed of saga phraseology and schoolboy slang. And soon after this, Weston produced a short verse play in which the two worlds are so confused that it is almost impossible to say whether the characters are epic heroes or members of a school O.T.C.

In the intervals of all this talk, we bathed, got mildly drunk at the village pub and sang hymns to the accompaniment of Weston's banging on the piano in our lodgings. Weston, despite the apparent clumsiness of his large pudgy hands, was a competent pianist. He could never resist the sight of a piano, no matter whether it was in the refreshment room of a German railway station or the drawing-room of a strange house: down he would sit, without so much as taking off his hat, and begin to play his beloved hymn tunes, psalms and chants—the last remnants of his Anglican upbringing. When he had finished the keyboard would be littered with ash and tobacco from his huge volcano-like pipe. He smoked enormously, insatiably: "Insufficient weaning," he explained. "I must have something to *suck*." And he drank more cups of tea per day than anybody else I have ever known. It was as if his large, white apparently bloodless body needed continual reinforcements of warmth. Although this was the height of the summer, he insisted, if the day was cloudy, on having a fire in the sitting-room. At night he slept with two thick blankets, an eiderdown, both our overcoats and all the rugs in his bedroom piled upon his bed.

When he had gone, I sat alone in my seaside lodgings and felt sorry: despite the fact that my most precious books were full of nicotine stains and dirty thumb-prints, that a hole had been burnt in my overcoat with a lighted cigar, and that I could hardly venture to show my face in the pub, since Weston had been practically turned out of it for loudly quoting the most lurid lines of Webster and Tourneur. With or without his hat, Weston was a most stimulating companion; and his short visit had excited and disturbed me profoundly. He had given me a badly needed shaking-up. Inevitably, I compared him with Chalmers. When Chalmers and I were together there were, and had always been, certain reticences between us: parts of our lives were common ground, other parts were not—and these, by mutual consent, we respected and left alone. The same thing was true of my other friends, Philip, the Cheurets, Eric. But Weston left nothing alone and respected nothing: he intruded everywhere; upon my old-maidish tidiness, my intimate little fads, my private ailments, my most secret sexual fears. As mercilessly inquisitive as a child of six, he enquired into the details of my dreams and phantasies, unravelled my complexes and poked, with his blunt finger, the acne on my left shoulder-blade, of which, since the age of eighteen, I had been extravagantly ashamed. I had found myself answering his questions, as one always must answer, when the questioner himself is completely impervious to delicacy or shame. And, after all, when I had finished, the heavens hadn't fallen; and, ah, what a relief to have spoken the words aloud!

Weston's own attitude to sex, in its simplicity and utter lack of inhibition, fairly took my breath away. He was no Don Juan: he didn't run round hunting for his pleasures. But he took what came to him with a matter-of-factness and an appetite as hearty as that which he showed when sitting down to dinner. I don't think that, even in those days, he exaggerated much: certainly, his manner of describing these adventures bore all the marks of truth. I found his shameless prosaic anecdotes only too hard to forget, as I lay restlessly awake at night, listening to the waves, alone in my single bed.

But one doesn't inherit a nonconformist conscience for nothing; and Weston had stirred up mine with a vengeance. During the next three or four months, I suffered all the acute mental discomfort of a patient who has been deserted by his psycho-analyst in the middle of the analysis: I couldn't bear to see anybody—either Chalmers or Philip or the Cheurets; and Weston least of all. I ran away from them to a cottage in Wales, where I sat at the window, looking down the road towards the mountains or trying to read the first volume of Proust. It rained without stopping. The stream at the bottom of the garden was like dark foam-flecked stout. The clouds were piled upon the hill like damp heavy bedclothes. I wrote in my journal: "I am alone." At the end of four days, I could stand it no longer and returned to London, where I bought a small Browning automatic pistol and made a will, leaving everything to Chalmers and requesting him to burn my manuscripts and diaries unread. Philip showed me how to use the pistol, with a certain professional relish: "Better not try the heart, boy. Too risky. Stick it in your mouth, that's the best way—but, for God's sake, be careful: if you tilt it too far back, you'll probably only be paralysed for life; and if it's too far forward, the odds are you'll just lose an eye or your sense of smell, or you mightn't even do any damage at all. . . . Far better get a nice big army revolver and blow the top of your head clean off. . . ." He knew perfectly well, of course, that I'd never have the nerve to do it. Even my family showed no undue alarm on receiving dark hints of what was locked away upstairs in my playbox. They knew me too well: everybody knew me too well—that was my supreme humiliation. In my journal, I raged extrava-

gantly against myself, as the fawning spaniel, the born para-
site, the masochistic self-confessor, the public lavatory that
anyone might flush. But I'd astonish them yet, I swore. Yes,
from that very instant, the change would begin. Screwing the
cap to my fountain-pen, rising from my chair, shutting the
bureau, I turned the handle of my sitting-room door and
opened it solemnly into the New Life. Descending the staircase of the dining-room I was Christopher Isherwood no
longer, but a satanically proud, icy, impenetrable demon; an
all-knowing, all-pardoning saviour of mankind; a martyr-
evangelist of the tea-table, from whom the most atrocious
drawing-room tortures could wring no more than a polite
proffer of the buttered scones. Exquisite politeness was the
most important feature of the new technique. At supper, instead of sitting cross and glum, I mildly surprised my family
by helping the ladies into their chairs, offering to carve the
joint, chatting amiably about the weather and the trees in
the parks. How were they to know that a sword transfixed
my entrails, that blood dripped steadily from my mental hair-
shirt? An aunt, who happened to be staying in the house,
remarked how well I was looking: my trip to Wales, she
added, certainly seemed to have done me good.

No. No No. It was hopeless. As long as I remained at
home, I could never expect to escape from my familiar tire-
some, despicable self. Very well, then: I would leave home.
I would start all over again, among new people, who didn't
know me. I would never see any of my old friends again—
well, at any rate, not for ten years. I would go to Mexico, to
Paris, to a mining village in Wales. Perhaps I would grow a
beard. (I sketched one to a photograph of myself, with my
fountain-pen: the effect was disappointing.) But one thing,
at least, was quite certain now: I really would go—even if it
was no farther than the next street.

My family, as usual, was reasonable, sympathetic and prepared to be helpful, if allowed. I had planned my departure
as the first of a series of staggering surprises—"he was next
heard of leading a revolution in Albania . . . a year passed
without news; then, by purest chance, a mutual friend caught
sight of him, for an instant, on the quayside at Lisbon, wearing the uniform of the Spanish Foreign Legion. . . . Seven
months later, came a letter on the notepaper of a little Dutch
hotel in Shanghai . . ." and so on. But, needless to say, within
twenty-four hours of my decision, the scheme was being dis-

cussed round our drawing-room hearth as the mildest and most respectable of domestic adventures: "We must try and find a nice bed-sitting-room . . . perhaps somewhere near the river . . . oughtn't to give more than thirty shillings. . . ." And the neighbours were told: "Christopher's decided to set up on his own for a little . . . better able to concentrate . . . naturally, at his age, one likes to be independent . . . bachelor's quarters . . ."

Since my leaving Cambridge, my family had been giving me an allowance of one hundred and fifty pounds a year, in addition to the pound a week sporadically earned at the Cheurets (who were now away on holiday in the south of France): so that I was very comfortably off, as long as I continued to live rent and board free, at home. Now, of course, I should have to look out for a full-time job. But what kind of a job? What—after twelve years at school and university, with well over a thousand pounds spent on my education—was I really qualified to do? Nothing whatever. As a result of my performance in the Tripos, I hadn't even the necessary credentials for schoolmastering—that last refuge of the unsuccessful literary man. Still, teaching of some kind it would have to be. Parents on the look-out for a private tutor were not so particular, I was told. I put down my name on the books of the scholastic agents, Messrs. Gabbitas and Thring.

If one were an eccentric dilettante of leisure and means, one might well take up this form of job-hunting as a sport, simply for the pleasure of prying into strange houses, studying at close quarters the habits of the rich, the neurotic, the silly and the mad, and getting fascinating glimpses of the astonishing tangles in which so many of our English upper-class families contrive to involve themselves and to live. The private tutor is, socially, a cross between a doctor and a domestic servant; and the future employer (almost always the lady of the house) will often speak to him with a freedom undreamed of when addressing her friends and equals: "I'd better tell you straight away, Mr. Isherwood: things are very difficult for me, just at present . . . at first you may find it rather strange. . . My husband has curious moods. . . ." "Of course, Douglas—that's my eldest boy—*is* a great anxiety to me in many ways. . . . Oh, Mr. Isherwood, isn't alcohol a terrible scourge? It's been the curse of our family for generations. . . ." "You're Church of England, I suppose? Yes. . . .

123

Naturally. . . . Well, I shall want you to help me struggle against certain *influences*. . . . You see, my husband's mother is a very strict Catholic. . . ." These, and even more intimate confidences, the applicant must be prepared to listen to ; tactfully, sympathetically, without the flicker of an eyelid. It is unwise to offer much comment. I once lost a job by brightly admitting that our own family skeletons bore a close resemblance to those displayed before me by a wealthy worried lady in Belgravia. Best of all is the grave silent all-comprehending nod. But don't be too solemn. Your interviewer is looking for someone who will amuse, as well as discipline, her children. Above all, air no educational theories: they are not welcome in the best houses. A very effective line is: "Look here, Mrs. Smith—will you let me talk to your son for five minutes, alone? Then, when I've gone, I want you to ask him if he'd like to have me for a tutor. It's no good whatever giving the boy a tutor he dislikes from the start." The beauty of this is that Mrs. Smith, utterly disarmed by your frankness, will almost certainly insist on engaging you, even if her son protests that he has never met anybody so unpleasant in his whole life.

Remember, you are a domestic servant: try to get on good terms with your future colleagues without delay. The butler or parlourmaid who opens the door to you may be a valuable potential ally: the ladies' maid, if she gets a down on you, won't miss an opportunity of saying something spiteful as she brushes her mistress' hair. And don't be proud or squeamish about your wages. Some employers will take a subconscious sadistic pleasure in forgetting to give you your week's money and manœuvering you into having to ask for it when visitors are present. Others will frankly tip you: "Never mind about the change." You may even receive the oddest perquisites: a half-empty box of cigarettes, a discarded pair of trousers, a slightly stale chocolate cake. Never, on any account, refuse.

If you are under thirty, and have an educated voice, a shaven chin and a clean neck, you should have no difficulty in getting a tutoring job at any time: it is the tragic elderly ex-army officers, with their excellent credentials and frayed shirt-cuffs, who are turned down again and again in favour of some plausible young ignoramus like myself. Everything is against the older man, and he knows it: sometimes he pathetically offers to reduce his terms. At one house, I saw the phantom trade union in action. A friend of the family, himself a preparatory-school master, had been called in to interview the applicants. "Don't worry," he told me, "I'll back you up. There was another chap here. Been in the navy. He only asked for two and a half guineas a week; so I soon put a spoke into *him*."

But there are jobs and jobs; and it would take a very bold or desperate man to accept some of them, however high the wages. A friend of mine, who had all but agreed to accompany a rich American family back to Arizona, hastily changed his mind on being asked, in peculiarly sinister tones, by his future ("highly nervous") pupil, if he was fond of poisonous snakes. I myself refused two offers before settling down, about the middle of November, with my first family. In both cases, the would-be employers were charming and the pay was good: it was the responsibility involved which I couldn't bring myself to face. A well-to-do, cultured, elderly married couple wanted me to relieve them of their delicate nephew for the next three years. The two of us were to take a cottage in the country, fish, shoot, buy a small car, go abroad whenever we felt inclined—live, in fact, like elder and younger brother, until the boy was old enough to matriculate for Cambridge. The idea was certainly tempting; but all my instincts were against it—I didn't want to bind myself for so long a time—and in the end, after much hesitation, I said No. I am very glad now that I did so; I think the arrangement would have been thoroughly bad, both for the boy and for myself. On the second occasion, however, I didn't hesitate for a moment. A widowed lady interviewed me in the lounge of a Kensington hotel. "I'm not looking for a tutor, Mr. Isherwood; I'm looking for a companion. Nobody could teach my son anything—he's a genius." And she went on to describe how the boy, who was only fourteen, spoke four languages perfectly, composed orchestral music, studied the calculus every night before going to sleep and had beaten some Polish champion, whose name I forget, at chess. I was engaged on the spot; but wrote next morning to say that I found I should have to be away from London for several months.

About this time, I came across Roger East, my friend of the Cambridge film society days, whom I hadn't seen, now, for more than a year. He had given up trying to get into films for the moment, he told me, and was doing free-lance journalism of various sorts. Also, he was just about to get married. His fiancée, Polly, was an artist. She had an enormous mass of bobbed hair, a Midlands accent, and the tiny face of an attractive Pekingese dog: I felt perfectly at home with her from the very first. Polly had a trick (which in almost anybody else would have been horribly disconcerting) of attending not to what you said but the way in which you said it. "You're ever so funny, you know, Bisherwood," she would tell me, at the end of a long and serious conversation between Roger and myself. "Do you always flap about with your hands, like that? Hasn't anybody ever told you how funny you are?" She invariably called me "Bisherwood"—a contraction of Bradshaw-Isherwood, my ponderous double-barrelled name, hitherto so carefully ignored in these pages.) "Oh, I do wish I could have seen Roger when he was at Cambridge!" she would add: "I bet he wasn't half a scream, with his high-necked jumpers and his silk scarves, and all!"

Roger was living in a furnished room in Romilly Road—a short rather dreary street leading out of the Fulham Road, with its crashing buses and shabby little shops, into the northern half of the art-slum district which lies between the Old Brompton Road and the river. The tall damp grey houses were inhabited by small-part actors, film supers, journalists, artists' models, and pupils from the Royal College of Music and the Slade. Most of the upper floors had been converted into studios: their grimy toplights blankly reflected the sky, beneath wireless masts which were like fishing-rods curved by the weight of a perpetual catch. Nevertheless, Romilly Road had a certain romantic charm, when you came to know it well. It was one of those streets of which people say, in bohemian circles, that "everybody" has lived in it, at some period or other: there are streets like it in every big city, and they represent a certain stage, either very early or very late, in the artistic career. You may pass through Romilly Road twice during your life: once on the way up, once on the way down—to the bottom. The work-house-infirmary, appropriately enough, is just round the corner. I was thrilled to discover that Kathy herself had spent some months in the Road, inhabiting a small basement flat. Had I lived there a few years earlier, I might actually have seen her opening the door in the morning to take in the milk or hurrying along the street to the confectioner's for some buns because D. H. Lawrence was coming to tea.

For, already, I had quite decided to settle in Romilly Road —or, as Roger put it, to "join the Romilly Group." I arranged to take over his room when he left it, at the end of the year, to marry and set up with Polly in a flat.

Meanwhile, my novel, *Seascape With Figures,* had been finished and revised. Our family friend had approved of it in general, wisely insisting, however, that the tempting but preposterous episode of the little girl's death must be cut out altogether. On her encouragement, I had sent the manuscript, already, to two well-known publishers. They had refused it, of course. One of them wrote saying that my work had "a certain literary delicacy, but lacked sufficient punch"—a pretty damning verdict, when your story ends with a murder. My friend advised me to persist: two refusals, she rightly said, were not enough. But I was pessimistic. Chalmers hadn't cared much for the book: I had failed, somehow to carry out our original scheme. And now I no longer felt—as I had felt a year earlier—that I wanted to see something of mine published at once, at all costs. There seemed, suddenly, to be plenty of time. I would put the thing away for six months, I decided, and try to rewrite it later.

Meanwhile, my head was full of new shadowy tremendous ideas for an immense novel: nothing less ambitious than a survey of the post-war generation. Its scene was to be Cambridge, bohemian London, the Alps and North Wales. All my friends were to appear: Chalmers, Philip, Eric, Weston, the Cheurets—and, of course, myself. I made elaborate plans —all of them, intentionally, a little vague: for the truth was, the subject seemed so exciting, so wonderful, that I hardly dared to begin. It was much easier to draw diagrams in coloured chalks, beautifully shaded, with arrows, numbers and wavy lines, and pseudo-technical terms invented for the occasion, such as "fifth static area" or "Tommy-roger Motif bridge-passage to Welsea." I would wake up in the middle of the night to scribble emotionally in my note-book. "The treatment must be nearly pure *Objective*. The Epic Myth. In a sense, there must be no actual 'development.' Like gossip. Very slow-moving maddeningly deliberate genre-packed scenes. People's attitudes to their own Coriolanus-myth."

But one thing, at any rate, I had definitely decided I knew what my novel—if it were ever written—would be called. Its title was to be *The North-West Passage.* I had had this

127

phrase in my head, already, for several months: it repeated itself again and again, usually in the most obscure connections. Like "lions and shadows" or "the rats' hostel," it was a private key to a certain group of responses; all, needless to say, related to the idea of "The Test." More rationally, it symbolized, in my mind, the career of the neurotic hero, The Truly Weak Man—antithesis of "the truly strong man" spoken of by the homicidal paranoiac whose statement is quoted by Bleuler:

> The feeling of impotence brings forth the strong words, the bold sounds to battle are emitted by the trumpet called persecution insanity. The signs of the truly strong are repose and good-will . . . the strong individuals are those who without any fuss do their duty. These have neither the time nor the occasion to throw themselves into a pose and try to be something great.

"The truly strong man," calm, balanced, aware of his strength, sits drinking quietly in the bar; it is not necessary for him to try and prove to himself that he is not afraid, by joining the Foreign Legion, seeking out the most dangerous wild animals in the remotest tropical jungles, leaving his comfortable home in a snowstorm to climb the impossible glacier. In other words, the Test exists only for the Truly Weak Man: no matter whether he passes it or whether he fails, he cannot alter his essential nature. The Truly Strong Man travels straight across the broad America of normal life, taking always the direct, reasonable route. But "America" is just what the truly weak man, the neurotic hero, dreads. And so, with immense daring, with an infinitely greater expenditure of nervous energy, money, time, physical and mental resources, he prefers to attempt the huge northern circuit, the laborious, terrible north-west passage, avoiding life; and his end, if he does not turn back, is to be lost for ever in the blizzard and the ice.

Unfortunately, my idea of "The North-West Passage" had very little to do with the scheme for the action of the novel which I did finally work out. As usual, I was trying to pack a small suitcase with the contents of three cabin trunks: my little comedy of bohemian life was, by this time, so overloaded with symbolism; the interplay of *motifs* (to use a very favourite word of mine, just then) was so complex and self-contradictory, that the book, had it ever been actually written, would have been merely a series of descriptions of the effects which I had hoped, in vain, to be able to produce. However, it wasn't written and never will be: so here is the plot.

A young man named Leonard, who is up at Cambridge, a great gossip and adroit organizer of tea-parties and social encounters, comes to London to listen to a concert by a well-known string quartette. After the concert is over, he goes round to the artists' room, where he is surprised to meet Roger Garland, an old school-friend. Garland explains that he is the quartette's secretary: he invites Leonard to come with him that evening to a studio party. At the party, a lot of celebrities and excitingly eccentric people are present, and they all talk to Roger Garland; indeed, he seems to enjoy quite an important status amongst them. Leonard is enormously impressed. He decides that Roger is far more interesting and intelligent than he had previously imagined, and determines to cultivate his society at all costs. He therefore invites Roger to visit him for the week-end at Cambridge. In the course of the evening, Roger also introduces Leonard to a girl 'cello student named Katherine Simmonds: and she and Leonard discover that they have some mutual acquaintances, the Llewellyns, who live in Wales.

We next see Roger Garland during his Cambridge visit: this part of the action is seen through Roger's eyes. Roger is amazing Leonard and Leonard's friends by his wit and general poshness at a big tea-party: and, all the while, he is a worthless sham. Oh, yes, he can tell funny stories and imitate Cortot and Casals and hold forth about Hindemith and Stravinsky and Delius; but he funked the high dive in his prep. school swimming-bath and now, in the profoundest, most irrevocable sense, it is too late. That evening, Leonard introduces him to Tommy Llewellyn. Leonard has no particular opinion of Tommy; he patronizes him because he is a Rugger Blue and because the Llewellyns have a good deal of money. But the meeting makes an extraordinary strong impression upon Roger. Prophetically, he imagines, in Tommy's face, the peculiar signs of the man doomed to a violent, epic death: "He is looking for his tragedy," Roger thinks. Tommy, so quiet and diffident, so ill at ease amidst brilliant behaviour and talk, is surrounded by an invisible aura of disaster: he is born to die. But Roger will never really die, because he has never really lived. (Guess where I got that from, reader.) Next

129

E

morning, Roger, still under the influence of this meeting, has a violent reaction from everything in his past life ; but even as he "repents" he knows, with a pang of self-hatred, that it is all quite useless. He will never change now. He leaves Cambridge in disgust. From Leonard's point of view, the visit has been an immense success.

Before leaving Cambridge, Roger has confided to Leonard something of his interest in Tommy ; and Leonard, delighted to be of use, has at once suggested that Roger shall join a holiday party at Tawelfan, the Llewellyns' house in Wales. Tawelfan belongs to Mrs. Llewellyn, Tommy's aunt, a rich Celtic-Twilight poetess : there are enormous mountains in the background and slate quarries which are blasted, at intervals, with terrific detonations. An atmosphere of violent springtime sexual vitality surrounds the guests. In addition to Roger, Leonard and Tommy, there is Beau, Tommy's younger brother, whom Mrs. Llewellyn calls her "mountain boy" : she is bringing him up to be "free" and "splendid," in the German Wandervoegel tradition. (I intended to build up a satirical sub-plot round Beau ; but this part of the story was never properly worked out.) And there are several other young men and girls, including Katharine Simmonds, the 'cello student. (For some reason which I have since forgotten, the idea of making her a 'cello student seemed specially and attractively spiteful.)

During this visit, Roger Garland becomes increasingly fascinated by the personality of Tommy. Indeed, he comes to feel that Tommy and he are united by some mysterious bond : there is even a certain physical resemblance between them— it is Katharine who remarks upon this. (What I was actually trying to suggest was that Tommy and Roger were two halves or aspects of the same person. Tommy is an embodiment of Roger's dream of himself as an epic character : in fact, both Roger and Tommy are The Truly Weak Man—but, while Tommy will one day be lost in trying to force the North-West Passage, Roger will never even dare attempt it.) Katharine and Roger talk about Tommy a great deal ; their interest in him draws them together. Both Katharine and Roger feel that they come nearest to Tommy when they are with each other ; and so a kind of love affair by proxy begins between them. Tommy, who is really in love with Katharine, but far too tied up and inhibited to be able to show it, is secretly very unhappy about all this. Leonard, the onlooker, enjoys himself as never before.

Back in London, the proxy love-making continues: a week or two later Katharine and Roger suddenly decide to leave together for the Alps. Their first night is to be spent on the Col des Aravis. It isn't till they are actually in bed together that the spell breaks: they discover that they aren't interested in each other as lovers, at all. They have an all-night talk, and return to England by the next available train.

In the autumn, Roger goes again to stay at Tawelfan. And now he finds that Tommy seems quite ordinary and dull. The mystic sign of doom has disappeared from his face. After a couple of days, Roger is heartily bored: he pines for London, the concerts and the studio gossip. If he is a sham, very well, he is a sham; he no longer cares.

Katharine now unexpectedly appears—evidently by arrangement with Tommy himself. Tommy and she are together a great deal: nobody quite knows what is happening between them. Then, one morning, Katharine comes, in a terrible state, to Roger. She and Tommy have had a violent quarrel. She has told Tommy about her trip with Roger to the Alps, and Tommy has rushed out of the house, jumped on to his appallingly powerful motor-bicycle and ridden away at full speed. "He might do anything," she sobs. But Roger refuses to share her alarm. He has seen through Tommy, he declares; their whole cult of Tommy has been a fake. He is a nice boy, of course, and will make a good husband; there is nothing in the least wild or dangerous about him; he is perfectly tame, Katharine needn't worry, and within half an hour he'll be back here, asking for forgiveness. His spiteful, witty dissertation is interrupted by some farm servants, bringing in Tommy's body on a shutter. He has crashed at the bend of the road and broken his neck. Katharine turns hysterically upon Roger, exclaiming: "You killed him!" And, thinking the whole affair over in the course of the months that follow, Roger comes to the conclusion that this is perfectly true. "After all," he reflects, not without a certain furtive conceit, "it is people like myself who are dangerous. We are the real destroyers."

Early in December, I went down to Oxford to visit Weston. I found him installed in some handsome oak-panelled rooms; in addition to the sitting-room and bedrom, he had a little closet, just big enough to hold a piano, to which he retired at frequent intervals, to play hymn tunes and Bach (just now "the *only* composer"). A cubist predecessor had painted the walls of this closet with a startling scarlet and black design, representing, apparently, a series of railway accidents and copulations between traction engines and pyramids. The University certainly suited Weston: he struck me as being, so to speak, several sizes larger than life. Talking his loudest, with the Oxonian modulations and accentuations more emphatic than ever, he showed me round the premises: there was no time to look at anything for long. On the mantelpiece was a Meccano model of a Constantinesco gear, made by Weston himself. Over the writing-table was a Picasso etching of two young acrobats ("*fright*fully *emo*tive"). Weston thrust into my hands an enormous book by Gertrude Stein ("my God, she's good!"), but I had barely opened it before I was told to "listen to this: she's absolutely the *only* woman comedian." Weston had put a record of Sophie Tucker, singing "After you've gone away," on to the gramophone, but I couldn't hear much of it, because he began, at the same time, to read aloud a poem by Morgenstern, despite my protests that I didn't understand a word of German. After this, it was time to go out to dinner. We dined, in great style, at the George. Weston insisted on ordering champagne ("the only *possible* drink. Except whisky, of course"). It occurred to me that evening, as often later, that he was one of the very few people I had ever met who ought to have been born a millionaire. (Philip was another.) And I was reminded of an absurd phrase I had once heard used by a French painter, a friend of the Cheurets: "*il n'a pas la nature riche d'artiste.*" Weston certainly *had* the "*nature riche*": he was lavish in every possible direction. During dinner, he held forth on the subject of amusements. The cinema, he said was doomed; we'd had nothing of the slightest use since *'Way Down East.* The only remaining traces of theatrical art were to be found on the music-hall stage: the whole of modern realistic drama since Tchekhov had got to go; later, perhaps, something might be done with puppets. As for the ballet— was I *sure* I wouldn't have a cigar? No? Frowning severely, Weston chose the largest on the tray—as for the ballet, well, it simply ought to be forbidden by *Act* of *Par*liament. The only decent way to amuse yourself in the evenings was to go to the dog races, or some boxing, or the dirt track. I'd never been to the dirt track? Oh, but I must. It was the modern version of the Epic Life: the saga world translated into terms of the machine age. On the whole, however, Weston thought he liked the dog races even better: they were marvellously *English*. "*English*," I soon discovered, was his latest term of approbation. "All this continentalism won't *do*," he declared. "It simply doesn't suit us. And we do it so frightfully *badly*."

However, as there were none of these spectacles available, Weston had decided to take me to a meeting of a college essay club: "You may as well see," he added, darkly, "what Oxford's really *like*." I was ushered into a large crowded room. Weston introduced me, brusquely, to about two dozen young men and several dons: the young men inspected me with unfeigned curiosity, and I wondered, uneasily, what on earth Weston had been telling them about me, in advance. (It was three or four years later that I discovered how, at this period, he had gone about proclaiming that *Seascape With Figures* (which he'd read in manuscript during our summer holiday) was "the *only* novel" since the War!) The meeting began with "private business"—an excuse, it seemed, for the members of the club to be as rude to each other as they knew how. I quite expected a free fight; but apparently it was merely the Oxford (or the "English") manner: they were all enjoying themselves enormously. Presently, one of the young men remarked that it would have been much better to hold the meeting on the following Saturday; whereupon Weston jumped to his feet and shouted: "I take that as a personal insult to my guest!" This protest was duly entered in the minutes of the club. I blushed and sat there feeling very silly.

The paper which followed was on "The Concept of Duty." Its author read it very fast, in a sulky, gobbling voice, as though he expected to be contradicted at any moment. It was all very abstruse, in the jargon of technical philosophy; I barely understood a single sentence. Nervously fingering the return half of my railway ticket in my waistcoat pocket, I was astonished to find how apprehensive and unhappy this university atmosphere still made me feel. It was now a year and a half since I had left Cambridge; but had I ever completely escaped? No, I had not. This room, these cultured voices still exercised something of their evil, insidious power; they made me feel, yes, competitive. Against my will, against

133

my better judgment, something inside me wanted to stand up, to declaim, to behave, to astound them all. And because I wouldn't, couldn't, I sat and sulked, trying to look distinguished and abstractedly helping myself to unwisely large quantities of bananas, mulled claret and preserved fruits. I returned to London next day, with the beginnings of a violent attack of influenza. Gargling my swollen throat, I cursed the Oxford climate: but Oxford wasn't to blame—it was Weston himself. Henceforward, I caught a bad cold nearly every time we met: indeed, the mere sight of a postcard announcing his arrival would be sufficient to send up my temperature and inflame my tonsils. During the next two years, these psychological attacks became one of our stock jokes: Weston, during his Homer Lane period (of which more, later) referred to them as "the liar's quinsey." I have never been able to explain them satisfactorily, even to myself. Were they due to cosmic composition of our respective auras? Or a manifestation of my tireless Sense of Guilt? Was the analyst-patient relationship between Weston and myself far more permanent and profound than either of us realized? Honestly, I can't say. Or perhaps I won't say. It makes no practical difference. I record my symptoms here, without further comment, for what they are worth to the professional psychologist—my modest exhibit in the vask freak museum of our neurotic generation.

Polly and Roger East were married on January the eighth, 1927, at the registrar's office in Marlowes Road. Rube, an art student friend of Polly's, and myself were the only witnesses. The extreme casualness of the ceremony made it rather impressive: it was a solemn thought that such a serious transaction could be carried through with such ease—I felt as though I had seen two people run over and killed while laughing and chatting in the street. Not that there was anything in the least tragic about the proceedings themselves: indeed, they nearly opened with a bit of slapstick farce. I was the first to arrive; very smart in my best suit, with buttonhole, hat and gloves. The other three turned up together, five minutes later. Roger ambled in, hatless, with untidy hayrick hair, wearing a floppy old greatcoat and rubber-soled shoes. Polly followed him, in a very arty blue cloak. Rube came last, like a page: he was dressed in a much-soiled fisherman's jersey and a pair of shapeless grey flannel bags. The registrar's clerk surveyed us with a disapproving eye: "You two come over here, please," he said, addressing Polly and myself: "We're late, as it is. We'd better start at once; there's another couple waiting." We explained and got ourselves sorted out, only just in time. Afterwards at the wedding breakfast—custard, Chianti and iced cake in the new flat—Polly seemed unnaturally quiet: several times, I surprised her regarding me with a thoughtful stare. "What's the matter?" Roger asked. "I was only thinking," she answered, quite seriously, "how awful it'd have been if I'd married Bisherwood, by mistake."

That evening, I felt in a mood to celebrate: Philip and I went together to see Sybil Thorndike and Henry Ainley in *Macbeth*. At that time Sybil Thorndike was my favourite tragic actress and *Macbeth* my favourite Shakespeare play. On the whole, I was very much disappointed. Sybil made a fine sinister entry with the letter; but later on she got much too noisy. Ainley stood about the place looking dazed, as well he might; for the producer had made his castle several times as big as Waterloo station, and the young men of the court ran up and down yelling like porters. Philip and I had blown the last of our money on stalls. During the interval, we turned round and saw Polly and Roger standing at the back of the pit. Philip was terribly shocked. According to his notions of propriety, the Easts, on such an occasion, ought to have taken the Royal Box.

Meanwhile, I had installed myself in Roger's old room at Romilly Road. Bill Scott, a friend of the Cheurets, helped me move in; Jean and Edouard were in and out all day long, sorting and arranging my books on the plank shelves which I had had fitted up at one end of the room. Madame Cheuret chose the material for my curtains and the cover on my divan bed. In the evenings, Philip would pop in for a chat, gloomier than ever, since he had just failed in one of his medical exams. Even Rose paid me an occasional visit: I had always plenty of company. And if, by any chance, I was alone for an hour or two and felt bored, there was my landlady, Mrs. Partridge, perpetually ready for a chat.

Mrs. Partridge was a thin lively youngish woman: a widow, with one little boy of eight, whose name was Billy. When she stopped talking for a moment and became thoughtful, her mouth drew down at the corners so that she looked suddenly very sad, and you wondered if she wasn't, perhaps, seriously ill—but she seldom stopped talking for long. She talked about anything and everything: the weather, the neighbours, the price of food, the Easts (whom she thought "an ideal pair"), the records I played on my gramophone ("the only thing with those classics," she complained, "is you can never tell when they're going to stop.") Mrs. Partridge cooked dinner for me in the evening: she was a good cook, though apt to be vague about meal-times—I occasionally had to wait until ten o'clock at night.

Mrs. Partridge often spoke of her late husband, who had been a builder. She described how she'd refused to have a honeymoon on the ground that "we'd better start as we mean to go on": in her dry, talkative way she seemed pretty tough. I wondered, nevertheless, whether she wasn't considering marrying again, because she had a regular male visitor, a bald gloomy man in brown boots, who turned up at the most unlikely hours of the day, and sat for long spells in the smelly little greenhouse which had been converted into a kitchen, sipping a glass of port. A certain air of mystery always surrounded his arrival. Mrs. Partridge was careful to shut my door before hurrying downstairs, patting her lank bobbed hair, to let him in. They conversed in low voices and stopped talking instantly if, on some excuse or other, I looked into the kitchen and disturbed them. Once or twice, they appeared to have quarrelled, because Mrs. Partridge, when she returned to my room, had visibly been crying. She and I never discussed these visits, but I often speculated about them with Philip. We both came to the same conclusion: Mrs. Partridge's admirer must obviously be a married man. "And I shouldn't wonder," Philip added, "if they haven't decided to murder his wife. They're just the kind of people you see at the assizes. And they're absolutely certain to make a mess of it, poor devils. For some inscrutable reason, they always *will* use arsenic. . . . God, how dreary it all is!"

In spite of the smell from the greenhouse-kitchen, and the worse smell from the bathroom drain, and a really filthy smell which haunted the staircase (ascribed by Mrs. Partridge, perhaps unjustly, to the Irish couple who lived on the ground floor) I felt, during those first weeks, very glad that I had settled in Romilly Road. My room, with its big win-

dows, was light and airy, my books made a fine show on the
plain wooden shelves, and there, in the evening, were my
two arm-chairs from Cambridge, waiting invitingly before
the glowing gas-fire. Yes, it was a nice snug little setting for
my cosy independent bachelor life; or at any rate for the
pleasing impression of that life which I wished to convey to
my visiting friends. For, to be honest, the room only really
came into being when I could see it through Philip's or the
Easts' or the Cheurets' eyes. Left alone in it, even for a few
moments, I couldn't sit still and hovered restlessly about,
touching the curtains, aligning the table with the bed, altering the position of a book, like a small shopkeeper who waits
for customers, uneasily arranging and rearranging his wares.
Every object, big or little, had its place in the pathologically
tidy scheme of my existence. Mine was the rigid tidiness of
the celibate: that pathetically neat room, as I now picture it,
seems to cry out for the disorderly human traces of cohabita-
tion—the hairbrush discovered among your papers in the
drawer, the unfamiliar queer-feeling garments in the dark
cupboard, the too small slipper you vainly try to pull on
when half awake, the wrong tooth-brush in your glass, the
nail paring in the fender and in the tea-cup the strange
lustrous single hair. But the room, as long as I occupied it,
remained virgin, unravished; and Philip said: "You've got
a nice place here, boy. God, I envy you, being on your own!"
And Jean and Edouard thought of me as leading a sort of
romantic Red Indian life, beside my own camp fire, and
envied me, too. Only Polly East, that merciless perceiver,
noticed that anything was lacking: "What's Bisherwood done
to this room?" She asked. "It's quite different from when you
had it, Roger. He's made it all sort of respectable—like a
public park."

Meanwhile, the Easts had moved into their flat, only a few
streets away, and had set about transforming it from top to
bottom. They were tireless art-workers: Roger, particularly,
seemed to practise every kind of decorative craft by sheer
instinct. All day long, he carpentered, carved, painted,
stencilled, stiched, experimented with varnishes, ornamented
the door-knobs, the mantelpieces, the tables, the lavatory
seat. Polly and he were gradually designing allegorical wool-
work backs for the chairs: Venus and Mars, the descent of
Hebe and the rape of Proserpine. In spare moments, Roger

wrote articles, stories and poems, while Polly drew female nudes, the fattest and flabbiest she could find. I envied their life: they seemed as busy and lively as birds. Their only tiffs were artistic, and I was frequently called in as umpire: "Come and look at Polly's new daub. Tell me frankly, don't you think it's absolutely bloody?" "Oh, Bisherwood, darling, do say you like it! I've been ever so depressed this morning. Roger's only jealous because he can't draw anything but trees." Roger, Polly always insisted, was a writer; he had no real business to be painting at all. When, a few months later, they both exhibited at a show, she was furious because he sold three pictures, while she sold only two.

Every week-day morning at a quarter to nine, I set off on the long bus-ride which took me to my employer's home, a large house standing inside its own garden, in St. John's Wood. My pupil's name was Graham. He was eight years old, an exceptionally nervous little boy, with a pale, lively, charming face, fair hair standing up in a tuft, and big steel spectacles which were perpetually getting lost. During lessons, he wriggled and squirmed continually, put his feet on the table, stood up on the chair, or wandered off round the room, moving in a kind of trance. Yet, all the time, he was attending to every word I was saying; indeed, he attended far too carefully, and frequently caught me out in the clumsiest self-contradictions and mistakes. The big nursery was overheated, and it was often as much as I could do to keep awake. The faint purr of the gas-fire, the far-off whine of the vacuum-cleaner in a distant room and the remote hum of traffic out of doors were deliciously soothing: luxury seemed to envelop us physically, like the pleasant oppression of a day in the height of summer. I hear myself speaking, consciously, deliberately, choosing every word, carefully modulating my voice, in order not to disturb the soporific calm: "All this, naturally, was before the—er—resurrection." I give my front teeth a smart rap with the knob of my sliver pencil, but fail to check a large lazy yawn.

Divinity was my favourite subject. I tried to teach it very flatly and prosaically, with a certain flavour of Lytton Strachey impudence. My history lessons were merely a pale reproduction of the methods and manner of Mr. Holmes. Maths I unexpectedly enjoyed: the kind of problems suitable for an eight-year-old boy were still just within my grasp, though Graham frequently solved them before I did. In geography and Latin, I clung firmly to the text-books and never ventured an inch without their protection. Graham knew much more French than I. My only contribution to his education in this subject was a single quotation: " '*C'est Lescaut*,' *dit-il, en lui lâchant un coup de pistolet, 'il ira souper ce soir avec les anges!*' " This phrase appealed to Graham so greatly that he repeated it on every possible occasion, to the mixed admiration and faint disapproval of his relations, who found it obscurely subversive.

Graham hated writing essays and made every possible excuse to void them. This was hardly surprising. The nursery governess who had preceded me had delighted in such themes as: "Duty," "Springtime," "Make Hay While The Sun Shines," "A Boy's Best Friend Is His Mother." And Graham, who was by nature extremely independent, had remained stubbornly suspicious of and antagonistic to the cut-and-dried schoolroom ideology. In his exercise book, I found the records of one such tussle between the governess and himself. This time, Graham had been told to "write *very neatly* a story with the title: Playing The Game":

There were once two boys who were brothers and they lived together and went to the same school. They both did very well at their school and became popular with everyone, but one was better at games than the other and this aroused some jealousy on the part of the boy who was worse at games than his brother. The brother who was best at games was a good sportsman but the other boy was not. The boy who was jealous of his brother got him expelled with a false charge, but his brother though expelled and numerous other troubles happened to him nothing prevented him from playing the game. He even got sent to prison again falsely by his brother but nothing hindered him from being a thorough sportsman and at last he proved that he had been falsely accused and his brother was sent to prison for five years.

Underneath this, the governess had noted: "A wrong idea. Playing the game is being honourable and truthful in spite of whatever trouble you may be in or whatever punishment you know is in store for you. Write another story over the page on the same subject."

So Graham had tried again:

Once upon a time there was a boy who had not done very well at his school but every time he was punished he always told the truth about what he had done and tried to do better. The result was that each time the punishment got gradually lighter till he did not have any at all. Then he began to pass all his examinations and he soon got high up in class and became very popular simply because he was a good sportsman and always played the game. Afterwards he developed a very good character and he got on very well for the rest of his life. His character and his good temper always made him popular and respected by everyone who knew him and afterwards he got a very high position for the rest of his life.

After this, the governess had given it up—and no wonder. She contented herself with remarking mildly: "Quite nice, but you have not grasped the real meaning yet!" Graham, I hope and trust, never did grasp it. He must be almost a man now. If he reads these lines, I am bound to confess to him that, when I left, I stole his exercise book and have kept it ever since.

One evening, when I got back from work, I was met by Mrs. Partridge on the stairs. Something in her gaunt silhouette against the twilit window warned me of disaster, even before she had opened her mouth: "I'm going to give you a terrible shock, Mr. Isherwood . . ." Darting back into the kitchen, she emerged, a moment later, with a cup of very strong tea—she must have been keeping it hot for me: it was intended, I suppose, as a kind of local anæsthetic: "Oh, dear, I don't know how I'm going to tell you. . . . I've been very foolish, I realize that now. . . . There's times I thought I should go out of my mind. . . ."

We went up to my room. Mrs. Partridge was sobbing. She refused to sit down. Gradually, I got the whole story out of her. The rent had been in arrears for months. She owed eighty pounds. The bailiff—her mysterious visitor—had been calling on her regularly since the beginning of December.

She'd made excuses, wheedled for little respites, put him off with promises she knew she'd never be able to keep—but now he'd finally lost patience. To-morow morning, if she couldn't produce the money, his van would come round and take away every stick of furniture in the house: "You're my last hope, Mr. Isherwood. I want to save my honour and the last bit of my happiness. If it wasn't for Billy, I'd throw myself in the river to-night. . . ."

There was nothing I could do, of course. But I remembered suddenly that the Easts had some money put aside for buying furniture. We went round to see them. Mrs. Partridge overflowed with promises. In a fortnight, in a week, they should have it all back, every penny. She had a brother-in-law who owned a public-house in Guildford. She would show us letters. She would go down to see him to-morrow—no, the day after to-morrow—and explain everything. If the Easts did this for her, she'd never forget it as long as she lived. Roger was ready to agree, on the spot. Polly was more suspicious; she asked searching, practical questions. But, at last, it was arranged. The Easts would guarantee to find the money within three days. It was in a bank in Leicester: Roger couldn't lay hands on it at once.

Everything seemed settled, and next morning I set off, as usual, for my job. While I was away, an extraordinary drama was enacted in Romilly Road. At ten o'clock, the bailiff and his van arrived. Mrs. Partridge met him triumphantly, waving the Easts' written guarantee. The bailiff, suspecting another trick, refused to look at it. He ordered his men to begin removing the furniture. Mrs. Partridge dashed out hysterically to fetch Roger. Roger drove up in a taxi and argued with the bailiff, who remained unimpressed. He must have cash down, he said, or nothing. By this time, Mrs. Partridge's sitting-room was empty. The men were starting on the bedroom. Roger sprinted to the bank at the corner and persuaded the manager to phone through to the Leicester bank for authorisation to pay out the money. There were arguments, explanations, papers to be signed, endless delays. At length, Roger emerged, shouting and waving the notes above his head, just as the removers were putting into the van my second armchair.

CHAPTER VI

AND now, at the beginning of that summer, here I was, back for the third time, at the Bay. Half an hour ago I had got out of the bus at the sweetshop corner which was the end of my pleasant, complicated, familiar journey: the quick train down from London, the slow train puffing through the forest, the voyage in the paddle-steamer (known as "The Workhouse," because of the excessive amount of brass-work her crew had to polish) along the shallow estuary, where saplings growing out of the water marked the many sandbanks, past fishing boats and private yachts owned by writers of adventure stories for boys, with a glimpse of the open sea and a great liner vanishing, in a smudge of smoke, towards America; the landing and the long walking race down Yarmouth Pier for the best seats in the bus, and finally the dangerous corkscrew drive, much too fast, through the deep twisting island lanes. The more dashing flashy types of village lad worked for the bus company: they formed a sort of *avant-garde* corps, with certain traditions of cheek, gaiety, bad manners and pseudo-American slang. They wore their caps over one eye, shouted noisily to each other, winked at the girls and punched tickets with a conceited smirk, affecting an insolent, lunatic-warder's patience when dealing with elderly female tourists. I recognised the conductor—last year he had been a half-time errand-boy, still at school—but he didn't recognize me.

Nobody recognized me. Mr. Peck, the coastguard, tapping out his pipe on the breakwater wall, regarded me with incurious bleached blue eyes. Bruiser was coming out of the pub. A new girl appeared at the sweetshop door: Ivy (nicknamed "The Soldier's Friend"), whom I'd known last summer had evidently found the Bay too small or too hot to hold her.

142

Even the curate, going somewhere in a great hurry, with a brown-paper parcel under his arm and his skinny red neck poked forward like a hen's, appeared to have forgotten our extraordinary evening conversation about television and Christianity, on the downs. Absolutely unnoticed, I carried my suitcase down the sandy lane, past Marine View and Ocean Villa, to the gate of Beach View, where I was staying. The low white gate stuck, just as it had stuck last year, and had to be lifted with both hands. The garden was full of lilac. And there, on the steps, beneath the veranda which was like an inverted green boat, Miss Chichester stood waiting to receive me. Nothing had changed.

One's first glimpse of Miss Chichester was so startling and shocking that I had always to prepare my friends for her appearance beforehand. Even Weston's clinical glance had blenched for a moment, when they were introduced; and Philip had exclaimed: "Phew, boy! That's nasty! Pernicious anæmia. She can't possibly live another six months." Nevertheless, Miss Chichester had lived. Indeed, she had looked exactly the same on the day when I had first seen her, two years before. I have never seen any other human being who so closely resembled a corpse. Although she cannot have been more than fifty years old, she had the face of a woman of ninety, parchment yellow, a network of tiny wrinkles radiating from her thin tight bluish lips. Her legs and arms were shrivelled to the size of walking-sticks; it was a wonder that she could move about at all. Only her hair, which was of the copper tint admired at the beginning of the century, seemed really alive. Yet Miss Chichester was no invalid. She was surprisingly active. With the help of a daily maid, she did all the housework, and I suppose she cooked my meals. (I never once penetrated to the back of the house, during any of my visits.) Occasionally, I saw her in the garden, weeding or pruning the borders, a cigarette between her corpse-like lips. There was something particularly disconcerting in the sight of Miss Chichester smoking; this habit of hers was much discussed, I later discovered, by her neighbours at the Bay. People said that she smoked hundreds of cigarettes a week, that she went over to neighbouring seaside resorts to buy them, in order that her curious vice should excite less comment. This was nonsense, no doubt. Yet nicotine, absorbed even in moderate doses, must surely have done her some harm; and I often had the impression, as I watched her blowing out the smoke through her withered nostrils, that she wasn't so much smoking the cigarette as that the cigarette was smoking her.

Miss Chichester welcomed me without the least animation, quite as though I had returned after an absence of a couple of hours. "Did you have a pleasant journey?" she asked, and barely waiting for an answer retired into the house to prepare my tea. Henceforward, we should exchange, perhaps, two dozen words a day: we were the perfect landlady and lodger.

I entered the sitting-room through the big window which opened to the ground, and, sitting down at the piano which Weston had so often thumped, played through my only piece, *The Merry Peasant*. Nothing had been moved. The frosted glass lamp still stood in the middle of the table-cloth with the woollen pom-poms. The Maiden's Prayer still hung over the fireplace and above the piano was the photograph of Lord Tennyson, described by the poet himself as "The Dirty Monk." How happy I felt, in this room! How absolutely at home. Morning after morning, I should sit out on the veranda in the plush armchair, with my block of ruled paper, my ink eraser and my fountain-pen, working away like an etcher, neurotically tidy, never crossing anything out, erasing every mistake, polishing the roughened surface over with my thumb-nail to prevent the ink from running, destroying ten sheets for every one I wrote. For I had made a vow: I wouldn't leave the Bay until *Seascape with Figures* had been completely rewritten from beginning to end.

After tea, I went out of doors. The Bay lay wedged between two immense masses of cliff; it was so tiny that, standing upon the steep shingle bank by the bathing huts, you were like an actor on the stage of a theatre—anybody at any of the windows in the little semicircle of boarding-houses and fishermen's cottages could follow your every movement. Men at work in the gardens on opposite sides of the valley shouted across to each other without effort. On the left, backed up against the steep slope of the cliff, stood the pub, which in summer was also an hotel; a biscuit-coloured building with small classical pillars, permanently shabby because the salt spray ruined each fresh coat of paint within a week. During the big winter storms, Mr. Peck had told me, the waves sometimes broke right over the shingle bank and swamped the low meadow behind the houses. Before the war, the Bay had had a miniature esplanade, but the sea had undermined it and, one night, smashed the entire structure to bits. Great chunks of concrete still lay scattered about the beach, as if flung apart by dynamite.

Leaving the shingle bank, I walked slowly up the path which led on to the downs, passing the big granite house which stood far too near the cliff edge; a slice of its garden had already slithered down to the beach. (There was a legend that, one night, during a gale, a maid in this house had been awakened by a man trying to climb in through her bedroom window—he was clinging to the rigging of a big sailing-ship which had just been driven ashore.) Then came a couple of new bungalows, standing amidst gorse bushes, inhabited only during the summer months. (At the Bay, "the summer" meant August and September—the sixty-one fat days during which the shop and lodging-keepers counted on making enough to see them through the lean remainder of the year.) And now, far ahead, against the sky, the monument appeared, a stumpy little moss-covered obelisk, barely four feet high, surrounded by an iron gothic railing, engraved simply with initials and a date: G.F. 1857. Very few of the Bay's inhabitants could tell you who had put it there, or why: even Mr. Peck was unusually vague; he knew only that it marked the spot where a boy had been murdered by two sailors and his body thrown over the cliff into the sea—for what reason, he couldn't really say.

From the obelisk, you could see the whole sweep of the island coast away beyond Blackgang, to the southern headland, with the waves creaming in over the great red deserted beaches; seeming, at this distance, to be frozen to the shore in scribbled overlapping margins of dazzling foam. Far out, the sea was a dull violet haze. There was a strong peppery smell from the gorse and the sheep droppings on the sunburnt turf. Below, on the hot cliff face, the gulls circled and squawked; one, in particular, seemed to utter a kind of mirthless laugh.

Suppose Weston were here, I thought, he would know the names of the different species of gull—and, by naming them, would dismiss them to their proper recognized unimportant place in the background of the poet's consciousness; of course, he would imply, one expects to be supplied with gulls during a seaside walk, just as one expects to be provided

145

with hot and cold water in an hotel bedroom. Very well, the gulls are there. One bestows a word of commendation upon them, passing; perhaps, even, a quotation from Tennyson (the only nature-poet Weston hadn't yet discredited) and then goes on to speak of something more interesting, something out of a book. No, at this particular moment, I didn't wish that Weston was here. And I didn't wish that Philip was here, either, or the Cheurets, or the Easts; they belonged to the town, and I didn't want to be reminded that I, too, was an intruder, a townee. Chalmers I should have been glad to see, as always; had he been with me now we should have immediately begun to reconstruct the scene of the murder, the Bay would have become yet another annexe of Mortmere, and the real Bay, as the tourists and the fishermen saw it, would have gradually grown invisible to my eyes. That's the disadvantage of travelling with Chalmers, I thought; wherever we are together is always the same place.

And so, finding that, for once, I was not sorry to be alone, I said to myself: I am happy. Perfectly happy, I repeated, as my eyes roamed wide over the brilliant desolate sea and the empty contours of the land. Were they, after all, searching for something that was lacking? I hardly knew. A tiny obstinate figure by the dwarf obelisk under an enormous sky, I declared for the third time: I am absolutely happy, absolutely content. And, increasingly overcome by a profound melancholy which I interpreted simply as an appetite for supper I began to walk downhill, towards my sitting-room, my holiday task and my lonely bed.

Every morning during the weeks that followed, round about eleven o'clock, I would break off my first session of work on the revised *Seascape*, put away my papers and start off on my tour of inspection round the Bay.

Mr. Peck, the coastguard, would usually be digging in his garden as I passed. Bandy-legged, stocky and agile, in his blue trousers and square-cut sailor's vest, he was still every inch the naval man. Even his gardening was an affair of exact measurements: "I dig three trenches like; eighteen inch by two foot. . . ." By talking to Mr. Peck, I acquired a considerable stock of useless but fascinating information, of the kind which no novelist can bear to waste. I learnt, for instance, that the part of a flagstaff which is driven into the ground and into which the pole is fixed, is called "the tabernacle." It is correct to speak of "dressing the staff." The big flagstaff at the coastguards' look-out was so strong that it would take a gale of one hundred and fifty miles an hour to break it. The coastguards' own flag is "envelope-shaped, red, blue, black and yellow." (I realized that Mr. Peck was describing it out of a text-book, although we were both looking at the flag as he spoke.) The Mayor of Southampton, he told me, had taken one of the bungalows on the downs for the summer, and was going to fly his own flag, bearing the city arms. Passing ships would be expected to dip their colours to it. (Mr. Peck seemed to find nothing at all funny in this.) But his conversation was not without its lyrical passages. One day, we were admiring his poultry: "Take that old hen now, that Rhode Island there. To-morrow I'll set her, like, on the eggs. Twelve eggs, I'll give her: that's ten like, and two to make sure. And then, in twenty-one days, maybe, I'll have nine, ten, eleven fine chicks. . . . And do you know what does it all?"

"No." I tried to keep this as non-committal as possible, uncertain whether Mr. Peck was going to say "God," recommend some particular kind of hen food or make a dirty joke.

"Warmth! Nothing but warmth!" Mr. Peck shook his head smilingly, as though compelled to admit himself baffled by the ingenuity of Nature. "It's wonderful, really. Just a little warmth . . ."

My next stop would be at the sweetshop, for a chat with Muriel, Ivy's successor. Muriel was a tall, pretty, simpering girl with a consciously refined voice, who wore flat-heeled shoes to conceal her height. (Her fiancé, I gathered, was considerably the shorter of the two, and she was sensitive about this.) All our conversations were on an elaborate and rather tiring note of facetiousness: I frequently reminded myself of Philip at the skating rink and reflected that at least seventy-five per cent. of my "personality" consisted in bad imitations of my various friends. Actually, Muriel was the only person at the Bay to whom I confided any facts about myself at all. One day, I told her, I should probably inherit an estate in the North of England, I had been to Cambridge, I had seen the Alps, I had owned a motor car, I had spoken to Betty Balfour, I was writing a novel. "Oh, you are awful!" she laughed; for thanks to my sarcastic tone she didn't believe a single word.

"But what do you *really* do?" she would insist.

"Well . . . I'm a kind of schoolmaster. . . ."

Muriel uttered a scream, and immediately put her hand over her mouth: screaming was not ladylike: "*You* a schoolmaster! How can you tell such dreadful fibs!"

"But it's not a fib. Honestly it isn't."

"Well then," Muriel challenged, "tell me what you teach."

"Oh, all sorts of things." (This with one of Philip's most suggestive smiles.)

"All *sorts* of things! Very likely! Tell me *one* thing!"

"Well, Latin, for instance. . . ."

"Latin!" This time she fairly shrieked. "The idea!" Whisking out her dainty little scrap of a handkerchief, she dabbed quickly at her eyes. "*How* can you!" she gasped.

"How can I what?"

"How can you . . . oh dear!" She was off again.

"You'd be surprised at all the things I can do." (At this point Philip would undoubtedly have given her a long glance in the celebrated "certain way," and perhaps produced his latest trick cigarette-case, with one of those infinitely sophisticated Noel Coward gestures which contrived, without the least ostentation, to display his gold cuff-links.) Muriel regarded me for a moment, literally panting with swallowed laughter.

"Latin!" The word exploded out of her, violently, almost angrily, like an accusation.

And so on, and so forth.

One morning, when I came out of the sweetshop, I found a charabanc full of trippers halted outside the pub. It was the first of the summer fleet. Henceforward, there would be a daily service of tours round the island. The trippers, packed tight into their seats (the driver had dashed into the pub for a moment to get a drink, feeling hoarse no doubt from shouting the names of the beauty spots), looked dazed: they were suffering from ocular indigestion ; they had seen far too much in too short a time. Also, they were being forced to listen, involuntarily, to an extraordinary kind of sermon. The preacher stood on the low wall at the end of the breakwater. He was a small stout red-faced man dressed in a suit of very loud check plus-fours and wearing an immense tartan bow-tie, which might once have been the ribbon off a big chocolate-box. He resembled a music-hall low comedian. Although his small audience was only a few feet away from him, he

148

was bawling at it with all the power of his lungs. Yet his attitude wasn't in the least degree threatening or aggressive. He seemed to regard his hearers with boundless, magnificent contempt. As I approached, he pulled something out of his pocket and flourished it in the air ; it was a dandelion, with earth still clinging to its roots:

"Look at this!" he exclaimed. "An aeroplane couldn't pick what I picked in a field this morning, could it now? Why, I tell you, my friends, in a hundred years' time, that charabanc of yours will be *withered away*, shrivelled like a blade of grass!" He paused triumphantly, as if waiting to be heckled—perhaps he was down here on holiday from Hyde Park—but the trippers merely looked uncomfortable ; one or two of them attempted sheepish grins, the rest studiously avoided the madman with their eyes ; they wished he would go away.

"And I'll tell you something else," bawled the little man: "If England can produce a black man, she can produce the sun. Ha, ha! That's got some of you, hasn't it?"

The charabanc driver now hastily reappeared and jumped into his seat. The madman greeted him with a deep ironical bow ; the driver laughed and shouted a greeting—they seemed to know each other quite well. The madman waved, gaily and ironically, as the charabanc drove away. Then he got down from the wall and strolled off quietly, pausing for a moment to tap the stone-work with his crooked fore-finger, as though he expected to find that it was hollow. The result of his experiment seemed to sadden him a little. "The man who built this," I heard him murmur to himself, "must have thought he was living in Ancient Egypt!"

After this the little man used to turn up quite often at the Bay. Sometimes he preached to the trippers, sometimes he walked backwards and forwards along the beach, with very careful deliberate paces, as though he were taking measurements. He seldom stayed more than half an hour. I made various attempts to get into conversation with him ; but, interviewed privately, he was unsatisfactory. He ignored my questions with the conceited secretive smile of a great politician who is being tactlessly pestered by a cub reporter. He wasn't going to waste his wisdom on an audience of one.

Staying at the big hotel on the downs behind the Bay was a young man to whom I had taken an immediate, unreasonable, savage dislike. He was large and handsome, with

149

crimped yellow hair and a prominent, well-moulded, cleft chin. I had never spoken to him; but I had once heard him remark, as he strolled past, in earnest conversation with the curate: "Of course, if one leads a pretty full life. . . ." From these words, I had reconstructed, most unfairly, his entire character.

One morning the madman and I were standing together outside the pub when I saw the "full-life" young man approaching. With him was a girl (also staying at the hotel) who was, at the moment, my female public enemy number one. She had a sing-song voice, an air of being deadly keen on everything and the kind of square-cut bobbed hair which made one long to give her a terrific, sadistic kick on the behind. She had once remarked, in my presence, that somebody or other was "fearfully stimulating." I only wished Chalmers could have seen her. His command of invective was so much greater than my own.

"Look at those two," I appealed to the madman. "Surely you'll tell us something about them, won't you?"

To my delight, the little man rose, most unexpectedly, to the occasion. He broke into peals of loud, stagey laughter; and as the couple passed, quite close to him, talking quickly and self-consciously, their eyes riveted to the horizon, he pointed his finger straight at them and shouted: "Look at them! There they go! Adam and Eve!"

There was much applause from the half dozen loungers who formed his audience. But neither the young man nor the girl looked back. They only seemed to stiffen, a little; their movements were suddenly and ridiculously speeded up, as in a quick-motion film; their two figures disappeared, with jerky rapidity, round the corner, down the steps which led to the beach.

The Full-Lifer, like the rest of the hotel guests, bathed in a tiny inlet of the Bay, right under the cliff, where the hotel had provided its own special bathing-cabins and raft. And I had taken to bathing there, too. It was my horrible, fascinating little aquarium, which I never tired of studying. I was passing through yet another of my pseudo-scientific phases of class hatred. For Chalmers' benefit, I took verbatim notes of the scraps of dialogue I heard on the beach—though nothing but gramophone records could have done justice to those special intonations and accentuations which seemed, to my hypersensitive ear, to convey the very essence of these people's lives:

"John proceeds to swim out to the raft. . . ."

"The stones are hard to the feet. . . ."

"He couldn't hit the town he was born in. . . ."

"Hi, you slacker, come on in!"

"Wha?"

"Come on in!"

"Is it cold?"

"Wha?"

"I said: Is it COLD?"

The coldness of the water was, of course, their inexhaustible joke. Indeed, there was, I thought, something profoundly significant in the hotel guests' whole attitude to the sea. They were very careful, I told Chalmers in my letters, not to take the sea too seriously. They were, in fact, afraid of it, as they were afraid of all the great natural forces. They were afraid of surrendering themselves to it, lest, in their exhilaration, they should do something silly, should give themselves away. This was why they bathed in a ridiculous little landlocked pool, which they could pretend was a kind of swimming-bath, instead of walking for a quarter of a mile over the downs to the enormous empty bay, where there were real waves which knocked you down even on the calmest day, and where you could shout out loud, if you liked, and scream and talk to yourself in nonsense languages and sing passages out of imaginary operas—in fact, behave like a human being. But no: bathing, for these people, was something rather childish, slightly to be ashamed of, to be got through quickly, just before lunch, so as to leave plenty of time for the ball games which formed the really serious business of the holiday. And so, even while they were in the water, their jokes tacitly apologized for what they were doing; some bathers even behaved with an elaborately parodied childishness, just to show that they were well aware that this wasn't, in any sense, proper adult "sport."

Also, of course, the majority of the men were secretly embarrassed at finding themselves practically naked in the presence of a lot of semi-naked and (presumably to them) attractive girls. And this subconscious embarrassment had the effect of bringing out, in each individual, some characteristic defect in carriage or stance; the scarcely visible limp became accentuated, the sloping shoulders drooped more miserably

151

than ever, while the stiffly muscle-bound torso bulged into a ridiculous caricature of itself and its owner trotted snorting into the water like an absurd little bull. Surprisingly few of them, it seemed, could swim more than a few yards. Many a young man would strike out, with powerful faultless strokes, as if starting for France, and then, as he passed the diving-raft, turn abruptly aside and grab hold of it, gasping violently for breath.

But beneath all my note-taking, my would-be scientific detachment, my hatred, my disgust, there was the old sense of exclusion, the familiar grudging envy. For, however I might sneer, these people *were* evidently enjoying themselves in their own mysterious fashion, and why was it so mysterious to me? Weren't they of my own blood, my own caste? Why couldn't I—the would-be novelist, the professional observer—understand them? Why didn't I know—not coldly from the outside, but intuitively sympathetically, from within—what it was that made them perform their grave ritual of pleasure ; putting on blazers and flannels in the morning, plus-fours or white trousers in the afternoon, dinner jackets in the evening ; playing tennis, golf, bridge ; dancing, without a smile, the fox-trot, the tango, the blues ; smoking their pipes, reading the newspapers, organizing a sing-song, distributing prizes after a fancy-dress ball? True, I wasn't alone in my isolation. Chalmers, had he been here, would have felt just as I did. Madame Cheuret would have said: "Not really very cosy." Weston, despite his enthusiasm for the English, would have made these bathers the text for a grandly patronizing psycho-analytical lecture. People like my friends and myself, I thought, are to be found in little groups in all the larger towns ; we form a proudly self-sufficient, consciously declassed minority. We had our jokes, we amuse each other enormously ; we are glad, we say, that we are different. But are we really glad? Does anybody ever feel sincerely pleased at the prospect of remaining in permanent opposition, a social misfit, for the rest of his life? I knew, at any rate, that I myself didn't. I wanted—however much I might try to persuade myself, in moments of arrogance, to the contrary—to find some place, no matter how humble, in the scheme of society. Until I do that, I told myself, my writing will never be any good ; no amount of talent or technique will redeem it : it will remain a greenhouse product ; something, at best, for the connoisseur and the clique. And I envied Philip, that amazing social amphibian. He alone, of all my friends, could have met the hotel guests in their own element; could have talked their language and observed their customs: could have been accepted by them as one of themselves. It was Philip, not Weston, who truly understood "the English"; it was Philip, not myself, whom nature had equipped to be their novelist. The most I shall ever achieve, I thought, will be to learn how to spy upon them, unnoticed. Henceforward, my problem is how to perfect a disguise.

I had a disguise, of sorts, already; but it wasn't intended for the hotel guests. Every morning, after bathing, I strolled along the shingle bank, to pay my daily visit to Bruiser and Tim, the fishermen, who looked after old Mr. Straw's boats. Bruiser was a big hearty man, tattooed all over his chest, who worked fifteen or sixteen hours a day, partly at the boats, partly in the quarry, getting up in the middle of the night to row out and attend to his lobster pots. The combined earnings of his various trades were just sufficient to keep himself, his wife and his five-year-old son alive in a tumbledown cottage, on meals of butcher's leavings, margarine and bread. Bruiser, despite his robust appearance, had something the matter with his lungs. He could neither read nor write. His sharp brown eyes twinkled with good-humoured contempt for all summer visitors, white-collar workers and for everybody who stayed in bed after six a.m. "Good evening," he would greet me, ironically: "Lovely day it's been."

"Why," Tim would exclaim, looking up from his net-mending: "If it isn't our Marmaduke! How fwightfully allurin'. Well, Marmaduke, and how's the trahsers?"

This was our stock joke. The truth was (it embarrasses me a little to have to admit this, even now) that, in my eagerness to make myself acceptable to Bruiser and Tim—and, no doubt, to dissociate myself from my class-mates on the bathing beach—I had half-consciously assumed a slight Cockney twang. Tim, whose vowels were from Portsmouth, had, of course, noticed it at once; indeed, he would probably have found my ordinary university accent much less remarkable and comic. But, having started, I couldn't stop; and, after a few days' practice, I found myself slipping quite naturally into my disguise-language whenever the two boatmen or any of the other villagers were present. It was all rather ridiculous, and I'm sure it didn't take in Bruiser for a moment. I never felt really at ease under his bright ironical eye. Tim was less critical. Having accepted me as a casual gossip and drinking companion, he asked no questions of any kind—not even my name.

The companionship of Tim seemed, to my violently inverted snobbery, the peak of my social ambition at the Bay; I had set myself to win it with all the wiles that the most assiduous climber could practise upon a millionaire or a duke. I was never so happy as when squatting beside him outside Mr. Straw's hut, drinking with him at the pub, or accompanying him to the dance-hall in the village. I did my best to acquire that slow insulting stare (so discomforting when directed upon oneself) with which Bruiser and Tim followed the movements of a tripper. I grinned obsequiously at Tim's favourite catch-phrases and jokes: "How fwightfully allurin' . . . Many moons ago, when the world was young . . . The man who killed the Dead Sea whitewashing the Last Post. . ." The greatest mark of favour ever (apparently) bestowed upon me by Bruiser was his suggestion, one Saturday afternoon when they were short-handed, that I should row some of the hotel guests out to sea for a view of the lighthouse. There was an unpleasant swell that day, and after half an hour in the glaring sunshine without a hat I began to feel distinctly seasick; but the visitors were all excellent sailors and determined to have their money's worth. They asked questions about place names, distances and the heights of the cliffs which I couldn't correctly answer, though I did my best, obstinately maintaining my cockney twang. They disembarked at last, not a moment too soon, without tipping me. Bruiser eyed my greenish face, grinned cynically but said nothing. I had the sensation of having failed yet another test.

It was during the evenings that I finally managed to earn Tim's esteem. Tim was extremely vain of his powers as a lady-killer. "You see, Marmaduke," he would explain, "I've got It." He was seventeen years old, had a good figure and the face of an attractive monkey. His snub nose was covered with innumerable black freckles, which he was never tired of admiring in the splinter of looking-glass nailed to the wall of the hut: "Handsome men," he assured me, "is slightly sunburnt." Apparently the girls thought so too. Tim's spare time was a round of assignations—he called it "spicket-drill." Together, we visited the local cinema, picked up a couple of girls and cuddled them throughout the performance. I found that I was particularly good at cuddling; especially after three or four "dog's noses" (gin and beer) at the pub. Indeed, my very inhibitions made me extremely daring—up to a point. Tim, who really meant business, was often curiously shy in the opening stages. Once or twice, having pushed things farther than I had intended, I was scared to find myself committed to a midnight walk over the downs. But, on these occasions, I always discovered an excuse for passing my girl on to Tim. Next morning, he would be grateful and suitably impressed. "You ought to have seen our Marmaduke last night," he would tell Bruiser. "Honest, I was surprised . . . Our Marmaduke's a dark horse—ain't you Marmaduke?"

One afternoon we seemed to be on the verge of a tragedy. Tim had set out that morning in Mr. Straw's big motor-boat with a party of schoolgirls for a trip down the coast. They were due back at lunch time: at five o'clock they still hadn't returned. A thick woolly fog was settling down upon the sea. Everybody in the Bay became mildly excited; and most of us were standing along the sea-wall or watching from the beach, when, shortly before six, the missing boat emerged unexpectedly from the dense coiling vapours, scarcely a stone's throw from the shore. The motor had broken down, hours before, and while Tim was vainly trying to repair it the launch had drifted slowly out to sea. At length, he had been forced to row the heavy boat home as best he could, with a pair of unequally sized oars.

Tim seemed very little the worse for his ordeal. With a couple of monkey-like bounds he reached the top of the shingle bank and began pulling off his rubber boots, humming, as he did so, his favourite song:

> Waitin' fer ther moon
> Ter shine, ter show me the way
> Ter get yer ter say
> I love yer . . .

But the schoolgirls were in a sorry condition. Most of them were in tears and some had been sick. A mistress who had not taken part in the expedition dramatically embraced her colleague as she disembarked, and joined her, after casting a furious glance in Tim's direction, in shepherding the frightened and shivering girls away to their hot tea, consolation and bed.

"How I wish they'd all drowned!" said a voice at my elbow.

I turned to find, standing beside me, a young man whom I knew by sight already. I had passed him several times in the village street, hurrying along, hatless, in gym shoes, with a heavy walking-stick and a powerful, curiously wooden stride which suggested some unseen injury. He was gawkily tall; his small untidy mobile head was set upon gaunt shoulders; the eyes nervous, alert and puzzled. His whole appearance was that of an overgrown nervy boy. He might easily have passed for less than twenty years old.

His name, he told me, was Lester—by this time we were having a drink together at the pub—and he lived in a tent, in a field behind the Methodist Chapel.

"Do you always live in tents?" I asked.

"Mostly. I had a caravan, for a bit. But I prefer tents. Got used to them in the Army."

In 1915, a few weeks after his sixteenth birthday, Lester had joined the H.A.C. Stationed at the Tower, he had had to guard condemned German spies. "I'm ready to swear one of them was innocent. He was a Dutchman. The night before we shot him, he made such a row that nobody could get any sleep. Kept yelling out at me, over and over again: 'Have mercy!' Seemed to think I could help him. In the end, I got so rattled I started cursing him. I felt bloody ashamed about it afterwards. . . ." Lester had had a fight with another boy, hardly older than himself, who was cocky and boastful because he had been chosen to go out to France on an earlier draft. The other boy had been killed within twenty-four hours of reaching the front. And Lester had survived to see the last drafts go out in autumn of 1918, escorted down to the station by military police, for fear of wholesale desertion.

After this, he and I met frequently; sometimes we sat together in the garden of Beach View, under the boat-shaped veranda; sometimes I trotted beside him as he strode stiffly over the downs, brandishing his heavy dangerous stick. Once, he told me, he had used it to knock out three members of a racetrack gang who had attacked him near Epsom with knives. "They could have got me, if they'd known anything about trench-fighting. There's a trick the Canadians were fond of. Like this . . ." Whatever we talked about, our conversation

156

returned, inescapably, to the war. Lester, obviously, could speak of nothing else for long.

He described his training: the bayonet practices, at which the sergeant had shown them how to twist the bayonet in the body and extract it with the help of your foot; the jumping of trenches in full equipment; the bombing course, with its accidents—one man had lost an arm, two had been killed. He described the first journey to France—the night crossing with darkened lights, the troop trains, the trenches, the first attack: "It's not so bad, especially if you've had some rum first. You just do what the others are doing. You mustn't think about it too much, that's all. . . ." People who "thought about it" went mad, or wounded themselves with their own weapons, or stood on the parapet until they were hit—according to their temperaments. Lester had seen a young officer shot "for cowardice" after being in the line for five days without sleep. Another officer, also found guilty of running away, was sent back to the front while awaiting sentence; two days later, a colonel who did not know of his record recommended him for the Victoria Cross. When the earliest tank units were being formed, Lester had volunteered. The first tanks had barely room for their crews; you crouched on boxes of ammunition with your shoulders against the roof, jarred sickeningly by every explosion, sweating in the heat and fumes of the motor, scarcely able to breathe. "The first thing we all did when we got out was to go and brush our teeth." Lester had been in one of them when a shell exploded beneath it, killing or burning everybody else, and throwing him out of the door with a small wound in his little finger. This was the only physical injury he had ever received.

He never suspected, I think, how violently his quietly told horribly matter-of-fact anecdotes affected me. I had heard plenty of war stories before, from older men, and the war novel was just coming into fashion; but Lester alone had the knack of making all those remote obscenities and horrors seem real. Always, as I listened, I asked myself the same question; always I tried to picture myself in his place. But here, as ever, the censorship, in blind panic, intervened, blacking out the image. No, no, I told myself, terrified; this could never happen to me. It could never happen to any of my friends. It was physically impossible. It wouldn't be allowed. Nevertheless, Lester had shaken my faith in the invulnerability of my generation; for, in his eyes, we were not invulnerable;

what had happened to him could easily happen to us. "Oh, you'd have been all right," he reassured me, when I tried to tell him something of my feelings: "We all had to go through it, you know."

Yes, they had all had to go through it; and one day, perhaps, it would be our turn—Chalmers', Weston's, Philip's, mine. Our little world which seemed so precious would burst like the tiniest soap bubble, unnoticed, uncared for—just as Lester's world had exploded, thirteen years ago. And now Lester had no world. With his puzzled air of arrested boyishness, he belonged for ever, like an unhappy Peter Pan, to the nightmare Never-Never-Land of the War. He had no business to be here, alive, in post-war England. His place was elsewhere, was with the dead. Alone in his tent, camping like a refugee on the fringe of society, he seemed too puzzled to be bitter, was grateful, even, for the grudging scraps we threw him, a few pounds of pension money and free tickets to London to report himself to the medical board. The doctors had agreed in certifying him as totally disabled; he was to live an open-air life, they said; avoid alcohol and all excitement. They couldn't cure his headaches, or his insomnia, or his chronic constipation; they couldn't even suggest one good reason why he shouldn't commit suicide immediately. But he continued to visit them because, if he didn't, his pension would probably be cut off altogether.

I came to regard Lester as a ghost—the ghost of the War. Walking beside him, at midnight, on the downs, I asked him the question which ghosts are always asked by the living: "What shall I do with my life?" "I think," said Lester, "that you'd make a very good doctor." His answer took me completely by surprise: I laughed. "Imagine me as a doctor! And, anyhow, that's hardly a compliment, coming from you!" Nevertheless, I felt obscurely flattered and pleased.

Ghosts need the company of the living—otherwise they cannot exist—but they are never intrusive or possessive; they can establish contact, if necessary, from a distance. Often, when I was writing under the veranda, Lester would pass the garden gate, noiseless on the toes of his gym shoes, raising his stick for an instant in salute. We seldom met except in the evenings, but I was vaguely aware of his benevolent presence, just out of sight, throughout the day. I knew that he liked to see me working, just as he liked to watch the fishermen or the men in the fields. He wished us well.

Since getting to know Lester I had felt, strangely enough, a renewed interest in my novel. I began to double and treble my daily output. I spent less time gossiping with Muriel and Mr. Peck, Bruiser and Tim.

Towards the end of July, I finished my revised version of the *Seascape with Figures*. I had improved it, I hoped. Certainly, it was livelier: what Chalmers called "stage-directions" ("he said," "she answered," "he smiled," "they both laughed,") had been cut down to a minimum—indeed, it was now very nearly impossible to guess which of the characters was supposed to be speaking: and there were several "thought-stream" passages in the fashionable neo-Joyce manner which yielded nothing, in obscurity, to the work of the master himself. The murder was cut—"tea-tabled" down to an indecisive, undignified scuffle ; and the ending was an apotheosis of the Tea-Table, a decrescendo of anti-climaxes. My two chief characters, the medical student and the dilettante artist, now resembled Chalmers and Philip more strongly than ever. For my nasty Cambridge undergraduate, I had received some valuable new hints from my observations at the hotel bathing-pool.

Rewriting the *Seascape* had taught me a great deal ; I had begun to discover my limitations, to know what I could do and what I couldn't. I was strongest on dialogue, weakest on abstractions and generalizations: I must never try to address the reader—whenever I did so, I uttered platitudes or tied myself up in knots ; I must stick to the particular and the special instance. My characterization was flashy but thin ; I was a cartoonist, not a painter in oils. Love scenes I had better avoid—until I knew something about them.

I thought of the novel (as I hoped to learn to write it) essentially in terms of technique, of conjuring, of chess. The novelist, I said to myself, is playing a game with his reader ; he must continually amaze and deceive him, with tricks, with traps, with extraordinary gambits, with sham climaxes, with false directions. I imagined a novel as a contraption—like a motor bicycle, whose action depends upon the exactly co-ordinated working of all its inter-related parts ; or like a conjurer's table, fitted with mirrors, concealed pockets and trapdoors. I saw it as something compact, and, by the laws of its own nature, fairly short. In fact, my models were not novels at all, but detective stories, and the plays of Ibsen and

Tchekhov. *War and Peace*, which I read for the first time a few months later, disarranged and altered all my ideas.

Lester came down to Yarmouth to see me off. The morning was blazing hot. Lester, standing a head taller than anybody else in the flannelled quayside crowd, his gaunt body draped in an immense military overcoat (he was always complaining of the cold), looked more than ever like a visitor from another world. As "The Workhouse" churned away from the pier, he raised his stick and shouted: "Remember!" It seemed to me, at the time, that I knew what he meant.

London was stifling; Romilly Road, in the sunshine, looked shabbier than ever. The heat had brought out the smells. The stench of yesterday's cooking, when you opened the front door, nearly knocked you down. I found Mrs. Partridge in low spirits. She was having trouble with her lodgers, an Irish couple; they wouldn't pay the rent, she complained, they kept their room like a pigsty, and the baby squalled all night.

She was right about the baby: it kept me awake for hours. It seemed to have lungs of leather and an inexhaustible supply of breath. I began to wonder whether its parents didn't keep pinching it, just to annoy Mrs. Partridge—for the difference about the rent had developed into an open feud, carried on by the lodgers with all the ingenuity and humour of their race. Their acts of domestic sabotage varied from making holes in the rubber feed-pipe of the kitchen gas-ring to unscrewing the handle of their landlady's bedroom door. One morning, coming into the bathroom half asleep and automatically pulling the lavatory chain (always a necessary precaution) I discovered, too late, that a blanket had been carefully stuffed into the drain. The resulting flood covered the floor an inch deep and immediately began to drip through into the kitchen below. Mrs. Partridge rushed out on to the staircase, crying: "This is more than I can bear!"

The end came, two days later. The Irish lodgers departed, while we were both out, taking with them in a taxi a selection of Mrs. Partridge's vases and pictures, a number of cooking utensils and my portable gramophone. Mrs. Partridge, not unnaturally, insisted on informing the police. The lodgers were traced, without much trouble—they had only gone as far as Pimlico—and the vases recovered, all smashed. The gramophone had been sold to a second-hand furniture dealer: I eventually got that back too, but something went wrong with the works and it would only play at twice the normal speed. The Irish husband was sent to prison, which did no good to anybody, and merely meant that I had to give his wife some money to live on until he was let out again.

The following week, I left Romilly Road for good, and returned to live at home. The New Life had ignominiously failed.

That autumn and winter, I pottered about unhappily, writing nothing, earning a little pocket-money at temporary half-time tutoring jobs and drinking a great deal of gin. Chalmers had approved of the revised *Seascape* but disliked its title. We toyed with several others: "The Family of the Artist," "The Old Life," "An Artist to his Circle." Finally, I remembered a quotation from a Shakespearian speech learnt at school:

All the conspirators save only he
Did that they did in envy of great Cæsar. . . .

All the Conspirators. . . . It sounded grand. True, there was no Anthony in my story, much less a Brutus, and the life of Julius Cæsar couldn't by any conceivable stretch of ingenuity be related to the squabbles of a middle-class family in North Kensington—but considerations of this sort weighed very little in 1927. *All the Conspirators* was duly sent off on its round of the publishers. By Christmas, two had already refused it, with polite regrets.

My gin-drinking was done chiefly in the company of Bill Scott, the Cheurets' friend. Bill was a painter—a great painter perhaps: I only know that his pictures excited me more than any other modern landscapes I have seen. He painted trees as monstrous, terrifying vegetables, pushing up out of the ground, with soft naked trunks. Two of them would confront each other, like vast mysterious personages, between whom all speech is unnecessary. A hillside would be built up out of coloured geometrical blocks, so that you seemed to understand its structure and looked into its very depth. If there were houses, they were square, like dice, and without windows, furiously white against a burning blue sky. There were never any human figures, or animals, or birds, or flowers.

Bill was a dark sunburnt little man agile and quick as a lizard, with naughty, prominent blue eyes. His smile had an immediate, touching warmth: he always seemed pleased to see you. He would take infinite pains over anything which might please or amuse his friends, a dinner, fireworks, charades. If there was to be a party at his studio, he worked all day, preparing salads, goulasch and Mediterranean fish soup. At charades he was brilliant, mimicking French generals, Russian aristocrats, opera singers, nuns, performing burlesque ballet, juggling with plates. He expended all his energy, all his resources lavishly, to the point of absolute exhaustion. After making us laugh the whole evening, he would suddenly drop down on to the sofa and lie there motionless, like a cast-off glove, too tired to speak.

Drinking with Bill was a unique, a kind of psychic experience, like passing gradually on to another plane of being. I don't think that he himself ever got drunk at all ; but he acted on those who were with him like a medium, transferring sensations, transmitting visions. After two or three of his special cocktails (he would never tell you how they were mixed) I used to wander about his studio examining different objects —an ink-pot, a paper-knife, the petals of a flower—and thinking: "How wonderful! This is glass, this is metal, this is alive. I see now, for the first time, its essential nature: I see why it is formed in this particular way: I see what it represents. Until this moment, I have merely known its name, its label. Until this moment, I have never really looked at it at all." I was, in fact, seeing through Bill's eyes. He was hypnotically directing my vision, even though he might be standing at the other end of the room, joking with the Cheurets or handing around a dish of fruit. He was well aware of his powers and of my suggestibility. It amused him, sometimes, to frighten me. He was an adept at inducing terror. He would tell ghost stories horribly ; or he would get us sitting round the big table, with the tips of our fingers on the wood, waiting for a "message" ; these séances always started half humorously, Bill deadly serious, the rest of us giggling, but it wouldn't be long before even the most sceptical members of the party quietened down, and, presently, the rapping would begin. Of course, we assured each other later, Bill had been kicking the table with the toe of his shoe ; but we had to admit that we had felt thoroughly uncomfortable, all the same. One evening, when he and I were alone together in the studio, he told me that he had noticed "something very odd" about the big oak cupboard which stood in the corner: "I think, if we sit quite still for a few minutes, the doors will probably open." "Really?" I nervously tried to laugh this off. "And what do you suppose will happen then?" "One never knows. . . ." Bill gave me one of his quiet, frightening smiles: "Something might come out. . . ." And so, in the gathering twilight, we sat together on the sofa, staring at the cupboard doors. My heart was making a noise like a big drum. At the end of three minutes, I could stand it no longer, and insisted on switching on all the lights, starting the gramophone and throwing the cupboard wide open. There was nothing inside, except a pile of canvases and some old clothes.

Bill had a big car which he drove expertly, at terrific speeds. Sometimes, towards midnight, he would exclaim: "Let us get out of here!" and we would leave immediately, roaring away through the suburbs, to find ourselves when dawn broke, already far on the road to Cornwall or Wales. These suddenly undertaken excursions exactly suited my escapist temperament; I could never see a train leave a platform for any destination without wishing myself on board.

One evening, we left Bill's studio even more abruptly than usual. "We'll drive down to Southampton," he said, "and take a boat to Greece." But, in the Cromwell Road, we found ourselves turning north. We didn't stop again until Catterick Bridge, where we had breakfast. By lunch-time we were in Edinburgh. I had never been in Scotland before; my mind was a blank screen for the projection of Bill's hypnotic suggestions. He showed me a city of steep crooked streets, mysterious archways and stone stairs, as foreign as Le Havre, above which the washing hung from the windows on horizontal poles, like flags. After dark, we tried to take a short cut to the top of Arthur's Seat, and soon found ourselves spread-eagled on a nearly vertical slope, clinging desperately to tufts of grass: Bill made our scramble seem as dangerous and exciting as an ascent of the Matterhorn. Later, we slithered down to the gates of Holyrood and had supper in an eating-house full of scarlet soldiers, and an argument about Art. Bill said that the pattern evolved from the reality is more important than the reality itself: I disagreed, partly because I didn't understand what he meant, partly out of perversity, because I was drunk.

During the next few days, I was drunk almost continuously. Drunk at Stirling, where we inspected the two martyred virgins under glass; drunk at Blair Atholl, where, pushing open a glass swing-door in the hotel, I thought, with a wonderful pang of joy: "My life is a journey. I can never go back. Whatever becomes of me, I shall never use this lavatory again." Very drunk indeed at Inverness. We drove out, next day, to Culbin Sands. The whisky at the hotel was like perfumed soap, the most delicious I had ever tasted: after drinking three-quarters of a bottle, I wandered away, muttering to myself, over the sand dunes. It was a brilliant sunny morning, with a high wind blowing off the Firth. As I fought my way down towards the sea, the wind assumed a physical shape. It was the Enemy, the Laily Worm, Cambridge; it was the embodiment of my most intimate and deadly fears. It was mocking me. No, it squealed, you shall never escape! You shall be my victim, my prisoner, my lover—always! "Never," I yelled, and flung myself upon it. We swayed for a moment, locked together; then I tripped it and we fell, rolling over and over, down a steep bank of shale. Bill, suddenly appearing at the top of a sand dune, cheered me on. I punched and kicked and tried to throttle my antagonist. "Come and help," I gasped, to Bill. Then, all at once, I was alone, sprawling on my stomach on the ground, with bleeding knuckles and my hair full of sand.

We drove on and on. In Helmsdale, we stopped at the Commercial Hotel for tea. In the parlour, there was a water-colour painting of a fish, against the background of a highland river and a little bridge. Bill, tremendously excited, exclaimed that it was a masterpiece; better than anything Matisse had ever done. The picture was signed: J. Mellis. The landlady, when questioned, told us that he was a local man and that he had been killed in the war. When Bill offered to buy the picture, she refused, laughing, thinking perhaps that he wasn't serious: "Oh, I wouldn't like to part with it. It amuses the travellers. Why, the fish is larger than the bridge!"

Mist and thin rain blew down the road to meet us, like the cold breath of the North itself. On the wall of a white farm, a heart had been cut out of living ivy. There were antlers above the farmhouse doors. The carts and fences and the shutters of windows were painted scarlet, as I had seen them, once, in a nursery book about Norway. Bill excited me by saying that this wasn't the north of Britain, but the extreme southern province of the Norse kingdom. Near Wick, at a house where we stopped to fill the cooler with water, a bearded farmer showed us coins of Edward the Second and of

Philip and Mary which he had dug out of his land; we walked out to the cliff edge to look at a Pictish broch. Long streamers of mucus flew out of the farmer's nose and fluttered on the breeze; so that Bill and I had to keep dodging around him to windward, roaring with laughter. The lean agile old man seemed quite aware of the joke; he even appeared to be joining in the game and deliberately trying to hit us. Soon we were all three waving our arms, shouting, laughing and jumping about in a kind of rustic dance.

Wick, entrenched behind its stone jetty, seemed a last outpost, a frontier fort against the savage, hostile sea. Exhausted gulls were blown down the main street, flapping weakly, like sheets of wet newspaper. The waves exploded like enormous shells, spattering the gleaming wet roofs. There was a first-aid station behind the pier. The inhabitants were curiously gentle, with soft intimate voices. "Come awake!" said the chambermaid at the hotel, bringing our morning tea. The barber's boy, at the shop where we went to be shaved, recited a hymn: "'When I am sad, He makes me glad. He's my friend.' . . . It's verra nice, that." "Ah," laughed one of the older customers, "ye're too saft-hearted!" The boy smiled and shook his head: "Would ye have hearts of iron, then; or what?" Down at the harbour, Bill painted one of his best pictures: the doomed white houses shrinking back against the brown land, and one terrible wave, olive green with a hanging lip of foam, like a gigantic mountain, rolling in to engulf the town for ever.

We drove on, across the misty bog-plains, striped black where the peat had been cut, in the direction of Cape Wrath. The coast was gashed into jagged fjords: under the cliffs, the water lay like ebony, with vivid jade shallows. The mountains were piled up in the west against an angry sunset. That night, we slept at Bettyhill, where the road turns south, along the shallow estuary, through dwarf birch forests, towards England.

Bill talked of the Orkneys, the Shetlands, the Hebrides, but we both knew that we were going back. One always has to go back, I thought, at the end of these little escapades. You may give your familiar everyday self the slip easily enough; for several hours, your absence won't be noticed, and if your car is fast and you can keep on the run you may even escape for a whole week. But, sooner or later, you will come to a halt; sooner or later, that dreary governess, that gloomy male nurse will catch you up; will arrive, on the slow train, to fetch you back to your nursery prison of minor obligations, duties, habits, ties. All at once, I felt deeply depressed and very tired. Bill, sympathetic as ever, prescribed a double whisky. But this time the cure didn't work, and the two which followed it merely made me maudlin. "It's no good," I told him. "I shall never try to run away again."

Back at home, in the depths of my reaction from the excitement of our Scotch journey, I remembered Lester's advice. Suppose I really did become a doctor? The idea seemed as absurd as ever; and—for that very reason—attractive. "After all," I told Philip, "I've got to do something. I can't be a tutor all my life. And I'm not such a fool as to imagine that I'll ever make a living out of writing. . . ." (Needless to say, this wasn't quite sincere.) Philip shrugged his shoulders. He was anything but encouraging: "Ah well, boy; I suppose you know best. . . . I believe there *are* people who enjoy it. . . . Shouldn't have thought you would, somehow. . . But you never can tell. . . ." He plainly thought me a little mad. But Chalmers was surprisingly enthusiastic. Hadn't Tchekhov been a doctor? It would be wonderful for getting copy: the ideal career for a novelist. What opportunities for hearing death-bed confessions, marital confidences; for tea-tabling the most horrible diseases and loathsome operations! "And at night, when the last patient has gone home, you'll light your peculiar-looking green-shaded lamp in the surgery, and sit down to write your masterpiece. It'll be called . . . let me see . . ." To these day-dreams, I added others, more intimate: the beautiful doomed sufferer, the last clasp of the hot dry hand, the murmured name. . . . Or, alternatively, the marvellous cure, the lifelong gratitude. . . . Thus, with the aid of a little imagination, do one's most fantastic projects become real.

Within a week, I had got to the point of confiding in my family. Within a fortnight, the thing was as good as arranged. It would be hardly possible, of course, to start until the autumn of next year; in the slight recoil from my first enthusiasm I was secretly rather glad of this respite. It would give me time to change my mind, supposing that anything were to happen in the interval. What kind of thing? Oh well, something wonderful, something that would alter the whole course of my life. A miracle, in fact? Yes—and why not? After all, everybody has the right to demand at least one miracle.

Early in January, I got a letter from Messrs. Jonathan Cape. Would I go round to see them at once? Mr. Cape himself received me in his office. I forget what he looked like. Indeed, I was too dazed to notice or understand anything beyond the first unbelievable sentences: "Well, Mr. Isherwood, I liked your book. . . . There are just a couple of points I might make. . . . We'll ask the printers to indent the type in those passages. . . . Would May be too late? We suggest ten per cent, royalties and an advance. . . ." I suppose I neither kissed his hand nor danced a jig before the typists. But I ran all the way to the tube station; and the massed bands were playing their loudest, and the streets were full of waving flags.

CHAPTER VII

*A*LL *the Conspirators* duly appeared, as Mr. Cape had promised, during the third week in May 1928. I was back at Beach View, with Chalmers, when the six advance copies arrived ; every time he went out of the room, I kept furtively opening them and peeping at my name on the title pages. We both agreed that a copy should be sent to Mr. Holmes, with a suitable inscription.

Chalmers had left his job in Cornwall. He had spent the spring term tutoring a boy in the North of England : there had been plenty of spare time, and he had used it to write the longest and most elaborate of all our Mortmere stories, *The Railway Accident*. This is the last contribution either of us ever made to the literature of Mortmere. Mortmere seemed to have brought us to a dead end. The cult of romantic strangeness, we both knew, was a luxury for the comfortable University fireside ; it could not save you from the drab realities of cheap lodgings and a dull, underpaid job. Gunball was a fair-weather friend ; when your money ran short, he blandly left you in the lurch.

But Chalmers needed Gunball, at all costs. I did not. That, as writers, was the essential difference between us. Chalmers had created Gunball out of his own flesh and blood ; he could never afford to abandon him altogether ; if he did so, he was lost. He was to spend the next three years in desperate and bitter struggles to relate Mortmere to the real world of the jobs and the lodging-houses ; to find the formula which would transform our private fancies and amusing freaks and bogies into valid symbols of the ills of society and the toils and aspirations of our daily lives. For the formula did, after all, exist. And Chalmers did at last find it, at the end of a long and weary search, not hidden in the mysterious emblems of Dürer or the prophetic utterances of

Blake, not in any anagram, or cipher, or mediæval Latin inscription, but quite clearly set down, for everybody to read, in the pages of Lenin and of Marx.

"Mr. Christopher Isherwood," wrote *Punch,* "is either badly troubled with that kind of portentous solemnity which so often accompanies the mental growing pains of the very young, or else he has written his novel with his tongue in his cheek. . . . Altogether, the book leaves behind it a faintly nasty taste. . . ." The *Natal Advertiser,* still more severe, considered that I had made a "bad start on the difficult paths of fiction." The *Sun,* Sydney, was crushing: "If we must have Freudian and psychological novels, dealing with people's insides . . ." The *Sphere* and the *Southport Guardian* accused me of "cleverness." The *Liverpool Post and Mercury* recommended leniency on the grounds of my obviously extreme youth. The *Morning Post* and *The Times Literary Supplement* were politely encouraging. Mr. H. I'A Fausset, in the *Manchester Guardian,* was kind and generous. I had practically no other Press notices at all. The book sold less than three hundred copies, and was duly remaindered and forgotten—until Sir Hugh Walpole, writing in the *Sunday Times* five years later, included it in a list of six novels which he considered to have been "unjustly neglected" since the War.

Again this year the Bay was full of new faces. Lester had gone off with his tent; nobody seemed to know where. Tim had joined the Army and was in camp on Salisbury Plain. Muriel had left the sweetshop to be married. There was a different barmaid at the pub. But the changes did not depress me unduly, for, as usual, I found Chalmers' company all-absorbing and sufficient. With our advancing years (I could remember the time when I thought twenty-five almost middle-aged) we seemed to have grown increasingly silly: our favourite game was to chase bits of toilet paper with walking-sticks over the downs. When the wind was in the right direction the toilet paper would sometimes provide us with a run of several miles; we followed it with yells and Starnese hunting-cries, whirling our sticks above our heads or flinging them, like javelins, at the quarry. In the evenings, after a visit to the pub to buy beer, biscuits and some packets of potato crisps, we would settle down with pencil and paper at the sitting-room table for "automatic writing." This amusement had nothing to do with spiritualism: you were merely required to put down, as fast as you could, the first words or sentences that came into your head. To reflect, to erase, to try to be literary, was cheating: we both cheated a good deal. Here are some of our results: Chalmers' first:

This is a tale of a man in Russian boots who pulled the arms off railway signals. Every morning he ate ensilage and prayed for the redemption of two very old cows who lived in the bath. You understand this coinage? I didn't, but now, after having achieved, I acknowledged it all at once as the bogus synthesis of our most diurnal bugbear, to wit, the worship of the past. That's to say, girls, anything that can be improperly be said to the old; old spades, old hair, old tools found in the boxroom under a ruined geyser. Well, when our Petrovitch of the hour fluked into the plumbers' of his noman's pellucid errand he was unconditionally met by the unvariegated stare of the counter-maid —the evening star is not current. Neuters are never happy. Watching all day the whey-sour sea vomiting on the broken esplanade. Weary whores in pale dream-brimmed straw hats, reminiscence of the randier eighties when disguise gave sauce and gust to forms now hackneyed and mawkish. Rubber statuary in gardens of ice-cream roses bearing every imprint of foot and belly. Kissing beneath the jangling clock before the cinema doors are opened. Plush seats unbarred between, mumbling hands convolved in calico. Steady, chaps, go slow. Where were we? This problem. How to present the never formulated in terms of the I never tried to formulate. Once more, whores feed on straw. Queerly, queerly. R.L.S. Soon.

And mine (I should explain that I was suffering that evening from the effects of too much sunbathing):

My black back streams with bleeding blood with blood with blood with blood. Victim of Nacktkultur, of cliffs, of degenerate parents, of schoolboy tiffs, all all gone. All gone. All gone. All gone. The tape-machine in the lounge couldn't spool out the news fast enough. Then there was no news. None. For hours. I have eaten all the news. I have swallowed whole Mrs. Pace, the railway disaster in Durham, the gift to the Exchequer. Writing here in the closed room by lamplight, with injured bowels, I represent all that is best in a modern consciousness already vitiated by the puppet-show, the dog-racing, the automatic organ. To be true, to be free, to be Proust, ah yes, ah no, ah, ah, far car, stop that, Trudy, drop it or I shoot. I am dying. Typical autoerotic impulse myth. I am dead. Specimen bogus statement of the pre-television age. Very, very important that the word I wanted here: decade, was censored for nearly twelve seconds. Why do I say twelve, not ten? Well, to explain that, boys, would be to write a history of my whole Cambridge life. Of the tea-shops and the hopeless longings for pleasure. Look here, we'll face this. Am I a Catholic? Yes. Am I a conservative? Yes. Am I Life? Yes. Very well, enter into my kingdom. My back. Blood. All blood. Must end.

Curiously enough, when we tried this game on Philip, it didn't work at all. Perhaps his mind was too literal and too uninhibited; perhaps the trouble was that, unlike us, he played fair. All we got was a formidable list of girls who had attracted him since leaving school, with businesslike and quite unprintable comments.

Philip had come down to stay with us for a weekend. It was too early in the year for many hotel visitors, so he had no opportunity to display his social prowess; but Chalmers and I got him drunk one night at the pub and egged him on to pursue one of the few available local "bits." The results were unsatisfactory; possibly because Philip's complicated and showy technique of approach was wasted on a girl accustomed to the extremely direct advances of the village boys. He left for London next day, deeply disappointed. Chalmers, who had heard of a new job, travelled up with him for an interview.

While they were both away, and without the least warning, Miss Chichester died. She had served my tea, that afternoon, as usual. I had noticed nothing odd in her manner or her movements. Only, as she set the tea-pot on the table she had remarked: "My sister's arriving to-day," and, pausing at the door, had added: "I hope you'll be comfortable." This, I realized later, had been her admirably restrained, heroic farewell. For she had known what was coming; had wired, as I heard afterwards, that morning, to her married sister on the mainland to join her at once. The sister, a rosy-cheeked, elderly lady in the prime of health, had entered Miss Chichester's sitting-room to find her stretched on the sofa, unconscious. Before midnight, Miss Chichester was dead.

I have had many landladies since that day, some of them excellent, and a few of them remarkable; but not one of them—not even my beloved Fri Schroeder—could rival Miss Chichester in tact. Unfortunately, I couldn't show my respect by attending her funeral because I had no clothes with me except the flannels I stood up in: the only tribute I could pay to her memory was to stay indoors during the ceremony—in accordance with that curious superstition which demands that a house shall not be left empty while the mourners are away at the graveyard.

When I got back to London, I had Weston to stay. He had finished with Oxford now, and was going off in the autumn to Berlin to improve his German. He had brought with him to show me the typescript of a story written by an undergraduate he had got to know during his last year at the University: "He's mad," said Weston, by way of preface: "I think it's very good indeed."

The story—which turned out later to be part of a large, loosely constructed novel—described a young man's visit to the home of some male and female cousins. The young man is almost incredibly shy, gauche, tactless and generally neurotic; and his social shortcomings are exaggerated by contrast with the elegance, beauty and grace of his hosts. They appear to him as beings from another world; and his hopeless adoration of them fills him with self-hatred and despair. The cousins, on their side, are amused by the young man; they make fun of him, lightly, without malice; exposed to their unconsciously cruel mockery, he suffers tortures of humiliation—culminating in an extraordinary scene, in which, being unable to understand the simple mechanism of a folding card-table, he breaks down altogether and bursts into tears.

Having finished it, I agreed with Weston: indeed the story was not quite like anything else I had ever read. True, its grammar was awful, its dialogue stilted and its style naïve—but it did something to you; you accepted the absurd situations without question; you really cared about the problems of the blundering, tormented young man. The hero was so absorbingly interested in himself, in his own sensations and in everybody who came into contact with him that you couldn't help sharing his interest. In fact, the experience was so vivid as to be quite painful. You blushed for him, you squirmed at his every faux-pas; you wanted, simultaneously, to kick and protect and shake him.

A few weeks later, Weston arranged a meeting with the author. He burst in upon us, blushing, sniggering loudly, contriving to trip over the edge of the carpet—an immensely tall, shambling boy of nineteen, with a great scarlet poppy-face, wild frizzy hair, and eyes the violent colour of bluebells. His name was Stephen Savage.

In an instant, without introductions, we were all laughing and talking at the top of our voices. Savage, as I was later to discover, had this kind of effect upon nearly everybody he met; in his company you naturally began to shout, if only in order to make yourself heard at all. Savage himself was noisy without effort. His beautiful resonant voice—inherited from a professionally political father—would carry to the farthest corners of the largest restaurant the most intimate details of his private life. Not that anything in his life could be properly described as private: he shared his experiences, like a banquet, with his friends. In any and every sort of company he would relate, with the same perfect simplicity, the circumstances of a quarrel, the inner history of his family or the latest developments of a love affair. He inhabited a world of self-created and absorbing drama, into which each new acquaintance was immediately conscripted to play a part. Savage illuminated you like an expressionist producer, with the crudest and most eccentric of spot-lights: you were transfigured, became grandiose, sinister, brilliantly ridiculous or impossibly beautiful, in accordance with his arbitrary, pre-arranged conception of your role. And soon—such is the hypnotic mastery of the born *régisseur*—you began to live up to his expectations. In Savage's presence, people frequently behaved with an extravagance quite foreign to their everyday natures. I have seen several, who were otherwise quiet and reserved, shed tears, pray, perform exotic dances or seize each other by the hair; one eminently respectable lady was even moved to attack her husband with a knife.

But if Savage compelled you to act in his life drama, he also rewarded you handsomely for your services. He was the slave of his friends. He was always planning little pleasures and surprises for your benefit; he seldom came to see you without bringing some present—a gramophone record, a pretty tie, a book. Even when, a couple of years later, we were living only a few streets away from each other in Berlin, and met several times a day, Savage would often arrive with a large specially chosen orange or a little bunch of flowers. His kindness was so touching and disarming that it sometimes made me quite irritable. I was cross with myself because I couldn't hope to compete with it ; because it somehow made me feel myself an inferior, unworthy mortal, a traitor to his friendship. All Savage's friends betrayed him, in some minor degree, sooner or later. He asked too much of them ; he trusted them absolutely— so that the blow, when it fell, was doubled in force. The pin-prick hurt him like a thrust from a two-edged sword. He stumbled off, by himself, utterly bewildered ; and his nose began to bleed. Savage's nose-bleeding (now long since cured) was famous, at this period: Weston called him "the fountain." Without the least warning, at all times of the day, the blood would suddenly squirt from his nostrils, as if impelled by the appalling mental pressure within that scarlet, accusing face ; and no keys, no cold water compress could stop it until the neural wound had, as it seemed, bled itself dry.

In thinking about Stephen as he was in those days, I like specially to remember one incident. During the spring of 1930, the authorities had temporarily erected in Hyde Park a carillon of bells, destined, eventually, for a war memorial in New Zealand. Every day there were concerts. One afternoon, I happened to be crossing the park and stopped for a minute at the edge of the crowd which surrounded the little wooden bell-tower. The absurdly sweet, sugary chimes had just finished tinkling out "The Bluebells of Scotland" ; and the crowd stood awe-struck, with slightly open mouths, like sea-lions awaiting their next meal. Suddenly, in the reverent silence, a wild silly laugh rang out: somebody, with more courage than myself, was sharing my amusement at the scene. All heads turned in his direction, some curious, some indignant, some really shocked. And there stood Savage, a head taller than any of them, hatless and wilder-looking than ever: completely isolated in his riotous, unrestrained mirth. I felt very strongly drawn towards him at that moment.

At the beginning of October, 1928, I began my career as a medical student—not without the darkest misgivings. It was like starting school all over again, not as the prize scholar, the scholarship candidate, but as the backward, overgrown boy who finds himself left behind in the infants' class. Nearly all my fellow students had just passed out of their public schools; I was five or six years older than any of them— amidst those pink unfinished faces I felt like a man of forty. Nor was it any good my trying to imagine myself their superior on account of my advanced years; in the one essential subject I knew far less than they did. At school, I had done little or no science, my mathematics were disgraceful, chemistry I had never even touched. The hospital authorities had assured us that no preliminary knowledge was necessary; the courses would all start from the letter A. But the fact remained that my fellow students were merely covering familiar ground, while I was setting out, alone, into an unknown country.

The courses at the medical school were, no doubt, admirably suited to their object, which was to get you, by hook or by crook, through the preliminary science examination, and on to the corpse-dissection and the beginnings of practical medical knowledge. They were never intended to provide an ignorant, imaginative, woolly-minded person like myself with a bird's-eye view, a general conception, of the nature and origins of matter. Yet without this general view I was lost. Brought up on the methods of Mr. Holmes, I expected all kinds of instruction to be condensed into epigrams, aphorisms, brilliant simplifications. Instead of which, wandering about in a fog, I stumbled upon signposts marked cryptically "Aluminium Hydroxide," or "H_2SO_4," and was none the wiser. Chemistry, to my bewildered ignorance, was merely cookery: a mad sort of cookery in which you mixed things or heated them, without knowing what they were, or where they came from, or how they came. Theoretically, of course, a cook could make a delicious omelette in the firm belief that butter was a mineral, that eggs grew on trees and that salt was laid by hens: but such misconceptions are likely, in the long run, to lead to trouble—possibly, even, an explosion. It is profoundly disconcerting to find yourself landed in a world where the labels have come seemingly unstuck. "Aluminium," to my lay ear, was inextricably associated with saucepans; "mercury" meant a thermometer; "magnesium" was something only used for lighting the insides of caves. Yet here they all were, on a shelf in the lab., leading isolated existences of their own: the whole physical universe was taken to bits and displayed in a row of bottles and little glass pots. The lecturer instructed us to pass sulphuretted hydrogen through a solution of copper sulphate. Copper sulphide, we were told, would be precipitated. "Copper sulphide," I repeated to myself, staring dully at the small brownish-black mess in the test-tube. I wasn't in the least surprised. This was purest alchemy, anyhow. I shouldn't have raised an eyelid if I had accidentally succeeded in manufacturing gold. But here was, apparently, copper sulphide. I had made it with my own hands, and now I hadn't the remotest idea what I should do with it. Neither, it seemed, had anybody else. We all poured our little messes down the sink.

Physics, by contrast, were dry and odourless and drearily clean. We measured bits of metal with the micrometer screw-guage, weighed them on scales or suspended them from springs. We proved Boyle's Law and learnt to construct the Polygon of Forces. The only things I had to cook here were my results: I seemed incapable of making any kind of measurement accurately. If you had questioned me as to the significance of what I was doing, I should have replied vaguely that I supposed all this technique might conceivably be useful to an engineer. As I wasn't going to be an engineer my enthusiasm for physics was faint.

Botany exposed my clumsiness most mercilessly. I could never cut a section which didn't look like a thick slice of bread and butter. Under the microscope, my specimens were usually quite opaque. And the names! How should I ever manage to stuff them all into my poor head? How should I ever remember the difference between epidermis and endodermis, metaxylum and protoxylum, collenchyma and parenchyma? The truth was that I was frightened by the mere sound of them: my brain shut its doors against them from the very start.

Zoology, on the whole, I disliked least. Here, at any rate, we were on the threshold of the animal kingdom: Man, our proper study, was already in sight. Even the earth-worm has intestines, blood-vessels and nerves. As for the dogfish, it seemed almost as good as human: and if its insides contained a whole new classical dictionary of anatomical names, you could comfort yourself with the reflection that quite a number of them would recur later on.

Later on. . . . Yes, at all costs, I must keep my objective steadily in view. At the moment it wasn't easy. The "peculiar-looking green-shaded lamp in the surgery" which Chalmers had described—how brightly and cosily it had shone six months ago! How faintly it glimmered now, far in the remotest distance, behind an immense and formidable foreground of lecture rooms, labs., alphabetically chalked blackboards, and all the sad armoury of microscopes, magnets, mirrors, Bunsen-burners and test-tubes which encircled my daily studies! "I shall never reach it," I thought, in moods of sudden panic: "I shall never learn to distinguish between the Pharyngo-, the Epi-, the Cerato- and the Hypo-branchials; I shall never make a decent dissection, or prepare a good slide! Was I really the stupidest, clumsiest member of the entire class? It seemed that I was. All these nineteen-year-old boys—not to mention the women students, the Indians and the three Chinese—were working placidly away, jotting down calculations, raising intelligent faces to answer the demonstrator's questions: their calm, their industry, their bright self-assurance fairly terrified me. I was slipping behind, hour by hour, day by day. This was Cambridge again, but worse. Worse, because this time, I was honestly trying, seriously doing my best. I couldn't flatter myself with conceited lies about my Art: my Art was a flop, a declared failure in the open market. And I couldn't hide myself in Mortmere: Mortmere had failed us, dissolved into thin air. The brutal truth was: I should never make a doctor. The whole thing had been a day-dream from the start. It was madness ever to have joined the medical school at all. But suppose I left it now—what was to become of me? Was I to go back to tutoring until I got too old to impress the parents? Was I to try for another amateur-secretary job, and spend the rest of my life messing about on the outskirts of Bohemia? Was I, indeed, a total misfit, a hundred per cent. incompetent? I couldn't, I daren't face such thoughts. I took refuge from them in my note-book; concentrating all my faculties upon a very beautiful drawing of helianthus (transverse section) which I didn't even begin to understand.

With my friends I was very bright and lively. I told them funny stories about the medical school, described my fellow-students, imitated the lecturers; casually letting drop, from time to time, one of my small stock of scientific words. The Cheurets, the Easts and Bill Scott were duly impressed. "How extraordinary Christopher is!" I could imagine them saying. "The very last person you'd expect would take up this kind of thing—and he seems to be settling down to it wonderfully!" Already, there were lots of jokes about my future career. Should I take up surgery, or psycho-analysis? Should I specialize? Perhaps I'd operate on the King and get a knighthood! Perhaps I'd discover the cure for cancer and become a lord! "I can just see Christopher in Harley Street!" Such is the magic of a label that, when our cook poisoned her thumb on a rusty bit of tin, my family seriously asked me to come down to the kitchen and take a look at it.

But there was one friend who, for obvious reasons, I avoided; and that was Philip himself. It would be impossible to pretend to him that my life at the medical school was a success. He would see through my false gaiety in a moment, and the truth would be out. I could just picture the melancholy satisfaction of his sympathetic, delicately implied "I told you so!" No, I would keep out of Philip's way, until . . . Until things got better, somehow—or worse.

On arrival at the medical school I had looked round, as a matter of course, for a pal. Students pair off like birds. There are always experiments which have to be done in couples, pieces of apparatus which must be shared. And it is depressing to eat your midday teashop meal alone. I knew exactly the kind of pal I wanted. He must be efficient, energetic, patient with me, good at mathematics, and generally of a helpful nature. Also, and this was most important, he must be a typical medical student who liked his work and wanted to stick to it: I wasn't keen to meet any more rebels, however interesting. I wanted to stop playing the rebel myself. I wanted to be absorbed in the crowd.

Platt had all, more than all, these qualities: he was in every way more than I deserved. From the moment I first caught sight of him, in the lobby, with his snub-nosed, sallow, good-natured face and stocky rugger player's figure, I knew that here was the unlucky Sinbad whose broad back was doomed to carry me, like an Old Man of the Sea, through the trials and ardours of the next three or four years. Platt, who was only eighteen and, no doubt, feeling lonely, seemed pleased at being spoken to. We made friends hastily, for it was past the hour already, and went into our first lecture together.

He little guessed what he had let himself in for that morning: perhaps, even if he had guessed, he wouldn't have minded. He was one of Nature's boy scouts. He loved bossing me, in the most friendly manner imaginable: and I, alas, was only too ready to be bossed. Our partnership, unequal from the first, rapidly became so lop-sided that Platt would only trust me with the very simplest jobs. "You clean that test-tube, old horse," he would tell me, "and I'll work out the results. You can have my book to copy, later." So I cribbed my way from one experiment to the next, completely in the dark ; and Platt, who managed everything, went from strength to strength.

We always ate together, choosing each day a different restaurant. Platt's favourite dish was sausage and mashed, mine was meat rissoles. Our conversation varied as little as our menu : the peculiarities of the lecturers, of our fellow students, of our respective schools, with occasional speculations as to the morals of the waitresses who served us, and, perhaps, a couple of dirty limericks with the dessert. Platt never asked me my age ; and I was careful never to say anything which would start him thinking of me as a person older and more experienced than himself—though often, in his company, I felt like a man of eighty. The subject of writing and writers I avoided like the plague. With Platt, it was not very difficult to avoid.

Yet Platt, for all his stolidity, his unruffled patience with my incompetence, his well-arranged school-prefect's conception of the universe, was by no means a dull companion. Sometimes he made me laugh a great deal. He could be startlingly catty about our neighbours and was capable of surprising flashes of wit. One afternoon, while we were doing qualitative analysis in the lab., Platt's experiment, for the first and perhaps the last time in his life, went altogether wrong. Too little or too much of something or other had been added, and the result was a thick, poisonous-smelling black liquid. Platt poured it into the sink on our bench ; but the drain was blocked and it wouldn't disappear. We were both distastefully regarding it when the demonstrator came round.

"What have you got there, Platt?" he asked.

"I don't quite know sir," a grin suddenly split Platt's sallow face from ear to ear: "I think it must be the Well of Loneliness."

It was Platt who insisted that he and I should go and watch some operations. "We've got to get used to them some time, you know, old horse," he argued, "and if you're going to throw a faint, you'd much better to do it now and get it over." This seemed unanswerable, and I agreed. Besides, I'd always

179

half wanted to see an operation myself. Any medical student, even in his first year, was allowed to visit the theatres of the big hospitals, provided he didn't make a nuisance of himself and the surgeon didn't object. Several of the other students had been already. I rang up Philip and we fixed our adventure for an afternoon when Philip himself would be acting as one of the dressers.

The operating-theatre was like an unnaturally clean kitchen. And the nurses and dressers were like cooks, in their white caps, goloshes and sexless overalls, chatting in groups, or scrubbing their hands at the sink, or busy at the gleaming silver oven doors of the sterilizers. The air was steamy. The atmosphere was expectant, yet somehow horribly domestic. Platt and I sat down on a little flight of marble steps, which formed a grand-stand before the operating-table, at one end of the room. In our dirty flannel trousers and highly septic tweed jackets we were as much out of place as if we had intruded upon a levée at Buckingham Palace. I began to feel rather queer, and Platt's face had already a greenish tinge.

One of the neuter cook-dressers approached us. It was Philip —a Philip I had never seen before and should scarcely have recognized. The only human thing about him was a tiny new-grown moustache, which looked dirty and reassuring against the stern whiteness of his overalls. We conversed across the silver railing which separated the septic and the antiseptic worlds. "Do you like it?" he asked. "I've only had it ten days. People call it the cricket match—eleven a side." "You're in luck to-day," he added, "We've got a sarcoma of the femur. MacDonald is going to amputate."

We were interrupted by the entry of the patient, wheeled in under blankets, attended by the anæsthetist and the surgeon himself. The groups broke up, the oven doors were opened, the cooks took up their positions around the table. But now they were no longer cooks ; they were acolytes and minor priests. This was a religious ceremony. A sister, in her triply disinfected, sacrificial robes, brought out the consecrated instruments and proffered them on a towel. The hot-water bottles were removed ; the victim's leg was bared to the hip. The surgeon had assumed his black rubber gloves of office. Bending over the table he pronounced the opening words: "Now, gentlemen, I want you particularly to notice where the incision is made . . ."

180

The scalpel approached the thigh. This was the moment I had most feared to see—the terrible, outrageous contact between metal and flesh. I wanted to shut my eyes, but I didn't. I had to watch. A wave of nausea dimmed, for an instant, the powerful electric lights. And, in an instant, it was over. A thin ring, drawn quick as lightning by the knife, in scarlet ink, encircled the leg: tiny blood-drops were flecked along the edges of the wound. The wound was like a tight-shut mouth which grinned suddenly, and gaped wide. The leg was no longer a leg, but something quite inhuman, not even disgusting—a joint of raw meat in a butcher's shop. They were tying up the arteries. The surgeon made a sign to the sister for the saw. "I never liked this thing," he told the students, "old Douglas of Edinburgh invented it, fifteen years ago." What followed didn't upset me in the least. I had seen it so often before, out shopping, as a little boy. The leg was dropped into a pail, and carried off. The bleeding jam-roll stump, before they stitched over the flap of flesh, was entirely without relation to the face at the other end of the motionless form under the blankets: an eleven-year-old girl, lying calm and remote, with a wonderful bluish moonlit beauty, in the depths of the ether, the tube between her lips. Her eyes were half open and gazing quietly at the ceiling, as though she were wide awake.

We had tea afterwards with Philip in the hospital canteen. He was grumbling because the surgeon had given him the leg to dissect in his spare time. "And Heaven knows what use they think the operation is, anyway. . . . It's pretty well dead certain to develop later, somewhere else. . . ." I regarded Philip with a new-found respect. He had long since surmounted all my obstacles. What if he had failed an exam. now and then? He had persevered; and this was his moment of triumph, his reward—to sit, blasé and weary with all the weariness of knowledge, opposite two gaping greenhorns who hung on his every word. Philip, I now felt, had really found his vocation. He would make an ideal doctor; so comfortably mondain, so soothingly bored. And if he had chucked up the medical school earlier on it would have been largely my fault. This was a sobering but not uninspiring thought. Perhaps I, too, should persevere: perhaps, if I made one more mighty effort, the dogfish and the helianthus and the acidic radicals would yield up their secrets. At any rate I'd try.

But when Philip, who obviously found Platt's presence a little cramping, suggested that we should dine together that evening, I made an excuse and declined. I wasn't strong enough to face him alone—yet.

The medical school had stimulated me in one direction, at any rate. No sooner had I joined it than I began to write a new novel. Every afternoon, about tea-time, when lectures were over for the day, I hurried eagerly home to my manuscript. During those autumn months I wrote like mad, as I had never written before, without hesitation, without pausing to correct, forgetting all my inhibitions, my neurotic etcher's neatness, intent only upon discharging my load of ideas. This was to be only a rough draft, of course. I simply wanted to get the bare outlines of the story down on paper, before they changed and became blurred again.

· The novel was to be called *A War Memorial, The War Memorial*, or perhaps simply *The Memorial*. It was to be about war: not the War itself, but the effect of the idea of "War" on my generation. It was to give expression, at last, to my own "War" complex, and to all the reactions which had followed my meeting with Lester at the Bay. Its private title (most novels have private titles) was of course, *War and Peace*. Like Tolstoy, I would tell the story of a family ; its births and deaths, ups and downs, marriage, feuds and love affairs—all "The Eternals," as Chalmers used, rather acidly, to call them, were to be stuffed into sixty thousand words. No more drawing-room comedies for me. I was out to write an epic ; a potted epic ; an epic disguised as a drawing-room comedy.

The worst of all epics, except the very greatest, is that their beginnings are so dull. Either the writer is going a long way back in time and doesn't know his stuff, or there are wearisome interrelationships to be disentangled and explained, or you have got to plough through the hero's childhood, which is almost certain to be a bore. Therefore epics, I reasoned, should start in the middle and go backwards, then forwards again—so that the reader comes upon the dullness half-way through, when he is more interested in the characters ; the fish holds its tail in its mouth, and time is circular, which sounds Einstein-ish and brilliantly modern.

But if you are to go backwards in Time, surely that means an "I remember" digression—a remedy infinitely worse than the original fault? Yes, it does ; as long as you stick to the idea of writing a continuous narrative. But why should the narrative be continuous? Why not write the story in self-contained scenes, like a play ; an epic in an album of snapshots? First snapshot: a group of men and women drinking cocktails in nearly modern dress, the fashions of the year before last. Second snapshot: an Edwardian tea-party. What charming, funny costumes! But, hullo—wait a minute! We seem to recognize some of the figures. That young girl in the enormous hat; surely she's the smart Eton-cropped woman of forty with the well-preserved figure? Yes, she is! And now, here's the third snapshot: the dresses still look queer, it's immediately postwar. Looking at it carefully, you can see what ten years have done to these men and women. Some of them have disappeared altogether from the earlier scene; and that little boy in the foreground has nearly grown up. The final, fourth snapshot (dated the present day) is, at first sight, something of a disappointment: it is, to all intents and purposes, identical with number one. But that only shows the exquisite subtlety of our method; because, if you look at these faces more closely, there is all the difference in the world. It is the difference made by knowledge. In the first snapshot, we saw these people merely as casual acquaintances: here they are our intimate friends. With the eyes of friends, we look deeply into their faces, reading, in Time's cipher, everything which is secretly written there. And this sends us back to the first snapshot. With how much more interest we examine it now! Every attitude, every gesture, seems charged with meaning, with reference to things past, with presage of things to come. And so we go through our album once again. And again and again and again. There is no reason, theoretically, why you should ever stop reading this kind of book at all.

I had planned to finish the first draft of *The Memorial* before the end of the medical school term. And I did finish it, after a fashion: the last twenty pages were a mere scribble. I put it away in a drawer—without even reading through it— and hurried off to take the terminal chemistry exam. I need hardly add that I came out bottom of the list.

Weston returned from Germany to spend Christmas at home. He was full of stories of Berlin, that astonishing vicious yet fundamentally so respectable city, where even the night-life had a cosy domestic quality and where the films were the most interesting in Europe. Also, it seemed, cigars were incredibly cheap. Weston had one continually in his mouth: he now looked more than ever like an exceedingly dirty millionaire.

But the most important experience of Weston's Berlin visit

had had nothing to do with Germany or the Germans at all. One evening, in a café, he had got into conversation with a stranger, an Englishman named Barnard. This Mr. Barnard—himself an anthropologist and a most remarkable man from all accounts—had first told Weston about the great psychologist, Homer Lane. Barnard had been a patient and pupil of Lane's, and now, since the master's death, he was one of the very few people really qualified to spread Lane's teachings and carry on his work. In Weston, he had found an intelligent listener who became, overnight, an enthusiastic disciple.

Every disease, Lane had taught, is in itself a cure—if we know how to take it. There is only one sin: disobedience to the inner law of our own nature. The results of this disobedience show themselves in crime or in disease; but the disobedience is never, in the first place, our own fault—it is the fault of those who teach us, as children, to control God (our desires) instead of giving Him room to grow. The whole problem, when dealing with a patient, is to find out which of all the conflicting things inside him is God, and which is the Devil. And the one sure guide is that God appears always unreasonable, while the Devil appears always to be noble and right. God appears unreasonable because He has been put in prison and driven wild. The Devil is conscious control, and is, therefore, reasonable and sane.

Conventional education (I am paraphrasing Barnard's own words, from a letter Weston once showed me) inverts the whole natural system in childhood, turning the child into a spurious adult. So that later, when the child grows up physically into a man, he is bound to try to regain his childhood—by means which, to the outside world, appear ever more and more unreasonable. If the conscious mind were really the controlling factor, God would remain in prison, the world would become a bedlam in a few generations, and the race automatically die out. So diseases and neuroses come to kill off the offenders or bring them to their senses. Diseases are therefore only warning symptoms of a sickness of the soul; they are manifestations of God—and those who try to "cure" them without first curing the soul are only serving the Devil. The disease of the soul is the belief in moral control: the Tree of the Knowledge of Good and Evil, as against the Tree of Life.

Lane, as will be seen from the above, had a good deal in common with D. H. Lawrence—particularly in Lawrence's *Fantasia of the Unconscious*. Lawrence, like Lane, exclaimed against the conception of the "right" kinds of feeling invented by professional moralists—meekness and forbearance and consideration for others—as opposed to the "wrong" kinds of feeling—anger and hatred and rebelliousness. Both of them were horrified by the ideal of self-sacrifice. Self-sacrificing Barnard had told Weston, only means, in the last analysis, the sacrifice of others to yourself: it is the subtlest and most deadly form of selfishness. One of the greatest evils of our civilization is the invention of the idea of pity. Pity, consciously induced, loveless and sterile, is never a healer, always a destroyer. Pity frustrates every attempted cure. If you find yourself beginning to pity anyone who is ill or in trouble, said Barnard, you cannot help him: you had far better abandon him altogether.

Lane's practice seemed to have been as sensational as his preaching. He detested the conventional pomposities of the psychologist: the solemn consulting-rooms and the shaded lights. If his patients needed it, he took them to night clubs, or tearing about the countryside in his car. A timid retiring young man he knocked down, to make him hit back. A child of rich parents who was "difficult" and smashed all his expensive toys became quite normal as soon as he had been allowed to play with his own excrement. Lane laughed hygiene and antisepsis to scorn (this item had particularly appealed to Weston): for how could you possibly contract blood-poisoning if you were pure in heart?

Weston had assimilated all these ideas with his customary zest and ease, adding to them a touch of extravagance which was peculiarly his own. His whole vocabulary, I found, was renovated and revised to include the new catchwords. We hadn't been together a quarter of an hour before he was reproving me for harbouring a "death-wish." I had admitted to feeling ill:

"You've got to drop all that," said Weston. "When people are ill, they're wicked. You must stop it. You must be pure in heart."

"What nonsense!" I retorted. "How can I stop it? There's nothing the matter with my heart. It's my tonsils."

"Your tonsils? That's very interesting. . . ." Weston's consulting-room manner was excessively irritating: "I suppose you know what *that* means?"

"Certainly. It means I've caught a chill."

"It means you've been telling lies!"

185

"Oh, indeed? What have I been telling lies about?"

Weston looked down his nose; provokingly mysterious. I could have kicked him: "You're the only person who can answer that!"

After this, Weston gave me a whole catalogue of ailments and physical defects, with their psychic causes: if you refused to make use of your creative powers, you produced a cancer, instead; excessive obstinacy—a refusal to "bend the knee"—found expression in rheumatism of the joints; deafness and short sight were attempts to shut out the exterior world ("Oh, yes, I know," Weston interrupted, before I had time to say anything suitably sarcastic, "that's how I have to pay for being an introvert. . . . Stephen's different. You know why he's so tall? He's trying to reach Heaven!". . .), deformities, producing a lop-sided body, were the result of a struggle between instinct and will; consumption represented a desire to return to early childhood, because the lungs are the first organs used by the new-born baby; epilepsy went even farther back—it was an attempt to become an angel, and fly.

And how, I asked, somewhat acidly, were all these misfortunes to be avoided? Quite simply, Weston replied—by being pure in heart. Even to-day, I am uncertain whether it was Barnard or Weston himself who was originally responsible for this annoying and priggish-sounding phrase. At any rate I could suggest no better one, and very soon, I, too, began to use it freely. The pure-in-heart man became our new ideal. He represented, indeed, our picture of Lane himeslf. He was essentially free and easy, generous with his money and belongings, without worries or inhibitions. He would let you brush your teeth with his toothbrush or write with his fountain-pen. He was a wonderful listener, but he never "sympathized" with your troubles; and the only advice he ever gave was in the form of parables—stories about other people which you could apply to your own problems, if you liked. He was entirely without fear: therefore he could never catch an infectious disease. And without sexual guilt: therefore he was immune from syphilis. Above all, he was profoundly, fundamentally happy.

Needless to say, I didn't accept the Lane gospel without a great deal of conscious and subconscious resistance. There was plenty in it to sneer at, and, in Weston's presence, I sneered. But when Weston had returned to Berlin and I was left alone, with the prospect of another medical school term ahead of me, I began to think things over seriously, with reference to my own life. And the more I thought, the more dissatisfied I became.

I hadn't advanced an inch, really, since those Cambridge days. "Isherwood the Artist" was still striking an attitude on his lonely rock. But his black Byronic exile's cloak failed to impress me any longer. I knew what was inside it now—just plain, cold, uninteresting funk. Funk of getting too deeply involved with other people, sex-funk, funk of the future. I was eternally worrying about what was going to happen to me— in 1930, in 1940, in 1950; eternally building up defences against attacks which were never launched. Why had I ever become a medical student? Largely, I had to admit, because of a vague, hardly defined fear—a fear that somehow, somewhere, I should one day be isolated and trapped, far from the safety of the nursery and Nanny's apron, and compelled to face "The Test." And I had thought of the career of medicine as being essentially safe: people respected your status: if there was a war, you didn't have to fight. With a medical degree in my pocket, I had fancied, I could face the world. Well, perhaps I could. But was that going to make things any easier for myself? Did I really want to sham my way through life, impressing other people, perhaps, but knowing myself for a coward, at heart? Of course I didn't. Besides, what was going to happen to my work? As long as I remained a sham, my writing would be sham, too.

Weston, needless to say, had told Barnard all about me, and about my doings. And Barnard (who, as I later discovered, had very little use for the woes and waverings of young literary neurotics) was said to have commented: "The only thing which interests me about Isherwood is the way he cleared out from Cambridge. . . . Perhaps there's something in him after all." What was I to make of this—the Master's only utterance with regard to myself? Did it mean that I ought to give up the medical school? I felt increasingly convinced that it did. I thought of writing direct to Barnard and asking his advice: but Weston had already warned me that Barnard never advised anybody. He only asked: "What do *you* want to do, yourself?" And when I asked myself what I did want to do, the answer was certainly clear enough: I want to leave. At the same time, I was only too painfully aware how disingenuous these self-examinations had become. Naturally, I *wanted* to leave the medical school. Who wouldn't want to wriggle out of difficult uncongenial work? If everybody were to argue like this, would anyone ever qualify for any professional career at all? Besides, as I had said to myself so often before, I had got to settle down, somehow. I had got to earn my living. I had made my bed, and now, by all reasonable standards, I must lie on it.

But here, Lane and Barnard promptly interrupted: "Reasonable? Aha, we were expecting that word! Isn't the Devil always reasonable? Didn't we warn you? Have you forgotten your lesson already—that the way to salvation always lies through acts of apparent madness and folly? What you call the voice of Reason is only the voice of Fear. You're afraid—afraid to trust in your deepest instincts, afraid to take the plunge! Don't flatter yourself even, that the world is on your side. The world really despises those who conform to its standards. The world is the first to applaud those who dare to break free! We know what you want, all right! The voice of your heart has told us already. You want to commit the unforgivable sin, to shock Mummy and Daddy and Nanny, to smash the nursery clock, to be a really naughty little boy. Well, why not start? Time's getting on. It's your only hope for ever growing up, at all. If you stick to your safe London nursery-life, you never *will* grow up. You'll die a timid shrivelled Peter Pan. At present, you're exactly seven years old. Never mind! There's still time. In 1942, if you start growing now, with luck, you'll come of age!"

And so the internal struggle continued—to its inevitable conclusion. Early in January I made my decision. I told my family that I wanted to leave the medical school at once. My family, patient but bewildered as ever, agreed sadly in principle, requesting only that I should stay on until the summer: "After all, it's been paid for." I compromised: I would leave at Easter, at the end of the coming term.

And what then? First of all I must leave England altogether —the break with the old life must be complete, this time—and I must talk to Barnard. I'd go to Berlin. Weston had already invited me to visit him there. Perhaps I'd stay on right through the summer. But this was plan-making, and plan-making, by the new rules, was wicked, like all other forms of worrying about the future. I should have to await the further commands of the inner voice. As luck would have it, I had just unearthed a forgotten War Loan certificate worth close on fifty pounds. One could consider it, if one liked, as the first-fruits of purity of heart. I have often wondered, since then, how Lane expected people to obey the inner voice when they hadn't any ready cash.

Now that I was virtually a free man, I could afford to regard the medical school with very different eyes. Indeed, I was actually glad to be back, to breathe again the rotten-egg smells of the lab. Platt I greeted like a brother. He was sallower than ever—for he had been working hard all through the Christmas holidays—and stockily self-confident: he had passed out top in the terminal exams. I didn't tell him of my decision. It would only have shocked him, and might even have damaged slightly his cast-iron morale.

I told the Cheurets, of course; and Chalmers and the Easts and Bill Scott and Stephen Savage, and finally Philip. For Weston I kept the news as a surprise, when we met in Berlin. The Cheurets were astonished but entirely uncritical: they had long ago ceased to pass judgment on the eccentricities of their friends. Chalmers wrote from the school at which he was working: he approved of this, as of every other anarchic, irrational act, but was inclined to mistrust the brief sketch I had given him of the Homer Lane philosophy—he had lost none of his old dislike of cults. The Easts were simply amused: "Bisherwood's off again!" Bill, rather unexpectedly, disapproved: he had nothing against my leaving the medical school, and what I told him about Lane interested him deeply (he was an ardent admirer of D. H. Lawrence); but he had a violent and, as it seemed to me, purely mystical prejudice against Berlin: "You're the very last person who ought to go there, Christopher. It isn't the right sort of place for you at all. . . ." On being pressed to explain what he meant, he would only repeat: "It's a bad place . . . I can feel it. . . ." I had the greatest respect for Bill's intuitions, and might have taken this one more seriously had not Bill admitted that he himself had never been in Berlin in his life. (Nevertheless, looking back, I can see clearly what he did mean: and, certainly, in a sense, he was right. I must refer my readers, here, to my novel, *Mr. Norris Changes Trains*!) As for Stephen Savage, he was as enthusiastic as I could wish. Viewed from his super-dramatic standpoint, my departure was an act of unparalleled daring, personal integrity and moral courage. At the end of half an hour he had succeeded in making me feel every kind of prig, fool and sham. It was overwhelming to be believed in by Stephen: it was like being hugged by an enormous bear.

Philip, whose gentle sarcasm I had so uneasily awaited, was tact and kindness itself. If he felt any bitterness at all he expressed it only in one mild, typically prosaic remark: "I envy you, boy. I'd have done the same thing long ago—if I'd had the cash." We parted rather sadly, at the hospital gate: I hurrying off to catch a bus into the sensational, unknowable future, Philip returning slowly to the boredom and unchanging wretchedness of the great whitewashed wards. (How I wish I could have comforted him at that moment—could have foretold, clairvoyantly, what lay ahead! Why was there no fortune-teller to murmur consolingly in his ear: "I see a ship . . . a long journey . . . blue sky . . . adventures . . . distant countries . . . some money . . . a dark woman . . . your novel in the bookshop windows . . . marriage . . . love. . . ."? Never mind, Philip: you deserved them, and you got them all.)

The Easter term passed quickly. At no other period of my life have I been so disgracefully and unashamedly lazy. I visited the medical school nearly every day, much as one drops into a club, made a few jokes with Platt, and sneaked out again, in the middle of a demonstration hour, to get a drink. My drinking companion was usually a charming, disillusioned young man named Lee, who had been at Oxford, and whose prospects of ever obtaining a medical degree appeared, at that time, to be dubious. One afternoon, Lee and I came in very drunk during a physics hour. For some reason or other, we had filled our pockets with tomatoes at the restaurant where we lunched: we now proceeded to distribute them among the female students. Some of the girls were amused; others rather huffy. The virtuous Platt was delighted: like most respecters of law and order, he enjoyed seeing other people misbehave. The demonstrator, vaguely aware of the commotion, came towards us. I dived for my note-book and opened it upside down. The demonstrator, evidently deciding to be tactful, passed our bench. But this didn't suit my drunken caprice. I went up to him, feeling chatty, and began to ask questions about the proper use of the oscillating magnet. The questions must have been rather odd, because he looked hard at me, and answered sharply: "Well?" Then, just behind me, I heard a terrible crash. I had knocked over a refractometer. Thank heavens, it wasn't broken! The demonstrator gave me another look; but all he said was: "I'd better take this away." We were lucky not to hear any more of this incident; and I am none the less grateful to the demonstrator for his charity because, in my own case, it was sadly misplaced.

In due course, I gave the college authorities formal notice of my departure. It was necessary to find a sensible excuse: I was leaving, I told them, to get married. The Principal was very understanding and kind; he wished me luck—urging me, however, to take up the courses again as soon as I and my wife had settled down.

On March the 14th, 1929, I left London by the afternoon train for Berlin. It would be easy to dramatize my emotions on this portentous but unexciting journey—easy, because I have forgotten altogether what they were. I remember only the externals, people and places: a German who asked me to admire the overcoat he had bought in Conduit Street; Dover quay, enveloped in clammy brown fog; the third-class steamer saloon crammed with soldiers going out to the Army of Occupation at Wiesbaden; two Cambridge undergraduates with enormous red wrists, who welcomed my old school tie (some obscure kind of insularity had caused me to put it on for the first time in several years). At Ostende the train stood waiting to leave for Warsaw and Riga: the undergraduates unscrewed a *Niet Spuwen* notice as a souvenir. I parted from them in the waiting-room at Köln, as an official marched down the platform carrying, like a sacred banner, the wooden signboard announcing the arrival of the Berlin express.

Throughout the ten hours' travelling which followed, huddled sleepily in my hard-backed corner seat, I thought, I suppose, of the future; but, if I did so, the view was limited. I could see no farther than that evening, when I should meet Weston, and, perhaps, Barnard himself. These two, between them, would take care of everything. I was in their hands, and content to be. One day, no doubt, I should start worrying again, making plans and patterns, trying to organize my life. One day I should rewrite *The Memorial,* and all those other books I'd planned. But for the moment I was only a traveller, given over, mind and body, to the will of the dominant, eastward-speeding train; happy in the mere knowledge that yet another stage of my journey had begun.